STUDIO PAPERBACK

James Stirling
Michael Wilford

Robert Maxwell

Birkhäuser Verlag
Basel · Berlin · Boston

Übersetzung aus dem Englischen/Translation from English: Andreas Simon
Archiv/Archivist: Laura Parker, Michael Wilford and Partners

A CIP catalogue record for this book is available from the Library of Congress, Washington D. C., USA

Deutsche Bibliothek - CIP-Einheitsaufnahme

Maxwell, Robert:
James Stirling, Michael Wilford / Robert Maxwell. [Übers. aus dem
Engl.: Andreas Simon]. - Basel ; Berlin ; Boston : Birkhäuser, 1998
  (Studio-Paperback)
  ISBN 3-7643-5291-4 (Basel . . .)
  ISBN 0-8176-5291-4 (Boston)

© 1998 Birkhäuser – Publishers for Architecture
Birkhäuser – Verlag für Architektur, P. O. Box 133, CH-4010 Basel, Switzerland

Printed on acid-free paper produced from chlorine-free pulp
Printed in Germany
ISBN 3-7643-5291-4
ISBN 0-8176-5291-4

9 8 7 6 5 4 3 2 1

Inhalt

Contents

Einleitung

Introduction

Die Architektur von James Stirling und Michael Wilford

The Work of James Stirling and Michael Wilford

«...Architektur sollte im Idealfall Humor haben, und in diesem Kontext bietet das ernsthafte puritanische Bauen der Moderne eine reichhaltige Fundgrube, die sich satirisch zitieren und kommentieren läßt. Allerdings ist mir klar, daß die Wechselbeziehung zwischen einem neuen Entwurf und Assoziationen der Vergangenheit eine heikle Gradwanderung ist, bei der man zur einen Seite leicht in Kompromisse, zur anderen in Sentimentalität abstürzen kann...»[1]

James Stirling

«...hopefully there might be some humour in modern architecture, and in this context there is a rich vein in serious puritanical modern that can be satirized and commented upon; I realize that an interaction between the design for a new building with associations of the past is a dangerous tightrope to walk, with compromise and sentimentality on either side...»[1]

James Stirling

Ich lernte James Stirling im August 1959 kennen, als er die Arbeit an seiner einjährigen Abschlußarbeit an der Liverpool School of Architecture begann. Ich wurde bald sein Bewunderer, und als er mich im folgenden Frühling bat, die perspektivischen Zeichnungen für seine Abschlußpräsentation zu übernehmen, fühlte ich mich geschmeichelt und sagte zu. Das war der Anfang einer lebenslangen Freundschaft.

Beide standen wir unter dem Einfluß von Colin Rowe, einem ehemaligen Kommilitonen, der nun unterrichtete und als Tutor Diplomarbeiten betreute. In seiner Beurteilung verglich er unsere Arbeiten und ließ keinen Zweifel daran, welche er für die interessantere von beiden hielt.[2] Rowe war ein brillanter Wissenschaftler und Lehrer, und was er uns am nachhaltigsten und eindrucksvollsten vermittelte, war, Architektur als ein ständiges Streben zu begreifen. Er war Architekturhistoriker, schätzte aber auch die Entwürfe der Moderne sehr, die für ihn eine Phase in der Entwicklung der Architektur war, die aus sich selbst heraus Bestand und Wert hatte, auch wenn sie in keiner Weise frühere Leistungen auslöschte. An Le Corbusier zum Beispiel gefiel ihm die formale Kühnheit seiner Bauten, er sah darin aber zugleich Analogien, die seine Architektur mit den Renaissance-Bauten des großen italienischen Baumeisters Andrea Palladio verbanden.[3]

Unter diesem Einfluß entwickelte James Stirling einen eklektischen Geschmack und lernte, viele Perioden der Architekturgeschichte zu bewundern. Seine besondere

I met James Stirling in the autumn of 1959, when he was beginning work on his thesis – a year-long study undertaken in the final year at the Liverpool School of Architecture. I soon became an admirer, and when in the following spring he asked me to draw the perspectives for his final presentation, I was flattered, and agreed. So began a life-long friendship.

Both of us had fallen under the influence of Colin Rowe, previously a fellow student, now a lecturer and Tutor for thesis. He was to write comparing our two theses in terms that left no doubt which was the more interesting.[2] Rowe was a brilliant scholar and teacher, and what he communicated most powerfully was a sense of architecture as an enduring pursuit: he was a historian, but he enjoyed modern design as a phase in the development of architecture, legitimate in itself, but in no way displacing earlier achievements. Le Corbusier, for example, was valued for the boldness of his formal structures, but at the same time analogies were found that linked his architecture to that of Palladio.[3] Under this influence, Stirling developed eclectic tastes, and was able to admire many periods of architecture, with a preference for the early years of the nineteenth century, when neo-classicism was evolving into romanticism. More particularly, he was seduced by Rowe's enjoyment of Mannerism[4]: the idea of setting up a set of formal rules and then contradicting them; and it could be said that this predilection underlay all his subsequent work, and perhaps even served as a theoretical structure for it.

Without Rowe, Stirling would no doubt have become fa-

Vorliebe galt dabei den frühen Jahren des 19. Jahrhunderts, als der Klassizismus in den Historismus überging. Insbesondere zog ihn Rowes Hochschätzung des Manierismus an: die Idee, eine Reihe von formalen Regeln aufzustellen, um sie dann zu durchbrechen.[4] Und man könnte sagen, daß diese Vorliebe die Grundlage seines gesamten späteren Werks bildete, vielleicht sogar dessen theoretisches Gerüst.

Stirling wäre ohne Zweifel auch ohne Rowe berühmt geworden, hätte aber sein Interesse an der architektonischen Form vielleicht nicht so geradlinig entwickelt, und dies zu einer Zeit, als die Funktion als einzige legitime Quelle der Form galt. Dies galt besonders in Großbritannien, wo der Glaube an den Funktionalismus noch durch die puritanische Kultur verstärkt wurde. Rowe weitete den Blick für eine europäischere Perspektive ohne puritanische Befangenheit. Er lehrte seine Studenten, ihren visuellen Sinn zu schärfen, indem sie sich wieder und wieder nicht nur Fotografien von Gebäuden, sondern die Bauten selbst ansahen – als immer zugängliche, dem

mous, but he might not have developed so forthrightly his interest in architectural form, in an age when function was thought to be the sole legitimate source of form. This was so especially in Britain, where the functionalist creed was reinforced by a puritan culture. Rowe brought in a more continental perspective, unmarked by puritan constraint. He taught his students to cultivate visual acumen, endlessly looking – not only at photographs of buildings, but also at the buildings themselves – as evidence always accessible, always under our eyes, to be scrutinized for the secrets it contained. Stirling learned to look. He particularly enjoyed the tough buildings produced in the industrial revolution, and used both industrial and village vernacular as sources for his own work. He had under his eyes, after all, the same industrial landscape that Schinkel had travelled miles to see. These sources seem to have contributed to Stirling's appreciation of power and presence in a building, whatever its style, and may even have affected his feeling for proportions. The thesis design already has this touch – tough yet sensitive, like his own

Blick stets gegenwärtige Zeugnisse, deren Geheimnisse durch genaue Betrachtung zu enträtseln waren.

So lernte Stirling zu sehen. Besonders gefielen ihm die harten Gebäude der industriellen Revolution, und er setzte in seinen eigenen Arbeiten eine industrielle und aus der dörflichen Architektur gespeiste Formensprache ein. Schließlich hatte er dieselbe Industrielandschaft direkt vor Augen, für deren Betrachtung Schinkel seinerzeit weit gereist war. Dieses Anschauungsmaterial scheint ein Grund für Stirlings Wertschätzung von Kraft und Präsenz in Gebäuden gleich welchen Stils gewesen zu sein, und mag selbst noch seinen Sinn für Proportionen beeinflußt haben. Bereits seinen *Diplomentwurf* kennzeichnet diese Eigenart: hart, aber doch feinfühlig, wie sein eigener Charakter – ein Kennzeichen, das sich in seinem gesamten späteren Werk findet.

James (Jim) Stirling ging nach London und arbeitete eine Zeitlang bei Lyons, Israel und Ellis. In seiner freien Zeit beteiligte er sich an Wettbewerben, schuf Entwürfe für Häuser und Wohnhausstudien, die nicht realisiert wurden, darunter ein Projekt für eine Wohnsiedlung, sein Beitrag zur Ausstellung von Team X beim CIAM (Congrès International d'Architecture Moderne). 1955 gründete er zusammen mit seinem Partner James Gowan ein Architekturbüro, um den Auftrag für den Entwurf einer *Wohnanlage in Ham Common* zu übernehmen. Die Apartments sind mit Ziegelwänden und Betondecken in einem ähnlichen Stil errichtet wie Le Corbusiers Häuser für die Familie Jaoul, die als «brutalistisch» etikettiert worden waren, eine Bezeichnung, der Le Corbusier heftig widersprach. Das englische Klima, das weiße Wände schnell angreift, rechtfertigte aus Sicht der Architekten die Verwendung von Ziegeln. Eine ähnliche Konstruktionsweise findet sich bei ihrer *Schulaula in Camberwell* (1958 – 1962) und mehreren anderen Gebäuden. In einem Land, wo für die meisten

personality, a distinctive character that appears throughout his later work.

Coming to London, Stirling worked for a time with Lyons Israel Ellis, doing competitions in his spare time, projects for houses that were not built, and some theoretical housing studies, including a Village Housing Project that he contributed to the Team Ten display at CIAM. In 1955 he set up practice in partnership with James Gowan, in order to undertake a commission for *Flats at Ham Common*. These were built with brick walls and concrete floors in a manner derived from Le Corbusier's houses for the Jaoul family, a style that led to the architects being labelled «brutalist», which they hotly denied. The use of brick was justified by their view of the English climate as unkind to white walls. A similar constructional method was employed for their *School Assembly Hall* at Camberwell (1958 – 1962), and several other buildings. Brick was also perhaps justified as a suitably contextual material in a country where most domestic work was in brickwork, and of interest here is the project for a group of *Three Houses for Basil Mavrolean* which Stirling and Gowan designed in 1957, which with their carefully studied elevations are clearly contextual, although veneered in stone. Also of interest is the project for a *House in Kensington* (1960), not in brickwork, which has a very controlled street elevation that approaches the neo-classical, a condition of the brief.

The partnership became world-famous after the construction of the *Engineering Building* at Leicester University. Brickwork as facing to a concrete frame is here combined with cheap patent glazing. There could be no doubt about the boldness of the concept, nor about its functionalist basis, with all the elements attributed to a logical analysis of the brief. But this was not an architecture that conformed to current ideas, it was modern in an orig-

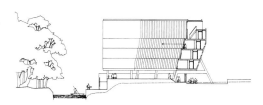

Florey Building, Oxford, Schnitt:
Studentenzimmer blicken auf einen Hof

Florey Building, Oxford, section:
Individual rooms address a courtyard

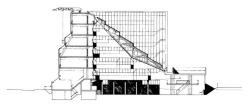

Geschichtsfakultät, Cambridge, Schnitt:
Die Zugänge zu den Büros blicken auf ein Atrium

History Faculty, Cambridge, section:
Office access addresses an atrium

Wohnhäuser Ziegel verwendet wird, war dieses Material durch den Kontextbezug durchaus angemessen. Ein interessanter Entwurf ist in diesem Zusammenhang die Gruppe von *Drei Häusern für Basil Mavrolean,* die Stirling und Gowan 1957 schufen und deren sorgfältig gestaltete Aufrisse deutlich auf ihren Kontext verweisen, obgleich sie eine Steinverkleidung haben. Ebenfalls von Interesse ist der Entwurf eines *Hauses in Kensington* (1960) ohne Verwendung von Ziegelstein, der zur Straße hin eine sehr kontrollierte, beinahe klassizistische Fassadengestaltung aufweist, die vom Bauherrn vorgegeben wurde.

Zu Weltruhm gelangte das Gemeinschaftsbüro mit dem Bau der *Ingenieursfakultät* der Universität von Leicester. Ein mit Ziegel verkleideter Betonskelettbau verbindet sich hier mit einer kostengünstigen Patentverglasung. Die Kühnheit des Konzepts, beruhend auf einem funktionalistischen Ansatz, bei dem sich alle Elemente aus einer logischen Analyse des Programms ergeben, stand von vornherein außer Frage. Aber es war eine Architektur, die nicht mit den gängigen Auffassungen übereinstimmte: Sie war auf eine originale Weise «modern», hatte historistische und europäische Anklänge – in diesem Fall an den russischen Konstruktivismus. Was Jim bei diesem Gebäude gerne seinen Freunden zeigte, waren die formalen Tricks: (an Melnikow erinnernde) Keramikfliesen an der Unterseite des vorspringenden Auditoriums, durch die alle Flächen in derselben Weise verkleidet sind, so daß die skulpturale Einheit des Gebäudes betont wird; oder die Fliesen an der Tür zum Installationsbereich im Gebäudesockel, die demselben Zweck dienen.

Nach dem Projekt in Leicester ging die Partnerschaft auseinander, und 1964 gewann Stirling mit seinem eigenen Büro den Wettbewerb um die *Geschichtsfakultät* der Universität Cambridge. Sie ist ebenfalls im «roten Backstein»-Stil gehalten, in Verbindung mit sonst in der Industrie eingesetzter Patentverglasung. Der fächerförmige Lesesaal entsprach mit seiner Übersichtlichkeit von einem Punkt aus genau den Anforderungen. (Es steckt eine gewisse Ironie darin, daß diese Anordung später durch die Einführung einer Magnetbandsicherung der Bücher überflüssig wurde.) Die Universität hatte Schwierigkeiten beim Erwerb eines Grundstücks, wodurch das Gebäude um 90 Grad gedreht werden mußte, ohne das für die erforderlichen Anpassungen mehr Zeit oder Geld bewilligt worden wären. Die für das Gebäude ungünstigere Lage führte dann zu Beeinträchtigungen, die sich durch ein anderes Vorgehen leicht hätten vermeiden lassen.[5]

Obwohl sein «roter Backstein»-Stil (wie Stirling bewußt war) Anklang gefunden hatte, ließ ihn der Architekt bei der folgenden Reihe von Gebäuden wieder fallen. Statt dessen arbeitete er nun mit vorgefertigten Teilen. Die Betonplatten, die er bei der *Wohnsiedlung Runcorn New*

inal way. It had historicist and continental resonances – of Russian Constructivism in this case – and the things about it that Jim enjoyed showing to his friends were the formal tricks: brick tiles applied to the underside of the cantilevered lecture hall (reminiscent of Melnikov), which allowed the same finish to cover all surfaces, reinforcing the sculptural unity; and the brick tiles set into the utility door that interrupted the podium, which performed the same service.

After Leicester, the partnership split, and in 1964 Stirling working on his own won a competition for the *History Faculty* at Cambridge University. This also was in the «red-brick» manner, with patent glazing. The assessors found the fan-shaped reading room an exact translation of their requirements for central supervision. Ironically, developments in book control, with the introduction of magnetic strips, were later to nullify this requirement. The University ran into problems with site acquisition, and required the building to be turned through ninety degrees, while refusing additional time or money for adjustment. The result was a series of complaints of environmental conditions that could well have been avoided.[5]

Stirling was well aware that the «red-brick» manner, once invented, had now become an adopted style, and he used it again for a third time in the *Florey Building* at Oxford, and then deliberately departed from it in his next series of buildings. These came out of an interest in pre-fabrication, as we find with the concrete panels used in the housing at *Runcorn* and in the residential blocks at *St. Andrews University.* St. Andrews developed some technical problems, and the Runcorn housing had its share of social problems, as did much technically innovative postwar housing. Prefabrication also governs the plastic panels used at the *Olivetti Training School* at Haslemere (1972), which was a brilliant success. The St. Andrews residences are now in good shape and are very popular with the students. However, it's to be noted that Stirling received no new commissions in Britain between 1973 and 1980, when he was asked to undertake the extensions to the Tate Gallery.

At the same time, the work itself was evolving and acquiring an ampler vision. The unbuilt designs for the *Dorman Long Steel Manufacturers Headquarters* (1965) and the *Siemens Research Centre* (1969) show a new formal sophistication, and presage the mature stage of Stirling's practice. Leon Krier worked for a time in the office, contributing to the competition design for *Derby Civic Centre* (1970). Krier may have acted as a catalyst in raising civic and contextual issues for consideration, reinforcing the search for social meaning already present in Stirling's work. Stirling now consolidated his practice by taking his principal assistant, Michael Wilford, as his sole partner,

Town und dem *Studentenwohnheim der St. Andrews Universität* verwendete, belegen dieses neue Interesse. Wohl wegen ihrer Neuartigkeit, aber auch, weil sie bei der Bauausführung die strenge Kostenkontrolle gefährdeten, wurden diese Entwürfe von technischen Problemen verfolgt. Vorgefertigte Teile beherrschen auch das gefeierte *Olivetti Trainingszentrum* in Haslemere (1972) mit seinen Plastikpaneelen. Trotz dieses Erfolgs erhielt Stirling zwischen 1973 und 1980, als er mit den Erweiterungen der Tate Gallery beauftragt wurde, keine weiteren Aufträge in Großbritannien.

In dieser Zeit entwickelte sich Stirlings Arbeit weiter und gewann einen breiteren Horizont. Die nicht realisierten Entwürfe für den Sitz der *Dorman Long Stahlwerke* (1965) und das *Siemens Forschungszentrum* (1969) zeigen eine neues formales Raffinement und weisen auf Stirlings reife Schaffensphase voraus. Leon Krier arbeitete eine Zeitlang in seinem Büro und beteiligte sich am Wettbewerbsbeitrag für das *Bürgerzentrum von Derby* (1970). Es mag auch Kriers Einfluß zu verdanken gewesen sein, daß Stirling nun der kontextuellen Einbindung und urbanen Gestaltung noch stärkere Beachtung schenkte – eine Intensivierung der Suche nach sozialer Bedeutung, die auch schon seine früheren Arbeiten kennzeichnet. Stirling konsolidierte nun die Arbeit seines Büros und machte seinen ersten Assistenten Michael Wilford zu seinem einzigen Partner. Mit der solchermaßen umstrukturierten Firma beginnt ein neuer Abschnitt in Stirlings Karriere.

Zwei Entwürfe aus dem Jahr 1972 künden von einem neuen Selbstbewußtsein: die Renovierung und Erweiterung der *Kunstfakultät der St. Andrews Universität* und der *Olivetti Firmensitz* in Milton Keynes. Die Wettbewerbsentwürfe für das *Wallraf-Richartz Museum* in Köln und die *Kunstsammlung Nordrhein-Westfalen* in Düsseldorf von

and with the firm so restructured, embarked on a new stage in his career.

Two projects of 1971 display a new assurance: the renovation and extension of the *Arts Centre for St. Andrews University,* and the *Olivetti Headquarters* at Milton Keynes. The competition designs for the *Wallraf-Richartz Museum* at Cologne and the *Museum for Northrhine Westphalia* at Düsseldorf, both of 1975, inaugurate not so much a new series of buildings as a new phase in design philosophy. Where expression had been confined to elementary volumes combined in an abstract way, it will now be possible to design so as to combine the abstract and the representational in all the elements of the composition, and achieve a richer synthesis.

Building form will derive not only from functional and constructional analysis, but from an intention to create social meaning, even if this means adopting reminiscences of traditional forms. In a little project for a *Hotel in Meinekestrasse* at Berlin, of 1976, the street facades reach a degree of elaboration approaching the mannerism of Michael Graves, and look «postmodern», as does the study for a group of *Townhouses in Manhattan* (1978); but more typical is the drastic separation of elements and their re-combination into a loose and sometimes deliberately disjointed composition, with a result that does not look postmodern. The project for the *Dresdner Bank* at Marburg (1977), where a sinuous colonnade creates a pedestrian route through the heart of the building, is thoroughly three-dimensional and sculptural in its method.

The theme of introducing a public footpath through the heart of the building proved to be sympathetic to democratic aspirations in the new Germany. It was adopted again in the competition design for the *Neue Staatsgalerie*

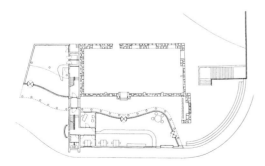

Dresdner Bank: Grundriß

Dresdner Bank: plan

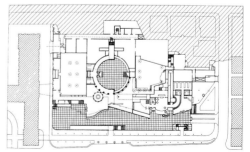

Staatsgalerie: Grundriß

Staatsgalerie: plan

1975 stellen weniger den Beginn einer neuen Reihe von Gebäuden als eine neue Phase der planerischen Philosophie der Architekten dar. Lag die Ausdruckskraft vorher allein in den elementaren, abstrakt kombinierten Volumina, verbinden sich im Entwurf nun Abstraktes und Repräsentatives in allen Kompositionselementen und gelangen zu einer umfassenderen Synthese. Die formale Gestaltung ergibt sich danach nicht mehr nur in erster Linie aus der funktionalen Analyse und den baulichen Erfordernissen, sondern orientiert sich verstärkt an der Absicht, soziale Bedeutung zu schaffen. Wenn dazu Anklänge an traditionelle Bauformen erforderlich scheinen, so werden sie ohne Zögern eingesetzt. Bei dem kleinen Projekt eines *Hotels in der Meinekestraße* (1976) in Berlin erreichen die Fassaden einen Grad der Ausarbeitung, der sie in die Nähe des Manierismus eines Michael Graves rückt. Sie wirken «postmodern», ebenso wie die Studie für ein Ensemble von *Stadthäusern in Manhattan* (1978). Noch typischer ist jedoch die schroffe Trennung der Elemente und ihre erneute Zusammensetzung in eine lose und zuweilen absichtlich zergliederte Komposition, die nicht postmodern wirkt. Der Entwurf der *Dresdner Bank* in Marburg (1977), wo eine geschwungene Kolonnade einen Fußgängerweg ins Herz des Gebäudes bildet, zeigt einen durch und durch dreidimensionalen und skulpturalen Ansatz.

Die Idee, einen öffentlichen Weg durch ein Gebäude zu führen, fand im neuen Deutschland Anklang, wo man mehr Demokratie wagen wollte. Stirling setzte sie erneut bei seinem Wettbewerbsentwurf für die *Neue Staatsgalerie* in Stuttgart ein, wo sich ein Fußweg kühn durch die zentrale Rotunde des Gartens schlängelt. Dieser Entwurf wurde allenthalben als Meisterwerk gerühmt. Die Kontextbezüge des Gebäudes zum alten Museum und den umliegenden Straßen werden hier durch einen frischen und dramatischen Einsatz moderner Technologie, durch eigenwillige Formen und leuchtende Farben ergänzt und verstärkt.

Stirling hat deutlich gemacht, daß seine Methode in der Collage alter und neuer Elemente besteht, die sowohl der jüngeren wie der ferneren Vergangenheit entstammen, die Assoziationen wecken und soziale Bedeutung schaffen.[6] Es ging ihm von Anfang an darum, Architektur als eine Kunst zu praktizieren, was für ihn bedeutete, eine geschlossene Einheit aus ausgewählten Elementen herzustellen.[7] Dies sowohl, wo sich die Gestaltungselemente aus einer funktionalen oder konstruktiven Analyse ergaben, als auch dort, wo sie sich einem eher intuitiven Verständnis ihrer möglichen sozialen oder urbanen Bedeutung verdankten. Wie er jedoch klarstellte, bedeutete dies nicht die Aufgabe von Modernität als solcher, sondern vielmehr die fortgesetzte Suche nach einer radikalen, der Moderne verpflichteten Architektur von größerem Asso-

at Stuttgart, where the footpath snakes boldly through the central rotunda. This design has been widely hailed as a masterpiece. Here contextual aspects relating the building to the old museum and the surrounding streets are invigorated by a fresh and highly dramatic use of modern technology, idiosyncratic forms and bright colours.

Stirling has made it clear that his method is to create a collage of old and new elements, taken from both distant and recent past, which will evoke associations and create social meanings.[6] He also admitted that, right from the beginning, he had always considered it proper to practise architecture as an art, which meant composing a unity out of selected elements.[7] This was true whether the elements arose from a functional or structural analysis, or from a more intuitive understanding of their potential social and civic meaning. However, as his subsequent remarks make clear, this did not mean an abandonment of modernity as such, but the continued search for a radical Modern Architecture, richer in associations, and free from the burden of utopia. It did allow him to treat architecture less solemnly, even to introduce a playful aspect, as with the car park ventilator in the podium at Staatsgalerie, which takes on the appearance of an accidental gap in the masonry. The playful aspect is given full rein in the next major commission, for the *Berlin Science Centre* (1979–1987). Here he breaks up the requirement for office space into a number of shapes that suggest a typology of historical elements – colonnade, hexagonal tower, apsidal hall, and so on. This creates a campus-like distribution very suitable for research activities, and it prevents the original palazzo, retained as the social core, from being overwhelmed by an administrative monster.

The mixture of boldness and discretion, balancing traditional and programmatic elements, continues now as a settled approach to design, an approach that always introduces surprise along with appropriateness. The extension to the *Rice School of Architecture*, in Texas, is so quiet that Philip Johnson, returning from a trip to view it, is reported to have said: «I couldn't find it». The *Sackler Gallery*, an extension to the Fogg Art Museum at Harvard, conceals a magnificent staircase and a set of harmonious galleries behind an office facade in striped brickwork. The project for a *Chemistry Building* at Columbia University bridges a site obstacle with structural panache.

In 1980 a further restructuring of the practice took place. So far the name *James Stirling and Partner*, while acknowledging Michael Wilford's unique status in the firm, evidently did not correspond to the reality of their relationship. The title now adopted – *James Stirling Michael Wilford and Associates* – better expressed the close collaboration between the two principals and the growth of

ziationsreichtum, die jedoch von allem utopischen Ballast der modernen Bewegung befreit ist. So konnte Stirling mit Architektur weniger feierlich und sogar spielerisch umgehen, wie etwa bei der Entlüftung der Tiefgarage im Sockel der Staatsgalerie, die wie eine zufällige Lücke im Mauerwerk wirkt.

Der spielerische Aspekt kommt bei Stirlings folgendem großen Auftrag voll zur Geltung, dem Berliner *Wissenschaftszentrum* (1979–1987). Hier bricht er den üblichen geschlossenen Büroblock in eine Reihe von Formen auf, die eine Typologie historischer Elemente suggerieren – Kolonnade, sechseckiger Turm, Apsidenhalle usw. Der Bau mag teurer als herkömmliche Büroblöcke sein, aber er schafft eine der Forschungsarbeit höchst angemessene universitäre Atmosphäre und verhindert, daß der Altbau von einem monströsen Büroturm erdrückt wird.

Die Mischung aus Kühnheit und Zurückhaltung, die traditionelle und programmatische Elemente ins Gleichgewicht bringt, ist nun eine konsolidierte Herangehensweise der Entwurfsarbeit, ein Ansatz, der Angemessenheit der Gestaltung und Überraschung zugleich schafft. Die Erweiterung der *Architekturfakultät der Rice University* in Texas ist so zurückhaltend, daß Philip Johnson, der von einer Reise zurückkam, gesagt haben soll: «Ich konnte sie nicht finden.» Die *Sackler Galerie*, eine Erweiterung des Fogg Art Museum in Harvard, verdeckt eine prachtvolle Treppe und eine Reihe harmonischer Ausstellungsräume hinter einer Bürofassade in gestreifter Mauerung. Der Entwurf der *Chemiefakultät der Columbia Universität* überbrückt ein Hindernis auf dem Grundstück mit einer kühnen Konstruktion.

1980 kam es zu einer weiteren Umstrukturierung des Architekturbüros. Bis dahin hatte es unter James Stirling and Partner firmiert und so zwar die herausgehobene Stellung von Michael Wilford angedeutet, war aber mit diesem Namen der Wirklichkeit ihrer Beziehung nicht gerecht geworden. Der neue Firmenname James Stirling, Michael Wilford and Associates umschrieb die Zusammenarbeit der beiden Chefs besser und spiegelte auch die Vergrößerung des Büros wider, die aufgrund der Auslandsaufträge notwendig geworden war. Das wichtigste Ergebnis dieser Neugliederung war, die Abhängigkeit von «Big Jim» zu vermindern: So konnte das Büro nach dem unerwarteten Tod Stirlings unter der Leitung von Michael Wilford mit bemerkenswerter Kontinuität weiterarbeiten. Stirling war nun weltberühmt und erhielt schließlich auch in seiner Heimat nach langen Jahren wieder einen bedeutenden Auftrag: Er wurde mit dem Entwurf der *Clore Galerie* beauftragt, einer umfangreichen Erweiterung der Tate Gallery of Modern Art (1980–1986). Man hätte meinen können, daß Stirling unter diesen Umständen mit

the practice resulting from the work undertaken abroad. This shaking down had one important result, since it reduced the dependence on Big Jim, and made it possible for the firm to continue under Michael Wilford's control after Stirling's unexpected death in 1992, with a remarkable degree of continuity.

Stirling now had a world-wide celebrity, and the British establishment finally came round to commissioning a major extension to the Tate Gallery of Modern Art – the *Clore Gallery* (1980–1986). As his first major commission in Britain for a number of years, Stirling might have been expected to exercise caution, but compromise was not in his nature. Instead, he proposed an entrance and staircase sequence that seemed aggressively formalistic, accentuated by feisty colours, and he showed himself indifferent to the cacophony of criticism that followed. He was helped by the fact that the galleries themselves were very effective, the relationship to the main gallery deferential, and that the result was praised by the doyen of architectural historians, Sir John Summerson, Curator of the Soane Museum. Summerson wrote approving the result as producing the kind of strange space that Soane would have enjoyed, and gave his article the title «Vitruvius Ludens», the architect at play.[8]

The design for the *Performing Arts Center* at Cornell University is one of Stirling's happiest. It is compact, built to a tight budget, yet breathes a generosity of spirit that makes it just right for a university building mediating between Town and Gown. The colonnade fronting Cascadilla gorge, and so making a full frontal gesture to the campus on the other side, is entered, not on axis, but at either end – from the street and from the car park. The arrangement works functionally, so that in effect the formal is used informally. The street front and the octagonal corner tower, while they shadow the image of a Florentine church, work functionally in an entirely informal way: the main window is not to light a nave, but to allow the dancers to appear momentarily to the townspeople; the tower is not a campanile, but an elevator shaft; and the octagon is not a baptistery, but a bus stop and information pavilion. Nothing could more clearly demonstrate the light-heartedness of the Stirling approach, while illustrating his continued commitment to practical planning. The little auditorium, he hoped, would be perfect for Mozart, and indeed, with its conical column caps stolen from industrial warehouses, it epitomises the gentle irony with which Stirling mixes old and new in a highly personal synthesis.

In a similar vein to Cornell, the project for a *Public Library* at Latina is one of the finest designs among Stirling's work, and it is greatly to be regretted that it was not realised. It shows a similar interest in the task of reconcil-

Vorsicht zu Werke gehen würde, aber Kompromisse waren seine Sache nicht. Statt dessen entwarf er, noch betont von schriller Farbigkeit, einen Eingang und eine Treppensequenz in einem aggressiv formalistisch wirkenden Stil und zeigte sich unbeeindruckt von dem Proteststurm, den er damit auslöste. Zu seinen Gunsten wirkte sich aus, daß die Ausstellungsräume selbst sehr effizient waren und die Beziehung der Erweiterung zum Hauptgebäude respektvoll zurückhaltend war. Zudem lobte der Doyen der britischen Architekturhistoriker, Sir John Summerson, Kurator des Soane Museums, das Ergebnis. Summerson schrieb zustimmend, daß Stirling die Art von seltsamem Raum geschaffen habe, den er sich für das Soane Museum gewünscht hätte, und betitelte seinen Artikel «Vitruvius Ludens», der spielende Architekt.[8]

Die *Fakultät für Darstellende Künste* der Cornell Universität *(Performing Arts Center)* gehört zu den glücklichsten von Stirlings Projekten. Sie ist kompakt und mit geringen Finanzmitteln verwirklicht, und doch atmet sie eine Freizügigkeit, die für eine Universität geradezu ideal ist und zwischen Stadt und Hochschule vermittelt. Die Kolonnade entlang der gesamten Campusfront gegenüber der Cayuga Schlucht, eine architektonische Geste zum Universitätsgelände dahinter, wird nicht von ihrer Querachse, sondern von den beiden Seiten betreten, von der Straße bzw. dem Parkplatz. Dieser informelle Einsatz funktionaler Gestaltung gilt auch für die Straßenfront und den achteckigen Turm, die das Bild einer florentinischen Kirche andeuten; nur daß das Hauptfenster kein Mittelschiff erleuchtet, sondern den Passanten für Augenblicke die Tänzer im Inneren des Arts Center zeigt. Und der Turm ist kein Glockenturm, sondern eine Bushaltestelle und ein Informationspavillon. Nichts könnte die Unbeschwertheit von Stirlings Architektur und gleichzeitig sein beständiges Bemühen um praktische Planung deutlicher machen. Das kleine Auditorium würde sich, so hoffte er, vorzüglich für Mozart eignen, und wirklich drücken die kegelförmigen Säulen, die der Lagerhausarchitektur entlehnt sind, die leichtfüßige Ironie aus, mit der Stirling Altes und Neues zu einer sehr persönlichen Synthese fügt.

Wie das Performing Arts Centre der Cornell Universität gehört die *Stadtbücherei in Latina* (Italien) zu den besten Entwürfen Stirlings, und es ist höchst bedauerlich, daß sie nicht realisiert wurde. Der Entwurf zeigt ein vergleichbares Bemühen, interne Erfordernisse und äußere Bedingungen in Einklang zu bringen. Erkennbar ist das wirkliche Interesse an der Stadt und der Wunsch, ihr einen bürgernahen Ort der Begegnung zu geben. Die Architekten unternahmen eine genaue Analyse der funktionalen Erfordernisse, die schließlich zu einer Trennung von Leihbücherei und der wissenschaftlichen Handbibliothek führte. Diese beiden Bereich wurden zu Zwillingstrom-

ing internal requirements and external site conditions. There was a genuine interest in the town and a wish to provide it with a social facility. The architects made a close study of the functional requirements, leading in the end to a distinction between the lending library and the science or reference library, and these two centres became twin drums marking the two main reading rooms. The adoption of the circular drum form is undoubtedly related to Asplund's famous library for Stockholm, which sanctified a modern return to the stark geometries of Ledoux. In the design for the *Bibliothèque de France* (1989), where the chosen design would become one of President Mitterand's *Grands Projets,* the interest in Ledoux is clear. But at Latina, such purely architectural ambitions are kept in check, and the result is much more modest. The charm of the design lies in the clarity of the geometry that reconciles drum and roof pitch. The drums marginally exceed the height of the roof ridge, so that they do not dominate it, but appear almost as undulations in the sloping flanks. This discretion is masterly – it is what gives the building its originality, imprinting it with a Stirling character and an economy of effect, while giving it a unique personality. But the rough sketches show that this solution did not come without trial and error. An early sketch shows a single drum on centre, another shows two drums associated with semi-circular ends to the building. The process is not one of applying a known solution, but of searching for compatibility between different forms and their functional implications.

There is a constant play between unity and variety. The treatment of the two libraries is not identical: in the science library the ascending tiers of book access move successively back to the edge, leaving a large central space, which has the effect of emphasising the public nature of science; while in the lending library the ascending tiers move progressively towards the centre, enclosing a quiet central space lit through the aperture left at the top, emphasizing the private nature of individual study.

Another feature worthy of comment is the loggia that embellishes the facade to the garden. The loggia is of a type that greatly preoccupied Stirling at this time. Throughout his work the loggia appears in various guises, but at the Wissenschaftszentrum (1979), at Cornell (1983), and at *Compton Verney Opera House* (1989) it adopts a singular character: the single roof pitch is turned through ninety degrees in the end bays, exposing the cross section as a terminal motif – cut off flush at Cornell, but in the other cases «carried around the corner» by one bay, as if defining the beginning of an enclosed courtyard. The actors' courtyard at Pompeii exhibits exactly this form, although there it is the result of the subsequent destruction of most of the colonnade; nevertheless, when

meln, in denen nach außen erkennbar die beiden Hauptlesesäle untergebracht sind.

Die Verwendung der Trommelform ist ohne Zweifel von Gunnar Asplunds berühmter Stadtbibliothek von Stockholm inspiriert, die eine moderne Rückkehr zur reinen Geometrie des klassizistischen französischen Architekten Claude-Nicolas Ledoux' einleitete. Beim Entwurf für die *Bibliothèque de France* (1989), eines von Präsident Mitterands Großprojekten, ist Stirlings Interesse an Ledoux deutlich zu spüren. Aber in Latina sind diese rein architektonischen Ambitionen kontrolliert, und so kommt bei diesem Entwurf eine weit größere Bescheidenheit zum Ausdruck. Der Charme des Entwurfs liegt in der Klarheit der Geometrie, die Trommelform und Schrägdach versöhnt. Die Trommeln überragen den First nur geringfügig, so daß sie es nicht dominieren, sondern beinahe wie Wellen an den abfallenden Dachseiten erscheinen. Diese Zurückhaltung ist meisterhaft – aus ihr bezieht das Gebäude seine Originalität, seinen «Stirling-Charakter», und erhält zugleich eine einzigartige Identität. Aber die Rohentwürfe zeigen, daß diese Lösung keine spontane Eingebung war, sondern erst durch viel Probieren gefunden werden mußte. Eine frühe Skizze zeigt eine einzelne Trommel im Zentrum, eine weitere zwei Trommeln, deren

employed as a motif, it suggests incompletion as well as the modern virtue of exposing the structure. This treatment emphasises the way the colonnade receives the outside space: at Latina it embraces the public garden, and regularises the relation of the building to its triangular site, stating clearly its civic responsibility, and entering it into the public realm.

The project for a *British Telecom Headquarters* (1983) is of special interest because of the way it recycles the elements invented for the Berlin Science Centre, now given the role of a central social nexus within a giant corporate layout. Layouts at this scale were proposed in the projects for Bayer and Siemens, so that the search for urban form was pursued outside of the city proper, in the desire to bring social meaning to the corporate colossus. The successfully completed layout for *Temasek Polytechnique* (1991–1996) has a similar resonance, although it is an educational campus and benefits accordingly.

The design which Stirling prepared for the competition to extend the *National Gallery* in London (1985) was close to his heart, and he was very disappointed not to win. In this case the general layout was comparatively neo-classical, with all the spaces organised around a north-south axis at right angles to the main frontage: the playfulness

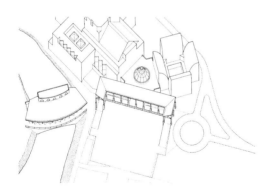

Axonometrie der Loggia des Opernhauses in Compton Verney

Axonometric drawing of loggia of Compton Verney Opera House

Hof der Schauspieler, Pompeji

Actors' Courtyard, Pompeii

Hälften das Gebäude an seinen Enden hablkreisförmig abschließen. Die Methode besteht nicht darin, eine schon bekannte Lösung anzuwenden, sondern nach der Vereinbarkeit von unterschiedlichen Formen und ihrer funktionalen Implikationen zu suchen.

Es gibt hier ein beständiges Spiel zwischen Einheit und Vielfalt. Die Behandlung der beiden Bibliotheken ist nicht identisch: In der wissenschaftlichen Bibliothek steigen die Bücherregale zur Rundwand hin an und lassen einen großen zentralen Bereich frei, der den öffentlichen Charakter der Wissenschaft betont. In der Leihbücherei dagegen erhöhen sich die Regale zur Raummitte und umschließen ein ruhiges Zentrum, das durch eine Öffnung in der Decke erleuchtet wird und den privaten Charakter individuellen Studierens und Lesens betont.

Ein anderes erwähnenswertes Element ist die Loggia, die die Fassade zum Garten ziert. Es handelt sich um eine Form, mit der sich Stirling damals sehr beschäftigte. In seinem ganzen Werk erscheint die Loggia in verschiedenen Gestalten; beim Wissenschaftszentrum (1979), der Cornell Universität (1983) und bei der *Oper in Compton Verney* (1989) sind die Loggien ähnlich: Hier wird sie jeweils von einem Schrägdach abgeschlossen, dessen letzte Felder abknicken und so den Dachquerschnitt in ein abschließendes Motiv verwandeln. Bei der Cornell Universität schließt es bündig ab, aber in den anderen Fällen wird ein Feld der Loggia «um die Ecke» geführt, als würde es den Beginn eines umschlossenen Innenhofs definieren. Der Hof der Schauspieler in Pompeji zeigt genau diese Form, obwohl sie hier Ergebnis der späteren Zerstörung eines Großteils der Kolonnade ist; als Motiv kommt darin jedoch die Idee von Unabgeschlossenheit ebenso wie das zeit-

comes in when the entrance is not allowed to share this axis, but joins it at right angles. In this way it faces sideways towards the main building in a manner analogous to the entrance at the Clore. In addition, the volume of the galleries is broken into three parallel volumes also running east-west, the front one of which is emphasized by an «Egyptian» cornice, similar to that on the main gallery at the Staatsgalerie. Stirling used to talk about the importance of *presence* in a building: the point where the building axis comes through to the front is marked here by a large window, similar to that at Cornell, and this elevation, facing south, has a magnificent presence that would have contributed in a major way to the London scene, while the city of Stuttgart is fortunate to have acquired the presence of the extraordinary tower of the *Music Academy*.

The *Braun Headquarters* building was commissioned in 1986 and completed in 1992, very shortly before Stirling's death. Walter Nägeli, who had worked on the Berlin Science Centre, became a collaborator of James Stirling Michael Wilford and Associates for this job.

This is a working environment, and the strategy here is to create a clean front. Across the valley floor runs a concrete wall, which screens most of the working complex from public view, and in particular the multi-storey car park, the use of which avoids the usual sea of parked cars. This wall is of double construction and contains a whole battery of staircases to allow of access down to the glazed bridge that fronts the wall and joins both sides of the layout.

This construction, with its canted timber piers, is extraordinary in itself. The corridor narrows and dips to the mid-

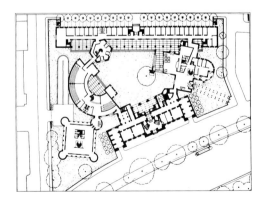

Wissenschaftszentrum Berlin: Grundriß

Berlin Science Centre: plan

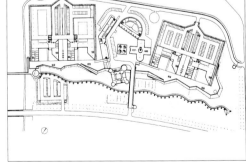

Sitz der British Telecom, Milton Keynes: Grundriß

British Telecom Headquarters, Milton Keynes: plan

genössische Bestreben zum Ausdruck, die Konstruktion sichtbar werden zu lassen. Die Behandlung betont die Art, wie die Kolonnade den Außenraum «empfängt»: In Latina faßt sie den öffentlichen Garten ein, reguliert die Beziehung des Gebäudes zum dreieckigen Grundstück und betont in der Öffnung zum Außenraum den urbanen Charakter des Gebäudes.

Der Entwurf für den *Sitz der British Telecom* (1983) ist von Interesse wegen der Art, wie hier die für das Berliner Wissenschaftszentrum entwickelten Elemente aufgenommen werden und nun einen zentralen sozialen Schnittpunkt innerhalb eines sehr großen Firmenkomplexes definieren. Planungen in dieser Größenordnung wurden auch für Bayer, Siemens und für das *Temasek Polytechnikum* (1991–1996) entwickelt. So läßt sich die Suche nach sozialer Bedeutung auch außerhalb der Stadt selbst fortsetzen.

Der Entwurf für die Erweiterung der *Nationalgalerie* in London (1985) lag Stirling sehr am Herzen, und er war sehr enttäuscht, als er den Wettbewerb nicht gewann. In diesem Fall war die Gesamtgestaltung verhältnismäßig

dle, directly over the water source to the lake. The lake and its adjacent landscape are designed to stress the formal aspects of the layout, and another water source feeds the canal which separates the two access roads – one for workers, one for visitors, so that these elements are tied together into a single sinuous line that seems like a parody of the English landscape tradition. Finally, the visitor's approach road rises on a cantilevered structure to set us down at the outer end of the administration block. Most dramatic of all is the nature of the supports to the administration building – a single row of columns with massive conical caps, running along the centre line of the block (reminiscent of the thesis design of 1950). The actual columns are concealed below the podium or in brick boxes, leaving only the caps visible, to support the three floors of offices above. The sense of power in reserve created by these supports makes for a strange atmosphere in the reception area, at the same time awe-inspiring and glamorous. The setting, the furniture, the lighting could well be appropriate for a fashion house. In the corridor which leads off to the glazed bridge natural and artificial

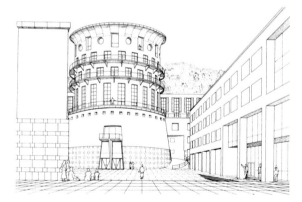

Musikakademie, Stuttgart:
Axonometrische Zeichnung des Turms vom Stadtpark aus

Music Academy, Stuttgart:
axonometric rendering of tower as seen from city park

«Die Qualität von Präsenz»
Nationalgalerie, London:
axonometrische Zeichnung des
Entwurfs der Straßenfassade

«The quality of presence»
National Gallery, London:
axonometric rendering of proposed
street elevation

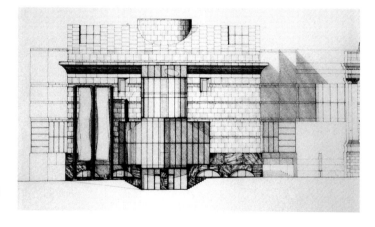

klassizistisch: Alle Bereiche gliedern sich um eine recht-winklig zur Hauptfront des Gebäudes verlaufende Nord-Süd-Achse. Die spielerische Qualität des Entwurfs rührt hier daher, daß der Eingang nicht auf diese Achse ausge-richtet, sondern rechtwinklig zu ihr angelegt ist. So blickt er seitwärts zum Hauptgebäude, ähnlich wie der Eingang der Clore Gallery. Zusätzlich ist der Baukörper mit den Ausstellungsräumen in drei parallele Volumina aufgebro-chen, die in Ost-West-Richtung verlaufen; das vorderste wird von einem «ägyptischen» Gesims betont, das Ähn-lichkeit mit dem Gesimselement der Staatsgalerie hat. Stirling sprach gerne von der *Präsenz* eines Gebäudes; der Punkt, an dem die Gebäudeachse auf die Gebäudefront stößt und durch ein Fenster markiert wird, ähnlich wie in Cornell, und diese nach Süden liegende Fassade der Er-weiterung der Londoner Nationalgalerie hat eine wun-derbare Präsenz, die eine große Bereicherung für das Stadtbild von London gewesen wäre – so wie heute die Stadt Stuttgart die Präsenz des außergewöhnlichen Turms ihrer *Musikakademie* schätzt.

Mit dem Entwurf der *Braun Werksanlagen* wurde Stirling 1986 betraut. 1992, kurz vor seinem Tod, wurden sie fer-tiggestellt. Walter Nägeli, der schon am Wissenschafts-zentrum in Berlin beteiligt war, arbeitete auch in diesem Fall wieder mit James Stirling, Michael Wilford and Asso-ciates zusammen. Der Ansatz war hier, eine glatte Front zu schaffen. Durch den Talgrund läuft eine Betonmauer, die einen Großteil der Produktionsstätten abschirmt, be-sonders das mehrgeschossige Parkhaus, mit dem das üb-liche Meer geparkter Autos vermieden wird. Die Mauer ist zweiwandig und enthält eine ganze Batterie von Treppen, die zur verglasten Brücke vor ihr führen, welche die bei-den Seiten des Komplexes verbindet.
Diese Konstruktion mit ihren geneigten Holzpfeilern ist für sich genommen schon außergewöhnlich. Der Korridor verengt sich und senkt sich zur Mitte hin direkt über die Wasserquelle zum See. Der See und die umliegende Land-schaft betonen in ihrer Gestaltung den formalen Aspekt des Ensembles. Eine weitere Wasserquelle speist den Kanal, der die beiden Zugangsstraßen – eine für die Mit-arbeiter, die andere für Besucher – voneinander trennt, so daß diese beiden Elemente zu einer einzigen gewunde-nen Linie verbunden sind, die wie eine Parodie der Tradi-tion englischer Landschaftsgärten wirkt. Schließlich führt die Zufahrtsstraße die Besucher über eine vorspringende Brücke zum äußeren Ende des Verwaltungsblocks. Den dramatisch wirkungsvollsten Eindruck machen die Pfeiler des Verwaltungsgebäudes – eine einzige Reihe massiver Säulen mit kegelförmigen Säulenköpfen, die entlang der Mittellinie des Blocks verlaufen (und an Stirlings Diplom-entwurf von 1950 erinnern). Die eigentlichen Säulen sind

lights like television sets arranged in a staggered pattern make a poetic transition to the central space from which the whole frontage can be viewed. These elements pro-ject the image of an unusual and powerful company.
So this building can be appreciated at different levels. First, it is a highly efficient computer-based industrial in-stallation. Secondly, it is a sophisticated public relations exercise. Thirdly, it is full of resonances and echoes that express an attitude about the state of architecture in our time. At a more abstract level, the building spans the val-ley as some combination of bridge and dam, uniting front and back, and placing the project simultaneously into na-ture and into culture. That all these resonances should exist in an industrial installation is something of a sur-prise, except that one may reflect that the industrial in-stallation was after all the very source of the ideology which has made modern architecture.
It is no surprise that this kind of architecture should ac-commodate easily to existing conditions. Two art gallery extensions illustrate this: the *Thyssen-Bornemisza Gallery* (1986) and the *Palazzo Citterio Art Gallery* at the Brera Museum in Milan (1987). They join effortlessly with the original buildings, but also introduce some stunning episodes (such as the single cupola support in the centre of the courtyard) that far exceed the demand for simple re-organisation. These designs are particularly sensitive to the landscape setting, and this is true also of the com-petition design for the extension of the *Glyndebourne Opera House* (1988), which uses a colonnade to frame the view out to the landscape, and retains the old play-house structure as a restaurant area. In the project for the Opera House at Compton Verney, the integration of gar-den layout with the building elements achieves a more dramatic resolution.
Accommodation with the city also distinguishes the Music Academy adjoining the Staatsgalerie at Stuttgart. Here it is not a matter of a single building, but of a co-herent shaping of the city. The urban design aspect of the project is as important as its architectural quality. The most striking feature is the substantial cylindrical tower in the middle of the building, intended to take its place as one of the many «stubby towers» that are characteristic of this city. From the roof terrace of the tower there is a splendid view of the park and the city centre, and the tower itself is visible across the park, so there is a strong sense of connection and fulfilment at the urban design scale. The tower terminates in a remarkable coved cornice that echoes the cornice on the Staatsgalerie. In response to the vegetation already engulfing the court of the Staatsgalerie in an atmosphere of Piranesian doom, it raises against the sky windowless openings that suggest a gutted interior, and that can just as easily be seen to

unter dem Sockel verdeckt und mit Ziegelstein ummauert. So sind nur die Säulenköpfe sichtbar, auf denen die drei Bürogeschosse ruhen. Der Eindruck verhaltener Kraft, den diese Pfeiler hervorrufen, schafft eine seltsame, zugleich ehrfurchtgebietende und berückende Atmosphäre im Empfangsbereich. Der Ort, die Ausstattung und die Beleuchtung wären auch für ein Modehaus angemessen. Im Korridor, der zur verglasten Brücke führt, schaffen künstliche und natürliche Lichtquellen, die wie Fernsehschirme wirken und versetzt angeordnet sind, einen poetischen Übergang zum zentralen Raum, von dem aus die ganze Gebäudefront zu überblicken ist. Diese Elemente geben einer ungewöhnlichen und bedeutenden Firma bildhaften Ausdruck.

So stellt sich dieser Komplex in verschiedenen Perspektiven dar: Als hocheffiziente, computergesteuerte industrielle Produktionsstätte; als raffinierte Repräsentationsstätte und drittens als Ensemble, in dem die Schwingungen und

speak of poetic retribution. Yet the way in which these openings invade the curve of the cornice projects an image which is far from neo-classical, has mechanical associations like a turbine housing, and is certainly unexpected and highly original.

The pace of work in the Stirling Wilford office quickened through the eighties. Invited competitions followed each other in quick succession. The project for a *Cinema Palace* for the Venice Film Festival was done in collaboration with Marlies Hentrup, and makes an enjoyable play between the regular columns, the zig-zag glazing that streaks between them, and the approach ramp. The *Biennale Bookshop* is a gem of a building, combining formal play with a sense of occasion, prompting the philosopher Richard Wollheim in his comments to utter the word *Beauty.*[9]

At the same time, the scope of the work was changing,

Kirche in Ravello in Süditalien

Church at Ravello in Southern Italy

Teilansicht des Wohnturms im Projekt für Canary Wharf, London

Detail of residential tower in project for Canary Wharf, London

Echos spürbar werden, in denen sich eine Position zur Architektur unserer Zeit mitteilt. In einer abstrakteren Perspektive bildet der Komplex eine sich durch das Tal ziehende, Vorder- und Hinterseite vereinende Brücke oder einen Damm, und darin rückt das Ensemble in einen Schnittpunkt von Natur und Kultur. Daß ein Industriegebäude all diese Resonanzen aufweist, ist überraschend; man sollte sich allerdings vor Augen halten, daß die Moderne schließlich ihre entscheidenden Triebkräfte aus der Architektur von Industriestätten bezog.

Kein Wunder, daß sich diese Art von Architektur ohne jede Schwierigkeit vorhandenen Bedingungen anpaßt. Dies machen zwei Erweiterungen von Kunstmuseen deutlich, die *Sammlung Thyssen-Bornemisza* (1986) und die *Kunstsammlung Palazzo Citterio* des Brera Museums in Mailand (1987). Mühelos verbinden sie sich mit den vorhandenen Gebäuden, setzen aber auch verblüffende bauliche Akzente (wie die Kuppelstütze im Zentrum des Hofes beim Palazzo Citterio), die weit über das Erfordernis einer Neustrukturierung hinausgehen. Diese Entwürfe reagieren besonders einfühlsam auf ihren räumlichen Kontext, und dies gilt auch für den Wettbewerbsentwurf für die Erweiterung der *Oper Glyndebourne* (1988), bei dem die Architekten eine Kolonnade einsetzen, um den Blick in die Landschaft zu rahmen, und die alte Spielstätte als Restaurant erhalten. Beim Projekt des Opernhauses in Compton Verney, erreicht die Integration von Gartengestaltung, Restaurant und – erneut – einer Kolonnade eine noch dramatischere Lösung.

Auch die Musikakademie neben der Staatsgalerie in Stuttgart paßt sich hervorragend in die Stadt ein. Hier geht es nicht allein um ein einzelnes Gebäude, sondern um eine kohärente Stadtgestaltung. Der stadtplanerische Aspekt des Entwurfs ist ebenso wichtig wie seine architektonische Qualität. Das überraschendste Merkmal ist hier der massive zylindrische Turm in der Gebäudemitte, der seinen Platz unter den vielen stumpfen Türmen einnehmen soll, die für die Stadt charakteristisch sind. Von der Dachterrasse des Turms bietet sich ein herrlicher Blick über den Park und das Stadtzentrum, während der Turm seinerseits vom Park aus sichtbar ist, so daß hier in stadtplanerischer Hinsicht ein hohes Maß an Kohärenz und Geschlossenheit erreicht wird. Der Turm schließt mit einem bemerkenswerten gewölbten Gesims ab, das an das Gesims der Staatsgalerie erinnert. In Reaktion auf die schon vorhandene Vegetation, die den Hof der Staatsgalerie in eine dunkle, an die Stiche des italienischen Barockkünstlers Giovanni Battista Piranesi erinnernden Atmosphäre taucht, strebt der Turm mit fensterlosen Öffnungen gen Himmel, die den Anschein eines ausgehöhlten Innenraums erwecken. Und doch schafft die Art, wie diese Öffnungen auf die Wölbung des Gesimses

with larger projects beginning to predominate. In the *Biological Sciences Library* in Irvine (1988–1992), we see an interesting hybrid where the strict neo-classicism of the outer surfaces is offset by the open, modernist facades to the courtyard. The distinction is not only a formal one, but relates to the degree of exposure to sunlight, and it also has social implications, in that the courtyard is full of people. In the *Stadium Development* at Seville (1988) the architects show great skill in channelling crowd movements within the substantial podium, while providing sites above the podium for two office blocks and a hotel, all defined by a powerful and varied geometry. A similar strongarm geometry appears in the projects for the *Disney Philharmonic Hall* in Los Angeles (1988), the Bibliothèque de France for Paris (1989), the *Tokyo International Forum* (1989) and the *Kyoto Centre* (1991).

The Seville hotel is remarkable for the way the geometry varies upwards in successive stages, superimposing cylinder upon hexagon, hexagon upon triangle, a diminishing series which reminds one of the Saracen churches to be found on the south-west shores of Italy.

This geometry is used with great effect in the project for a large *Residential Development at Canary Wharf* (1988). Here the facades are organised on a unit of glazing derived from Mies van der Rohe's Lake Shore Apartments, so they have a unitary character which, however is not allowed to inhibit the assertive geometrical variations. The perspective drawing gives some idea of how this riverside garden would have addressed the Thames westward, affirming its presence to the city of London, just as the courtyard in the Florey Building for Oxford University addressed the older colleges to which it related.

The vigorous way with large layouts is evident in three recent projects: *Temasek Polytechnic*, in Singapore, is already complete; the *Lowry Centre* at Salford has received Millenium funding from the British government and is expected to be complete in 2000; and the *Abando Passenger Interchange* at Bilbao is, hopefully, only delayed by the stringency imposed on European budgets by the Maastricht conditions. All of these exhibit an energetic control of complex layouts using clear geometrical units, each element marked both by its immediate function and by the part it plays in the total composition, with no trace of routine development clichès.

Stirling had played a varying role in these projects before his untimely death in 1992 left their completion in the hands of Michael Wilford. The faithfulness with which this has been done is evident in the Music Academy in Stuttgart, and above all in the offices at *No. 1 Poultry*, in the City of London, the design of which was begun in 1986 and the construction of which is now complete: in

stoßen, ein Bild, das alles andere als klassizistisch wirkt, sondern – überraschend und sehr originell – dem Turm fast das Aussehen eines Turbinenhauses gibt.

Das Arbeitstempo im Architektenbüro von Stirling und Wilford erhöhte sich in den achtziger Jahren. Einladungen zu Wettbewerben folgten rasch aufeinander. Der Entwurf für einen *Filmpalast* für die Filmfestspiele in Venedig entstand in Zusammenarbeit mit Marlies Hentrup und zeigt ein ansprechendes Spiel zwischen gleichmäßigen Säulen, den Fensterstreifen, die in Zickzacklinie dazwischen gesetzt sind, und der Zugangsrampe. Der *Biennale Buchladen*, bei dem Stirling eng mit Thomas Muirhead zusammenarbeitete, ist ein architektonisches Kleinod, ein Gebäude, das formales Spiel und Taktgefühl vereint und den Philosophen Richard Wollheim von *Schönheit* schwärmen ließ.[9] Gleichzeitig änderte sich in den Achtzigern die Art der Projekte, und größere Entwürfe gewannen langsam die Oberhand. Die *Biologiebibliothek der Universität von Kalifornien* in Irvine (1988–1992) weist mit ihren streng klassizistischen Außenfassaden, die mit der offenen, modernistischen Hoffassade kontrastieren, eine interessante Hybridität auf. Bei dem *Stadionskomplex* in Sevilla beweisen die Architekten großes Geschick, die Menschenströme durch einen massiven Sockel zu kanalisieren, und schaffen darüber Raum für zwei Büroblöcke und ein Hotel, die sich durch eine kraftvolle und abwechslungsreiche Geometrie auszeichnen. Eine ähnlich kraftvolle Geometrie erscheint im Entwurf für die *Disney Philharmonie* in Los Angeles (1988), der Bibliothèque de France in Paris (1989), dem *Tokio International Forum* (1989) und dem *Kyoto Centre* (1991).

Das zum Stadion gehörende Hotel in Sevilla sticht durch die sich in aufeinanderfolgenden Stufen nach oben abwechselnde Geometrie hervor, bei der ein Zylinder auf ein Sechseck und ein Sechseck auf ein Dreieck gesetzt sind, eine abnehmende Reihe, die an sarazenische Kirchen erinnert, wie man sie an der Südwestküste Italiens findet. Diese Geometrie setzen die Architekten mit großer Wirkung bei der *Wohnanlage Canary Wharf* (1988) ein. Hier sind die Fassaden mit einem von Mies van der Rohes Lake Shore Apartments herrührenden Glasmodul gestaltet, so daß sie ein einheitliches Erscheinungsbild gewinnen, das jedoch die kraftvolle Wirkung der geometrischen Variationen nicht beeinträchtigt. Die perspektivische Zeichnung gibt eine Ahnung davon, wie sich dieser Wohnpark am Flußufer auf die Westseite der Themse ausgewirkt und sich gegenüber der City von London behauptet hätte, so wie das *Florey-Gebäude des Queen's College* in Oxford mit seinem Hof auf die älteren Colleges Bezug nimmt.

Die kraftvolle Durchgestaltung ausgedehnter Komplexe zeigt sich an drei jüngeren Projekten: dem bereits fertig-

the eyes of this critic, another masterpiece. It holds up superbly in a confluence of famous buildings by Lutyens, Cooper, Dance and Soane, a city building at a meeting of city streets, modern, classical, and romantic all at once. Stirling's hand will also be evident in the *Apartments at 5–7 Carlton Gardens*, designed in 1988, on which construction has finally started.

Now we have a series of designs which Stirling never saw, but such is the closeness of the Stirling-Wilford collaboration that this fact hardly shows. Michael Wilford's hand is fully revealed in the *Architecture School* at Newcastle, Australia, a spirited exercise in steel construction that owes nothing to anyone. But in the *Sto AG Headquarters and Manufacturing Plant* at Weizen and Hamburg, and the *Cinemaxx and Music School* at Mannheim, it seems as if Stirling's voice is still heard in the office.

The design for the *British Embassy in Berlin* will establish Michael Wilford's serious reputation as a worthy successor to a man that many would have found it difficult to follow. This design necessarily defers on the exterior to the solemnity of Berlin planning controls, but achieves within the building envelope a lively sequence of spaces that mixes surprise with decorum. The Stirling philosophy is surely alive and well when Wilford can affirm, with an eloquence not evident before:

«I am interested in exploring the combination of function and economy with new strategic permutations of the monumental and the informal … as part of a broader and more profound search for a robust modern architecture which contributes to the evolution of the city and contemporary culture.»[10]

gestellten Temasek Polytechnikum in Singapur; dem *Lowry Centre* in Manchester, das Gelder aus dem «Millenium»-Fonds der britischen Regierung erhielt und voraussichtlich im Jahr 2000 fertiggestellt wird, und der *Abando Umsteigebahnhof* in Bilbao, dessen Realisierung sich hoffentlich nur aufgrund der Sparmaßnahmen zur Erfüllung der Maastricht-Kriterien verzögert. Alle drei Projekte zeigen eine energische Kontrolle komplexer Entwürfe auf der Basis klarer geometrischer Einheiten, deren einzelne Elemente ohne eine Spur von stereotyper Entwicklungsroutine sowohl durch ihre unmittelbare Funktion wie als Teile der Gesamtkomposition charakterisiert sind.

In verschiedenem Maße beaufsichtigte Stirling die Ausführung all dieser Projekte bis zu seinem vorzeitigen Tod, als Michael Wilford ihre Fertigstellung übernehmen mußte. Wie gewissenhaft er seine Aufgabe erfüllte, zeigt die Musikhochschule in Stuttgart, vor allem aber der *Bürokomplex Poultry Nr. 1* in der City von London, ein Meisterwerk in meinen Augen, dessen Entwurf 1986 begann und der heute nahezu fertiggestellt ist. Inmitten berühmter Gebäude von Edwin Lutyens, Thomas Edwin Cooper, George Dance und John Soane behauptet sich dieses Stadtgebäude an einer städtischen Straßenkreuzung souverän und wirkt modern, klassisch und romantisch zur gleichen Zeit.

Eine Reihe von neuen Entwürfen hat Stirling nicht mehr erlebt, aber daß dies kaum auffällt, belegt, wie eng die Zusammenarbeit von Stirling und Wilford war. Michael Wilfords Handschrift zeigt sich vollends in der *Erweiterung der Architekturfakultät* in Newcastle, Australien, eine kühne Stahlkonstruktion, die keinem Vorbild etwas schuldet. Aber bei den *Werksanlagen der Sto AG* im badenwürttembergischen Weizen und in Hamburg sowie beim *Cinemaxx* und der *Musikschule* in Mannheim scheint es, als vernehme man noch Stirlings Stimme.

Der Entwurf der *Britischen Botschaft* in Berlin wird Michael Wilfords Reputation als würdiger Nachfolger eines Mannes bestätigen, in dessen Fußstapfen nicht viele hätten treten können. Dieser Entwurf orientiert sich notwendigerweise an den Berliner Bauauflagen, aber er schafft innerhalb der Gebäudehülle eine lebendige Raumfolge, die eine überraschende und dezente Gestaltung in sich vereint. Stirlings Überzeugungen sind zweifellos noch lebendig, wenn Michael Wilford selbstbewußt feststellt:

«Ich interessiere mich für die Kombination von Funktion und Wirtschaftlichkeit mit neuen Verwendungen monumentaler und informeller Elemente... als Teil einer breiteren und tieferen Suche nach einer robusten zeitgenössischen Architektur, die zur Entwicklung der Stadt und der zeitgenössischen Kultur beiträgt.» [10]

Apartmenthaus Carlton Gardens 5–7, London

Apartments at 5–7 Carlton Gardens, London

Bürokomplex Poultry Street Nr. 1, London

Offices at No 1 Poultry, London

1 Vgl. *Casabella*, März 1975.
2 Vgl. Colin Rowes Einleitung in *James Stirling – Buildings and Projects,* London: Architectural Press und New York: Rizzoli, 1984, S. 19.
3 Colin Rowe, «The Mathematics of the Ideal Villa», in *The Architectural Review,* 1947. Deutsch: «Die Mathematik der idealen Villa», in Colin Rowe, *Die Mathematik der idealen Villa und andere Essays,* Basel/Berlin/Boston: Birkhäuser, 1998.
4 Colin Rowe, «Mannerism and Modern Architecture», in *The Architectural Review,* 1950. Deutsch: «Manierismus und die Moderne», in Colin Rowe, *Die Mathematik der idealen Villa und andere Essays,* Basel/Berlin/Boston: Birkhäuser, 1998.
5 Persönliche Mitteilung von Moses Finley, Jurymitglied, später Direktor des Darwin College: Seiner Ansicht nach wurden Stirling ungerechtfertigt Mängel vorgeworfen, die er zu vermeiden versucht hatte.
6 Vgl. Stirlings Rede anläßlich der Verleihung der Royal Gold Medal, veröffentlicht in *Architectural Design,* Nr. 7–8,1980.
7 Vgl. Stirlings Rede anläßlich der Verleihung des Pritzker Preises für Architektur: «For me, right from the beginning, the art of architecture has always been the priority», veröffentlicht in *Architectural Design Profile,* London: Academy Editions, 1982.
8 Sir John Summerson, «Vitruvius Ludens», in *The Architectural Review,* März 1983; ebenso, vom selben Autor: «Vitruvius Ridens, or Laughter at the Tate», in *The Architectural Review,* Juni 1987.
9 Richard Wollheim, Kommentar in *Modern Painters,* Winter 1992.
10 Vgl. *James Stirling + Michael Wilford,* in *Architectural Monographs* No.32, London: Academy Editions, 1993.

1 See *Casabella* March 1975
2 See Colin Rowe's introduction to *James Stirling: Buildings and Projects,* London: Architectural Press and New York: Rizzoli, 1984, p. 19.
3 Colin Rowe, «The Mathematics of the Ideal Villa», in *The Architectural Review,* 1947. Reprint: Colin Rowe, *The Mathematics of the Ideal Villa and Other Essays.* Cambridge: MIT Press, 1976.
4 Colin Rowe, «Mannerism and Modern Architecture», in *The Architectural Review,* 1950. Reprint: Colin Rowe, *The Mathematics of the Ideal Villa and Other Essays,* Cambridge: MIT Press, 1976.
5 Moses Finley, a member of the assessment panel, and later Master of Darwin, told me he considered that Stirling was unfairly blamed for problems he had sought to avoid.
6 See his acceptance speech for the Royal Gold Medal, published in *Architectural Design,* No. 7–8, 1980.
7 See his acceptance speech for the Pritzker Prize in Architecture: «For me, right from the beginning, the art of architecture has always been the priority», published in *Architectural Design Profile,* London: Academy Editions, 1982.
8 Sir John Summerson, «Vitruvius Ludens», in *The Architectural Review,* March 1983; also, by the same author: «Vitruvius Ridens, or Laughter at the Tate», in *The Architectural Review,* June 1987.
9 Richard Wollheim, comments in *Modern Painters,* Winter 1992.
10 See *James Stirling + Michael Wilford,* in *Architectural Monographs* No. 32, London: Academy Editions, 1993.

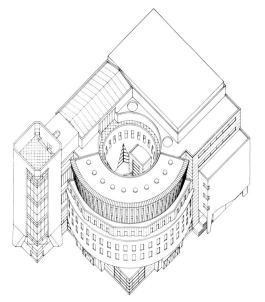

Cinemaxx und Musikschule, Mannheim:
Isometrie und Modellfoto

Cinemaxx and Music School, Mannheim:
Axonometric and model view

Diplomentwurf von James Stirling

Architekturschule Liverpool
James Stirling
1950

Stirlings Diplomarbeit in Liverpool war eine einjährige Studie über ein selbstgewähltes Thema, in diesem Fall ein Gemeinschaftszentrum für die städtische Neugründung Newton Aycliffe. Stirling erstellte ein Modell des neuen Stadtzentrums und setzte sein Gebäude an den Rand der urbanen, aus Gründen des Windschutzes abgesenkten Piazza. Das Gebäude ist ein schlichtes Rechteck mit zwei auf Pfeiler gesetzten Geschossen und zwei Lichtschächten von unterschiedlicher Größe. Mit einer komplexen Erschließung vermeidet Stirling die Aufreihung der Büros entlang eines zentralen Korridors, zu einer Zeit, als klimatisierte Bürolandschaften noch unbekannt waren.

Die regelmäßige Konstruktion wird von tiefen horizontalen Bändern geprägt, die an Lubetkin erinnern, aber die Art, wie einige der Elemente aus diesem Rahmen herausfallen, ist typisch für Stirling. Am auffallendsten ist die Verwendung von sich nach unten verjüngenden Pfeilern, die Le Corbusiers Unité in Marseilles viel verdanken, aber bereits auf Stirlings späteren Einsatz kegelförmiger Formen vorausweisen, auf seine oft verwendeten pilzförmigen Kapitelle und sogar auf die mächtigen Säulenköpfe bei den Werksanlagen von Braun, wo der Säulenschaft selbst unsichtbar ist.

Entsprechend einer Liverpooler Sitte wurden die perspektivischen Zeichnungen von einem anderen Studenten erstellt, in diesem Fall von mir.

James Stirling's Thesis Design

Liverpool School of Architecture
James Stirling
1950

The thesis at Liverpool was a year-long study of a self-selected subject, in this case a Community Centre for the new town of Newton Aycliffe. Stirling made a model of the new town centre, and set his building on the edge of a civic plaza lowered to reduce the wind exposure. The building is a simple rectangle, two storeys raised up on stilts, with two light wells of different sizes allowing a deep plan to be developed, in the years before office landscape and air-conditioning.

The regular frame is contained within deep horizontal bands that give a certain Lubetkin-like quality, but the way in which some of the elements escape from this frame is very Stirling. Most notable is the use of downward tapering stilts, that owe a good deal to Le Corbusier's Marseilles Unité, but presage Stirling's subsequent use of conical forms, his frequent mushroom capitals, and even those powerful capitals at the Braun Headquarters, where the column itself disappears. Following a tradition at Liverpool, the perspectives were drawn by another student, in this case, myself.

Perspektivzeichnung

Perspective

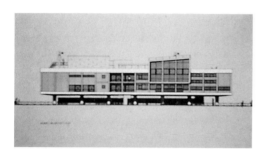

Ansichtsstudie

Elevational study

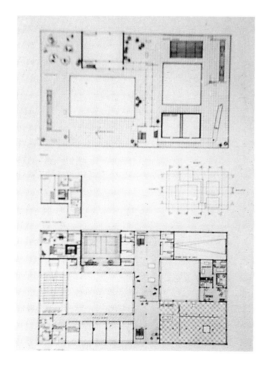

Grundrisse

Floor plans

Drei Häuser für Basil Mavrolean
Projekt für beschränkten Wettbewerb
Stirling and Gowan
South Kensington, London
1957

Zusammen mit James Gowan entwarf Stirling diese drei Häuser für drei Mitglieder einer Familie, ein Ensemble auf einem einzelnen, von einer Mauer abgeschirmten Grundstück an einer Straße, das aus zwei nebeneinanderstehenden Volumina und einem Baukörper an ihrer Rückseite besteht. Leicht über das Niveau der Straße erhöht, bilden sie zusammen ein Mehrfamilienhaus. Wie es sich für einen bedeutenden Auftraggeber wie den Schiffsreeder Basil Maveolean schickt, sind die Häuser aus Stein, auch wenn der Stein hier aus einer Verkleidung mit weißem Marmor besteht.

Trotz einer gewissen Ausgefallenheit der Familie sind die Häuser sorgfältig gestaltet und nicht übermäßig prunkvoll. Sie fügen sich auch recht gut in die Umgebung, ein vornehmer Teil von South Kensington in der Nähe der Stadtvilla, die Winston Churchill damals noch bewohnte. Marmor harmoniert nicht mit Ziegelstein, aber er paßt sehr gut zu weißem Putz. So sind die Häuser ein interessantes Beispiel für Einfühlungsvermögen in die Anforderungen der Auftraggeber und die Erfordernisse des Kontextes – Eigenschaften, die sich im späteren Werk von Stirling und Wilford voll entfalten sollten.

Three Houses for Basil Mavrolean
Limited competition
Stirling and Gowan
South Kensington, London
1955 – 1958

Designed with James Gowan, these are separate houses for three members of the same family, arranged as a composition sharing a single territory off the street, one at each side, one at the back, screened by a wall. Slightly raised above street level, they made a family compound. As befits a shipping magnate, they were stone houses, although the stone was a white marble facing.

In spite of the mild family obsession, the houses are carefully designed and are not particularly ostentatious, but fit into the area rather well: they are in a select part of south Kensington, close to the town house occupied at this time by Sir Winston Churchill. Although marble does not tone with brick, it goes very well with white stucco. In this way the houses represent an interesting example of sensitivity to the needs of both client and physical context – qualities that were to unfold in the later work of Stirling and Wilford.

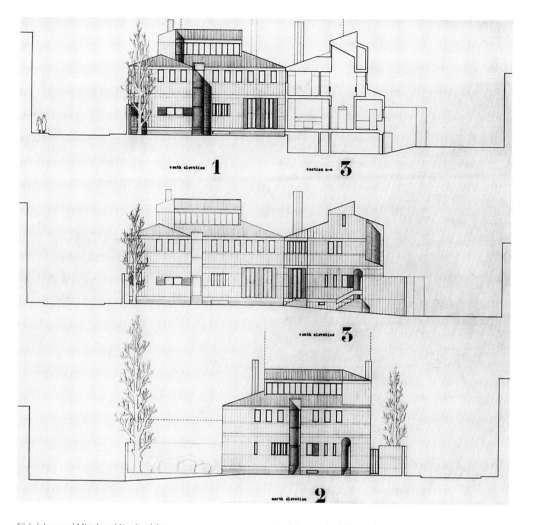

Süd- (oben und Mitte) und Nordansichten

South (top and middle) and north elevations

Wohnanlage in Ham Common

Stirling and Gowan
Richmond, London
1955–1958

Das Baugrundstück liegt im langen, schmalen Garten eines Hauses im georgianischen Stil gegenüber Ham Common – zwei Elemente, die den Entwurf wesentlich prägten. Sowohl von der Vorder- wie von der Hinterseite mit einer Zufahrt versehen, bot sich die Gelegenheit, eine verkehrsfreie Zone in der Nähe der Grundstücksmitte zu schaffen, die sich mit einigen aufgeschütteten Hügeln und Bepflanzung in einen Landschaftsgarten verwandelte.

Ein dreigeschossiger Block mit den Wohnzimmern an der Seite steht im vorderen Teil, während ein zweigeschossiger Block im schmaleren Grundstücksteil liegt, dessen Wohnzimmer auf die Längsseite des Gartens blicken. Der Bau ist aus Ziegelstein mit Betondecken und Betondach errichtet. Die Behandlung der Fassade mit den sichtbaren Betonstürzen und den U-förmigen Wasserspeiern schafft eine sehr skulpturale und einheitliche Wirkung, die von den schönen Proportionen aufgelockert wird.

Das Ergebnis wurde als «brutalistisch» und sogar «grausam» gebranntmarkt. Die Architekten wiesen diese Kritik vehement zurück und ließen das Brutalismus-Etikett nicht gelten. Unzweifelhaft ist hier aber der Einfluß des rohen Stils zu spüren, den Le Corbusier bei seinen Häuser für die Familie Jaoul in Paris einsetzte. Seine Abweichung von den weißen Fassaden der Moderne ebnete für Stirling und Gowan den Weg zu einem Backstein-Modernismus, der dem englischen Klima angemessener war. Auf diese Weise übten sie einen großen Einfluß auf viele soziale Wohnungsbauprojekte in Großbritannien aus.

Ham Common Flats

Stirling and Gowan
Richmond, London
1955–1958

The site was in the garden of a Georgian house facing Ham Common, using its long narrow back garden, and this determined the layout. Road access was available from both front and back, so that a road-free zone could be created near the centre, and with some mounding and planting, a landscape could be made there.

A three-storey block is sited in the front part, with living rooms facing the sides, and a two-storey block in the narrower part, with living rooms facing the length of the garden. The construction is of brick with concrete floors and roof, and the treatment, in exposing the concrete lintols, together with the emphasis on U-shaped rainwater outlets for the recessed balconies, creates a highly sculptural effect, unified by the beautiful proportions.

The result was criticised as «brutalist» and even bloody-minded, a criticism that was vigorously rebutted by the architects, who were forced to write to disclaim the brutalist tag. What is undeniable is the debt owed here to the earthy style in which Le Corbusier had made his houses in Paris for the Jaoul family. His modification of the white-walled modern movement image opened the door for Stirling and Gowan to propose a brick modernism more suitable for the English climate. In this way they were to greatly influence the character of much public housing in Britain.

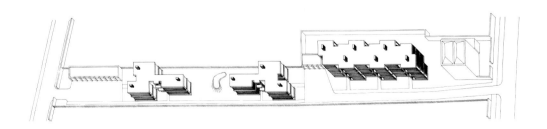

Lageplan   Site plan

28

Ansicht von Süden
Blick auf Balkone und Treppenhaus des
dreigeschossigen Wohnblocks

View from the south
View of balconies and staircase of the
three storey block

Schulaula
Stirling and Gowan
Camberwell, London
1958 – 1961

Mit dieser Arbeit setzten Stirling und Gowan ihre Reihe von Backsteingebäuden fort – für sie ein angemessenes Material im feuchten englischen Klima.
Die Aula ist Teil der Brunswick Park Primary School in South London. Sie dient einer Reihe von Aktivitäten: für die morgendliche Versammlung, als Speisesaal, als Halle für Gymnastik, Spiele und Empfänge, gelegentlich auch als zusätzlicher Unterrichtsraum. Das Arrangement, bei dem sich drei Volumina mit quadratischem Grundriß um eine Küche gruppieren, wobei sich ihre niedrigen Seiten berühren, ermöglicht ihre Trennung, wenn Bedarf an Klassenräumen besteht. Jeder Bereich hat jedoch ein hohes Fenster, durch das Licht in den gesamten Raum einfällt.
Die so entstandene Formation strahlt eine große Intensität und skulpturale Eindringlichkeit aus, was noch dadurch betont wird, daß die «gewöhnlich» wirkenden Ziegelwände teilweise hinter Erdwällen begraben liegen und das Gebäude so zu einem Objekt wird, das mit der Landschaft verschmilzt.

School Assembly Hall
Stirling and Gowan
Camberwell, London
1958 – 1961

This work of the Stirling-Gowan partnership continues their use of brickwork as the proper material for building modern architecture in a wet climate.
The hall is part of Brunswick Park Primary School in South London. It has to provide for a number of activities: morning assembly, dining room, gymnastics, games, and receptions, and on occasion provide additional classrooms. The arrangement whereby three square volumes are assembled around the kitchen, with their low sides touching, allows them to be separated when classroom use is required. Each space, however, has a high window throwing light across the whole floor area.
The resulting formation has great intensity and sculptural richness, accentuated by the fact that the «ordinary» brick walls are buried behind earth banks, thus making the building into an object engaged with its landscape.

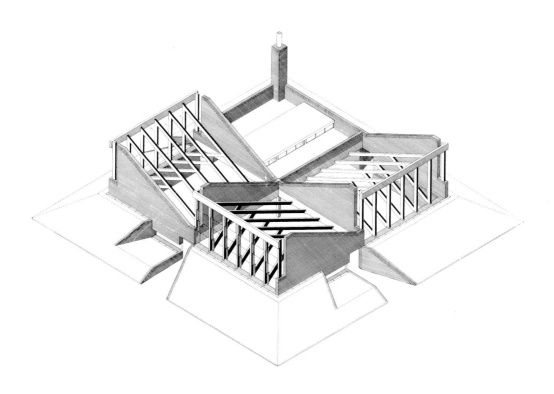

Isometrie
Gesamtansicht

Axonometric
View

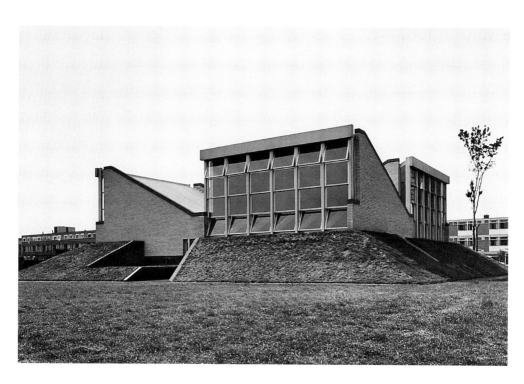

Studentenwohnheim für das Selwyn College

Projekt
Stirling and Gowan
Cambridge
1959

Dieser Entwurf von Stirling und Gowan für das Selwyn College sah eine «Kette» von Gebäuden um den Rand des College-Areals vor, die Abgeschiedenheit geschaffen und den Hintergrund des Gartens gebildet hätte. Auf einen durchlaufenden Erdwall gesetzt, wäre das Gebäude das erste in der Reihe von «roten Backstein»-Gebäuden in der altehrwürdigen College-Umgebung gewesen.

Die Erschließungstürme mit den Treppenhäusern sind von der Rückseite des Gebäudes abgesetzt und geben ihr ein erhabenes Flair. Im Kontrast dazu sind die Räume, die auf den Garten blicken, mit einer durchgängigen, facettierten Glasfassade versehen, die auf jedem Stockwerk doppelt vorspringt, so daß das Gebäude als Ganzes einen abstrakten und sogar expressionistischen Charakter gewinnt, der am Ende des Jahrhunderts, also heute, sehr modisch wirken würde.

Student Residences for Selwyn College

Project
Stirling and Gowan
Cambridge
1959

This design by Stirling and Gowan for Selwyn College proposed a «necklace» of buildings around the edge of the college grounds that would have afforded them privacy, and formed a backdrop for the garden. Set on a continuous grass mound, the building would have been the first in the series of «red-brick» interventions in ancient college environments, of which both Oxford and Cambridge later acquired examples.

The service towers are withdrawn from the back of the development, in association with the staircases, where they acquire a certain baronial look. In contrast, the rooms facing the garden are totally glazed, and the glass wall is faceted on plan, and sets forward twice with each storey, so that the building as a whole is given an abstracted and even expressionist character that would be very modish by the end of the century, where we are today.

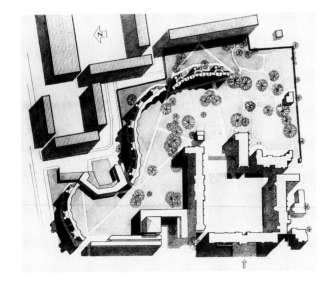

Lageplan

Site plan

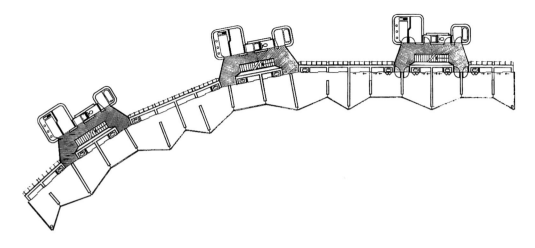

Grundriß Normalgeschoß

Typical floor plan

Schnittansicht

Section elevation

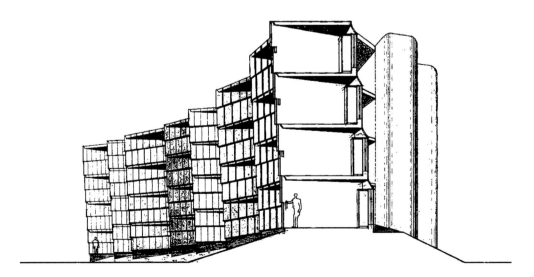

Ingenieursfakultät der Leicester Universität
Stirling and Gowan
Leicester
1959 – 1963

Da die Grundstücksgröße begrenzt war und die Labors im Erdgeschoß Vorrang hatten, waren die Planer einverstanden, den Rest der Nutzflächen in einer Gruppe von Türmen unterzubringen, die den angrenzenden Park überblicken. So entstand ein eindrucksvolles Gebäude, das Stirling und Gowan über Nacht berühmt machte.
Die Hochhauselemente umfassen einen Turm mit Forschungseinrichtungen, einen Verwaltungsturm, den Erschließungsturm und den Heizungsschacht, der ebenfalls Teil der Komposition ist. Jedes Element findet einen angemessenen Ausdruck: Glaswände beim Verwaltungshochhaus, abgeschirmte horizontale Fensterbänder beim Forschungsgebäude, reine Ziegelverkleidung des Erschließungsturms und Betonteile für den Heizungsschacht. Die Volumina sind eng auf einem gemauerten Sockel zusammengefaßt, und die Vorlesungssäle «hängen» an den Ecken eines der Volumina, ein stark an Melnikov erinnerndes Element. Sie wurden mit roten Ziegelfliesen verblendet, und dies auch an den Unterseiten der Vorsprünge, so daß der Komplex zusammen mit den roten Backsteinwänden visuelle und skulpturale Geschlossenheit und Einheitlichkeit erreicht. Die Konstruktion des Gebäudes ist ein Stahlbetonskelett.
Die ausgedehnten Laboratorien der Ingenieursfakultät reihen sich geradlinig entlang der Grundstücksgrenzen, aber die gut isolierende Industrieverglasung des Daches orientiert sich an den günstigsten Lichtverhältnissen. Die Unterteilung dieser Geometrien ist intelligent und skulptural zur gleichen Zeit, und, wie man hinzufügen sollte, auch optisch sehr ansprechend.

Engineering Building for Leicester University
Stirling and Gowan
Leicester
1959 – 1963

As the site area was constricted and the requirement for ground level laboratories was predominant, the planners accepted that the rest of the accommodation could be stacked up as a group of towers overlooking the adjoining park. The result created a memorable image that made Stirling and Gowan famous overnight.
The high-rise elements comprise a research tower, an administration tower, a staircase tower, and the flue stack, which plays its part in the composition. Each element has an appropriate expression: glass walls for the administration tower, shaded horizontal window bands for the research tower, sheer brickwork for the service tower, and concrete units for the flue. The group is collected tightly together on a brick podium, and the lecture theatres impend on the edges of the group in a highly Melnikov way. They are clad in red tiles, even on the undersides of the cantilevers, so that with the red brick wall surfaces, the whole ensemble is given visual and sculptural unity. The building is constructed on a reinforced concrete frame.
The large expanse of the engineering laboratories is aligned to the site borders, but the industrial glazing that forms the roof is aligned to the orientation, the exposed surfaces being heavily insulated. The resolution of these geometries is ingenious and sculptural at once, and also, it must be said, highly decorative.

Blick auf das Ensemble:
links Forschungsgebäude, rechts Verwaltungshochhaus,
im Hintergrund die Laboratorien
Verwaltungshochhaus von unten mit roter
Ziegelfliesenverkleidung

View of the overall complex:
left research tower, right administration tower,
laboratories in the background
Administration tower with
red tile cladding from below

Dachverglasung der Laboratorien

Roof glazing of laboratories

Geschichtsfakultät der Cambridge Universität

Eingeschränkter Wettbewerb
James Stirling
Cambridge
1964 – 1967

Der Entwurf für dieses Gebäude gewann den ersten Preis bei einem Wettbewerb auf Einladung. Hinterher stellte sich heraus, daß etwa die Hälfte des Grundstücks nicht verfügbar war und der Komplex um 90 Grad gedreht werden mußte, um noch auf das Baulos zu passen. Den Architekten wurde jedoch vor Baubeginn keine Gelegenheit gegeben, den Entwurf noch einmal zu überdenken.

Das Gebäude beherbergt einen großen Lesesaal mit 300 Plätzen und 1200 m² Stellfläche für die Bücher. Der übrige Teil der Fakultät setzt sich aus Räumen für den Lehrkörper, Seminar- und Gemeinschaftsräumen zusammen.

Den Lesesaal betritt man von der Ecke des Raumes, wo die Eingangskontrolle untergebracht ist. Der fächerförmige Grundriß, durch den sich von hier aus die Regale und Tische leicht überblicken lassen, fand die Zustimmung des Auswahlkomitees und war im Hinblick auf die Funktionalität der Hauptgrund, sich für diesen Entwurf zu entscheiden. Allerdings machte die Einführung von Magnetbandstreifen zur Sicherung der Bücher diese Anforderung im nachhinein obsolet.

Indem Stirling den Lesesaal als Quadranten eines großen Kreises entwarf, entstand der Eindruck eines riesigen Raumes von der vierfachen Größe, eine Erinnerung an Säle aus dem 19. Jahrhundert, die der Architekt bewunderte. Der kleine Baukörper umschließt den Lesesaal, in den man von seinen Korridoren Einblick hat. Eine Belüftungsanlage auf der Spitze des Glasdaches zwischen Innen- und Außenhaut schwebt über dem Saal und macht die Bibliothek als einen Raum des 20. Jahrhunderts erfahrbar.

History Faculty for Cambridge University

Limited competition
James Stirling
Cambridge
1964 – 1967

The design for this building was the winner in a limited competition. After the competition it was found that about half the land was not available and the building had to be turned through 90 degrees to fit on to the site. The architects were not given the opportunity to reconsider the design before construction had to begin.

The building provides a grand reading room for 300 readers, and 1200 square metres of book space. The rest of the accommodation is made up of staff, seminar, and common rooms. The reading room is entered at the corner, where the control desk is situated. The layout, with shelves and tables radiating from the control point, was approved by the selection committee and represented the idea of functionality for which the design was chosen. Ironically, the introduction of magnetic strip tell-tales has made this requirement obsolete.

By shaping the reading room as a quadrant of a great circle, the architect was able to created the impression of a huge circular reading room, four times the actual size, reminiscent of the nineteenth century readings that he admired. The smaller accommodation embraces the reading room on two sides, and allows people in the corridors to look down into the grand space. Air extract machinery at the apex of the glass roof, situated between the inner and outer skins, looms over the space and designates it as a twentieth century experience.

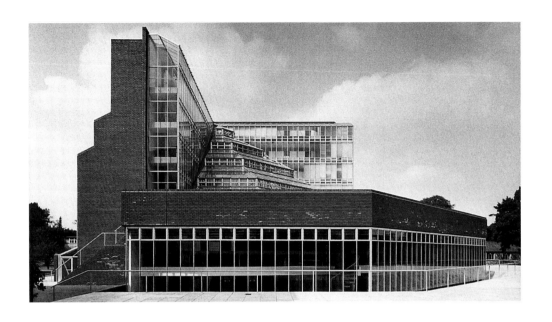

Ansichten					Views

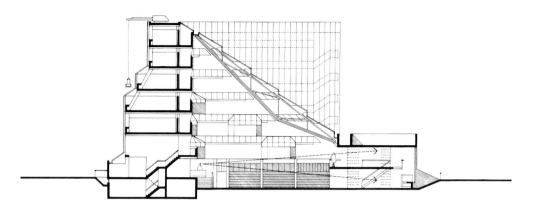

Schnittansicht

Section elevation

Blick in den Lesesaal

View of the reading room

Studentenwohnheim der
St. Andrews Universität
James Stirling
St. Andrews, Schottland
1964 – 1968

Aufgrund der Abgelegenheit des Grundstücks und des Mangels an technisch genügend versierten örtlichen Baufirmen entschloß sich Stirling, mit industriell vorgefertigten Betonpaneelen zu arbeiten, die zur Baustelle transportiert wurden – eine heute vertraute, damals jedoch ungewöhnliche Methode. Trotz technischer Schwierigkeiten blieb das Gebäude erhalten und erfreut sich heute unter den Studenten, die dort leben, großer Beliebtheit.
Das Grundstück durchzieht ein baumbestandener Hang, und die Studentenwohnungen, die in zwei abgewinkelt auseinander strebenden Flügeln untergebracht sind, liegen an diesem Hang wie an einem Dock vertäute Schiffe. Der Eingang auf höherem Niveau scheint in ein bescheidenes eingeschossiges Gebäude zu führen. Erst wo das Terrain abfällt, wird die Höhe der Baukörper erkennbar.
In den beiden Wohnflügeln sind 250 Studenten und Studentinnen in Räumen untergebracht, zu denen man über Treppen von einem gemeinsamen verglasten Korridor gelangt. Der Korridor führt auch zu den Gemeinschaftseinrichtungen an der Schnittstelle der beiden Flügel. Die Dachterrassen sind abgestuft, so daß die Gebäudehöhe auf vier bis fünf Stockwerke beschränkt bleibt; der verglaste Korridor liegt in unterschiedlicher Höhenrelation zu den Wohngeschossen. Die Zimmerfenster sind einheitlich aus der Fassade herausgedreht, um mehr Sonne hineinzulassen und einen besseren Blick auf die Landschaft zu erlauben. Dadurch entsteht eine Art industrielles «Sägezahn»-Profil, ein strenger Eindruck, der zumindest für die Bewohner weitgehend durch den großzügigen Raum der Glaspassage und die eleganten Bullaugenfenster zu den Zimmern ausgeglichen wird, die sich an ihr entlang reihen.

Student Residences for
St. Andrews University
James Stirling
St. Andrews, Scotland
1964 – 1968

Because of the isolation of the site, and the absence of a local building technology capable of undertaking a major contract, the architect decided to use prefabrication, bringing to the site pre-cast concrete panels manufactured in a factory. This approach was unusual at the time, but has become familiar since. Despite some technical problems, the building has survived and is now popular with the students who live in it.
The site is traversed by a tree-lined bank, and the unit of residential accommodation, consisting of two wings diverging at an angle, is attached to this bank somewhat as a pair of ships might be moored at a dock. The entry, at the higher level, appears to be into a modest one-storey building: as the ground falls away the full height of the building is revealed.
The residential unit of two wings accommodates 250 students of both sexes, the rooms being approached by stairs from a shared glazed corridor, which in turn leads back to the communal facilities at the junction of the wings. Roof terraces on top step down in stages, so that the building remains within a four to five-storey limit. The glazed concourse is thus in a varying heigth relation to the residential floors. The room windows are uniformly canted towards the sun and the view, giving a somewhat industrial «saw-tooth» profile, an impression of dourness that is largely offset, for the occupants at least, by the generous spaces of the concourse and the stylish porthole windows that line it.

Lageplan

Site plan

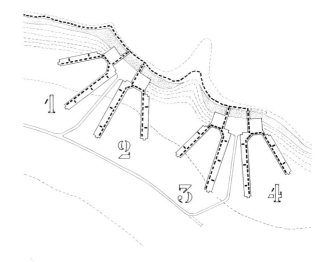

Grundriß

Floor plan

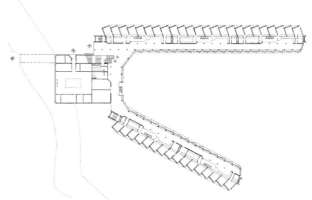

Perspektivische Darstellung eines
Wohnheimflurs mit Aufenthaltsbereich

Cutaway perspective of
corridor with lounge areas

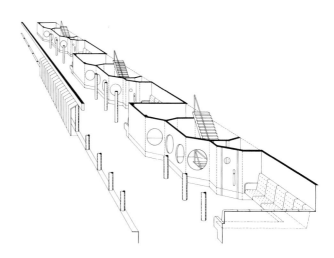

Ansicht

Elevation

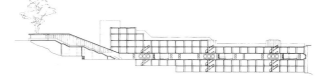

Blick auf den
Eingangsbereich

View of entry

Blick in den Hof der Anlage

View of courtyard

Blick auf Dachterrasse und Eingangstrakt

View of roof terrace and entry wing

Hoffassade

Court facade

Firmensitz der
Dorman Long Stahlwerke

Projekt
James Stirling
Middlesbrough, Yorkshire
1965

Als Stahlproduzent konnte Dorman Long für seinen Firmensitz kein anderes Material als Stahl wählen. Das Gebäude hat 14 Geschosse, ist mehr als 300 Meter lang und bietet viele kleinere Räume für Direktoren, Manager, Sekretärinnen und Stenotypistinnen sowie größere Bereiche, darunter Groß-raumbüros, ein Computerzentrum, eine Bibliothek und eine Kantine. Diese Unterschiedlichkeit der Raumgrößen ist der Grund, daß sich der Querschnitt des Gebäudes unten verbreitert – außen als abgeschrägte Front sichtbar. Die wuchtige Wirkung dieser Form wird auf der anderen Seite des Gebäudes durch die abgesetzten vertikalen Erschließ-ungsschächte, die das Gebäude stützen, ausgeglichen.

Da die Kosten der Konstruktion nur eine geringe Rolle spielten, wurde diese von rein ästhetischen Gesichtspunkten bestimmt, um eine möglichst beeindruckende und denkwürdige Architektur zu schaffen.

Headquarters for
Dorman Long Steel Manufacturers

Project
James Stirling
Middlesbrough, Yorkshire
1965

Dorman Long as steel producers could not build their headquarters of anything but steel. The building is fourteen storeys high and over 300 metres long. The accommodation contains many small rooms for directors, managers, secretaries and typists, and also requires larger spaces for typing pools, computer centre, library, and canteen: this disparity of size accounts for the thickening of the building section towards the ground, visible as a splayed frontage. The visual thrust created by this shape is counteracted by the shafts of vertical circulation exposed on the other side, to buttress the building.

As cost proved to be a small factor in the choice of structural design, it was governed in the end by a purely visual judgement of what would be striking and memorable. It shows Stirling to be capable of a single strong idea from an early stage of his practice.

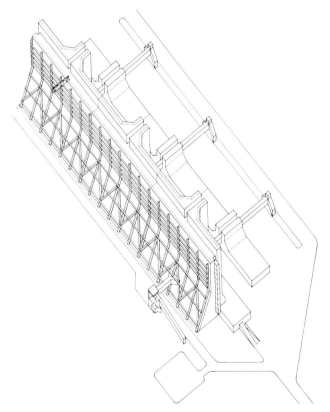

Isometrische Darstellung des Büro- und Laborgebäudes
Modellfotos

Axonometric view of the office building and laboratories
Model views

44

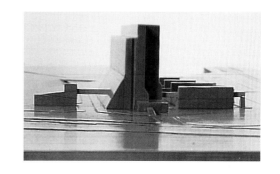

Florey-Gebäude des Queen's College

James Stirling
Oxford
1966 – 1971

Am Ufer des Flusses Cherwell gelegen, blickt das Gebäude über eine baumbestandene Wiese auf die alten
Colleges, bleibt aber, getrennt durch die Magdalen
Bridge, von ihnen abgerückt auf der Seite eines eher ge-
sichtslosen Stadtteils. Diese Lage erklärt, warum die beiden Seiten des Gebäudes so unterschiedlich sind, mit den
Studentenzimmern, die sich die Front zum Gemeinschaftsbereich teilen, auf der Vorder- und den Treppen
und Korridoren an der Rückseite. Dieser Unterschied wird
noch durch die offen sichtbaren Pfeiler hervorgehoben,
auf die sich das Gebäude «zurücklehnt».

Den Gemeinschaftsbereich gestaltete Stirling nach dem
Vorbild der traditionellen gepflasterten viereckigen Col-
lege-Höfe mit Rasenflächen. Hier bildet er jedoch einen
angehobenen Sockel, in dem auf einer Seite der Früh-
stückssaal untergebracht ist. Das Dach des Saals ist erhöht, so daß eine Terrasse zum Sitzen entsteht, von der
aus sich ein besserer Blick über den Fluß und die Wiese
dahinter bietet. Der Ventilator, der den Geruch von ge-
bratenem Schinken und Spiegeleiern fortbläst, wird über
den Wetterhahn vom Wind in Gang gesetzt und nimmt im
Hof die Stelle ein, die auf traditionellen Höfen von einer
Statue besetzt wird.

Die Räume, die auf den Hof blicken, sind völlig verglast
und mit Jalousien ausgestattet, die sich individuell aus-
richten lassen und von unten aus einem Rolladenkasten
im Fußboden nach oben gezogen werden. Die Pfeiler,
welche die Korridorseite stützen, sind abgewinkelt und
ein wesentlicher Grund, warum das Gebäude von Kriti-
kern in die Nähe des russischen Konstruktivismus gerückt
wurde. Es ist das letzte in einer Reihe von «roten Backsteingebäuden», die Stirling mit Erfolg in die Umgebung
altehrwürdiger Universitäten «einschleuste».

The Florey Building for Queen's College

James Stirling
Oxford
1966 – 1971

Sited on a branch of the river Cherwell, the building looks
out across tree-studded meadows towards the ancient
colleges. Yet it is removed from them, separated by Magdalen Bridge, and relegated to an undistinguished part of
town. The siting explains why the two sides of the building are so different, with the student rooms sharing the
front to the common space, and the stairs and corridors
arranged on the back. The difference is accentuated by
the way the building leans back on exposed struts.

The common space was conceived to resemble the traditional quadrangle paved with stone and grass, but is in
effect a raised podium that contains in one corner the
breakfast room. The roof of this is raised to form a sitting
terrace, with an advantageous view of the river and the
meadows beyond. The ventilator which disperses the
smell of bacon and eggs is geared to the wind by a
weathercock, and forms an object in the quad analogous
to the traditional statue.

The rooms facing the court are totally glazed, and
equipped with venetian blinds that can be adjusted to
suit the individual occupant. They pull upward from a
housing beneath the ground-level cill. The struts that support the corridor side are angled, and are the principle
feature to justify the Russian Constructivist look ascribed
to the building by critics. It is the last of the series of three
«red-brick» buildings which Stirling succeeded in infil-
trating into the hallowed environment of the ancient uni-
versities.

Hofansicht mit Gemeinschaftsbereich

View of court with common space

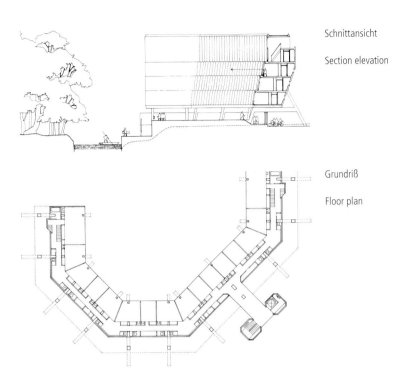

Schnittansicht

Section elevation

Grundriß

Floor plan

Rückansicht mit Erschließung

Rear facade with stairs and corridors

Wohnsiedlung Runcorn New Town

James Stirling and Partner
Runcorn New Town, Cheshire
1967 – 1976

1967 boomte in Großbritannien der öffentliche Wohnungsbau. Die Architekten, die Aufträge von den Gemeinden erhielten, wurden jedoch von strengen Bauauflagen und engen Finanzierungsrahmen geknebelt, so daß sich viele der im wesentlichen billigen Bauprojekte in sozialer Hinsicht als Fehlschläge erwiesen. In Runcorn, eine der städtischen Neugründungen *(New Towns)* auf der grünen Wiese in der Nähe von Manchester, versuchte Stirling den Zwängen des kostensparenden Wohnungsbaus zu entgehen, indem er große vorgefertigte Betonteile einsetzte und auf Methoden der industriellen Massenproduktion zurückgriff. Sozialen Entfremdungserscheinungen versuchte er dabei durch die Anlage von Plätzen und Reihenhäusern mit Terrassen zu begegnen, die sich zu früheren Zeiten als so erfolgreich erwiesen hatten.

Die Wohnsiedlung ist aufgrund ihrer regelmäßigen Anlage zu ihrer Zeit einzigartig. Die Nähe zum Stadtzentrum veranlaßte Stirling, sich durch die Verbindung von traditionellem Platz und modernem Straßengitter um einen urbanen Charakter der Anlage zu bemühen. Wo traditionell alle Fronten unabhängig von der Himmelsrichtung auf den Platz ausgerichtet waren, sucht der zeitgenössische Entwurf die ideale Orientierung: So blicken die Vorderfronten der Häuser an zwei aneinander grenzenden Seiten auf den Platz, während sie ihm an den anderen beiden den Rücken zukehren, um die optimale Lage der Wohnzimmer zu gewährleisten. Die Terrassen sind auf zwei Himmelsrichtungen ausgerichtet, wobei die Wohnzimmer auf der Gartenseite und die erhöhten Zugangswege an der Seite zur baumgesäumten Straße liegen. Die Zugänge der Wohnungen um eine gemeinsame Erschließungsgalerie anzulegen, war eine Auflage der Baubehörden. Damit verletzte der Entwurf unwissentlich jene Angemessenheit seiner räumlichen Gliederungen, die bis dahin der sozialen Kohäsion förderlich gewesen war.

Von den 1500 Wohneinheiten sind ein Drittel Wohnungen, ein Drittel Maisonnettes und ein Drittel dreigeschossige Wohnungen, zusammengefaßt in fünfgeschossigen Volumina, so daß eine gleichmäßige Traufhöhe gewährleistet war. Die Mischung der unterschiedlichen Wohneinheiten erlaubte eine ausgewogene Verteilung unterschiedlich großer Familien, wodurch eine Konzentration von sozialen oder Altersgruppen vermieden wurde. Der Bandenbildung unter Jugendlichen konnte mit diesem Mittel jedoch nicht begegnet werden.

Kritiker sahen im klassizistischen Erscheinungsbild der Anlage den Grund für die sozialen Probleme, doch gibt es

Low-Cost Housing Runcorn

James Stirling and Partner
Runcorn New Town, Cheshire
1967 – 1976

In 1967 Britain was in a period of massive expansion of the housing stock. Architects who received commissions from municipal authorities found themselves ham-strung by building regulations and cost restrictions, and much of the essentially cheap housing built in this period has proved to be a social failure. At Runcorn near Manchester, one of the New Towns on fresh greenfield sites, Stirling tried to overcome the problem of building cheaply by utilising the principles of mass production with large precast panels, and the problems of social alienation by adopting the forms of square and terrace that were so successful in an earlier age.

The layout is unique at this time because of its regularity. Situated close to the city centre, it sought an urban quality, combining traditional square with modern grid. Where the traditional square had its «fronts» facing the space, whatever the orientation, the modern layout had to refer to ideal orientation, and here the square is faced on two adjacent sides by fronts and on the other two by backs, maintaining correct orientation for all the living rooms. The terraces had dual aspect, with the living rooms on the garden side and the elevated walkways facing the tree-lined roads. The arrangement with gallery access was imposed by the housing authorities. Thus, unknowingly, the architect broke with the propriety which had formerly worked to preserve social cohesion.

Of 1500 dwellings, a third were flats, a third were maisonettes (duplexes) and a third were houses, on three storeys. These types were stacked in a building envelope of five storeys, ensuring a regular height. The mix of types allowed larger families to be dispersed evenly, avoiding a concentration of social or age groups. This, however, did not engage with the gang behaviour of the adolescents, however dispersed their homes.

Critics tended to blame the neo-classical appearance for social problems, but there is ample evidence to show that architectural style as such played no part in the isolation of young families and the other social problems that plagued the official housing programme at this time.

genügend Hinweise, daß der Architekturstil keine Rolle bei der Isolierung junger Familien und bei anderen sozialen Problemen spielte, an denen die öffentliche Wohnungsbauprogramme der Zeit krankten.

Blick auf eine Reihenhauszeile

View of terrace houses

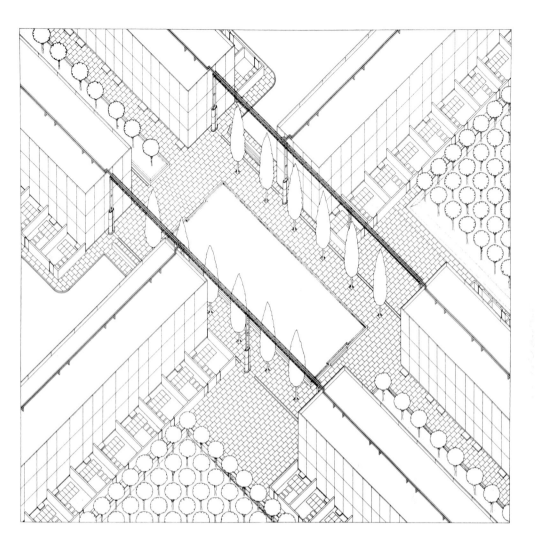

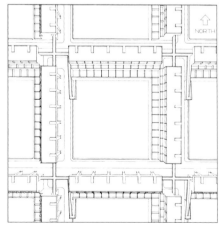

Perspektivische Darstellung der Reihenhäuser
Lageplan
Luftperspektive der Gartenplatzgestaltung

Perspective of terrace houses
Site plan
Aerial perspective of garden square layout

51

Siemens Forschungszentrum

Projekt für beschränkten Wettbewerb
James Stirling
München
1969

Der Entwurf zeigt eine streng lineare Gliederung des Komplexes auf einem großen Grundstück, um eine spätere Erweiterung zu erleichtern. Der Querschnitt ist also der Schlüssel zu diesem Aufbau, auch wenn es sich hier nicht einfach um die Vervielfältigung eines Musters handelt, sondern die Anlage den Charakter eines wirklichen Ensembles hat.

Es gibt zwei Hauptelemente: einen ausgedehnten Sockel, der auf dem untersten Niveau die Produktionsstätten enthält. Darüber befinden sich die Zufahrtswege und der Parkplatz der Direktion, Testlabors und Laderampen. Auf den nächsten beiden Ebenen liegt die Computer-Forschungs- und Entwicklungsabteilung, deren Dach eine Art Boulevard mit Service-Einrichtungen bildet, die nicht in der Ausschreibung gefordert, sondern von den Architekten vorgeschlagen wurden: Kolonnaden zu beiden Seiten, Baumreihen, Restaurants, Imbisse, Tabakwarenladen und Drogerie. Darüber waren Einrichtungen für das Management, soziale Einrichtungen und die Abteilung für Öffentlichkeitsarbeit, eine Bibliothek, eine Registratur und der Empfang vorgesehen. Diesen linear angelegten Park nannten die Architekten «soziales Tal».

Das zweite Element ist eine Abfolge von zylindrischen, zu Paaren gruppierten Bürogebäuden, die sich über den Sockel ziehen. Diese Türme fügen den vorhandenen weitere acht Geschosse hinzu und sind mit Fahrstuhlschächten in ihren zentralen Lobbies ausgesprochen großzügig ausgelegt. Eine vertikale, computergesteuerte Verblendung, die jeden der vollverglasten Baukörper umschließt, bietet Schutz vor der Sonneneinstrahlung.

An einem Ende des Komplexes verteilt sich auf seiner Hauptachse eine Gruppe von Gebäuden, die das Trainingszentrum, Management und Ausstellungsräume beherbergen. Auf jeder Seite des Komplexes liegen Parkplätze, die von einem durchlaufenden, in langen Terrassen abgestuften Wassergarten von ihm getrennt sind. Über Rampen gelangt man durch die Wassergärten zu den Büros.

Siemens Research Centre

Limited competition project
James Stirling
Munich
1969

Situated on a large site, the building was given a strict linear organization that would be easy to expand. The cross section is the key to the organization, although this is not a continuous «extrusion» but has the quality of an aggregation.

There are two main elements: a wide podium containing the production hall at the lowest level; above this are service roads and the directors' car parking, experimental workshops, and vehicle delivery bays. Above again are two floors of computer research and development, capped by a sort of boulevard containing additional amenities proposed by the architects: flanking colonnades, lines of trees, restaurants, snack bars tobacconists, drug stores, and at a higher level management facilities, social and public relations, library, registry, reception areas. This linear park the architects called the «social valley».

The second element is a succession of cylindrical office buildings arranged in matching pairs along the length of the social valley, and carried on the podium building. These towers have a further eight storeys in height, and are laid out on a lavish scale, with the lift cores organised in a central lobby. A vertical screen shaped to the window walls moves around each building to shield it from direct sun, all controlled by computers.

At one end of the complex there is a group of buildings arranged on the main axis, to accommodate the training school, management and an exhibition hall. On either side of the complex are car parking terraces, separated by a continuous water garden stepped in long terraces. Access from the parking zone to the offices is provided by ramps crossing the water.

Modellfoto
Isometrie
Ansicht der Bürogebäude

Model view
Axonometric
Office building elevation

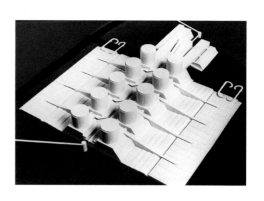

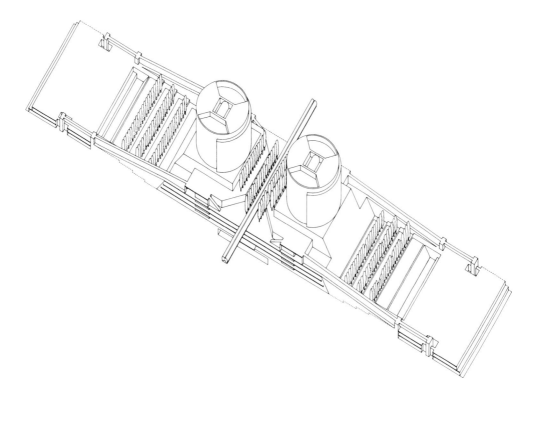

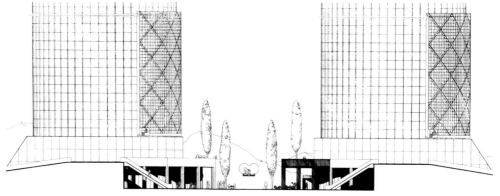

Olivetti Trainingszentrum

James Stirling
Haslemere
1969 – 1972

Ein Herrenhaus im Arts-and-Crafts-Stil inmitten eines 17 Hektar großen Guts in Surrey bildete den schon vorhandenen Kern eines ländlichen Zentrums, dem die Architekten einen Flügel für Schulungszwecke hinzufügen sollten. Der Flügel gliedert sich in zwei Teile, einen für Techniker und einen für Verkäufer. Sie liegen hinter dem Altbau auf einer baumfreien Fläche. Den Zugang vom Haus bildet ein doppelstöckiger verglaster Durchgang, von dem aus zwei gerade Rampen und eine Wendeltreppe zu den beiden Geschossen mit den Schulungsräumen führen. Am Schnittpunkt befindet sich eine quadratische Mehrzweckhalle, die sich durch Trennwände unterteilen läßt, die nach oben in den kreuzförmigen Dachstuhl gezogen werden können. Die Halle läßt sich durch eine flexible Membran, die auf zwei vertikale Rollen aufgewickelt werden kann, von den Erschließungsbereichen abschirmen.

Die Schulungsräume sind aus einem vorgefertigten Betongerippe errichtet, das mit ebenfalls vorgefertigten glasfaserverstärkten Polyesterpaneelen in vier verschiedenen Größen verkleidet ist. Sie sind auf einen Ziegelsockel in alternierenden hell- und dunkelgelben Bändern montiert. Die ursprünglich geplanten leuchtenden Farben stießen auf den Widerstand der örtlichen Behörden.

Die modellierten Formen der Paneelverkleidung besonders an der Mehrzweckhalle schaffen in Verbindung mit der eleganten Verglasung des wintergartenartigen Durchgangs und seinen raumhohen Heizkörpern eine fast feierliche Atmosphäre. An der geschwungenen Ecke der Halle gegenüber der Bühne stehen zwei erhaben wirkende Säulen mit übertrieben großen pilzförmigen Kapitellen – eine Vorahnung späterer Entwürfe.

Olivetti Training School

James Stirling
Haslemere
1969 – 1972

An arts-and-crafts manor house at the centre of this 17 hectare estate in Surrey already formed the residential nucleus of a rural centre, to which the architects were asked to add a teaching wing.

The wing divides into two parts, one for technicians and one for salesmen. They are sited behind the parent building on ground clear of trees. They are approached from the house by a double height glazed concourse where two straight ramps and one spiral stair serve two levels of classrooms. At the point of intersection is situated the multi-purpose hall, square in form, which can be subdivided by partitions that can be withdrawn upward into a cruciform roof housing, and can be shielded from the circulation areas by a flexible membrane that winds away on two vertical rollers.

The classrooms are constructed from pre-cast concrete framing, to which are clipped prefabricated panels of glass-reinforced polyester. These are manufactured in four panel sizes. They are assembled on a brick plinth in alternating bands of light and deep yellow: earlier proposals to have them in bright colours were vetoed by the Local Authority.

The moulded forms of the facing panels, particularly on the multi-purpose hall, and the elegant glazing of the conservatory-concourse with its full height radiators combine to create an almost festive atmosphere. At the point where the curved corner of the multipurpose hall answers to its stage across the space stand two noble columns with exaggerated mushroom caps – somehow an augury of great things to come.

Blick in die Erschließungshalle

Interior view of concourse

Blick auf verglaste Erschließungshalle

View of glazed concourse

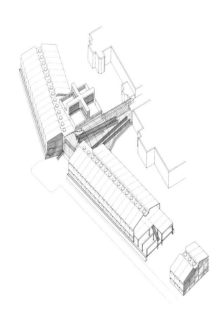

Isometrie der Gesamtanlage
Luftbild

Axonometric of complex
View from above

Bürgerzentrum Derby
Projekt für beschränkten Wettbewerb
James Stirling mit Leon Krier
Derby
1970

Dieser Wettbewerbsentwurf entstand unter Mitwirkung von Leon Krier und markiert den Beginn von Stirlings Interesse an städtischen Bauten.

Der Komplex ist in einer Hufeisenform entworfen, dessen Innenfläche einen öffentlichen Platz und ein informelles Freilichttheater bildet, eine Arena für Aktivitäten unter freiem Himmel. Die Hinterseite der Bühne wird von einer akustischen Wand abgeschirmt, an deren Rückseite die Fassade eines historischen Gebäudes aufgebaut ist, die den Krieg überstand. Die Fassade ist geneigt, ein Zeichen, daß dieses Zitat nicht allzu ernst gemeint erscheinen soll. Der Platz ist außerdem mit einer Reihe monumental wirkender Telefonzellen und öffentlichen Toiletten unter dem Platzniveau ausgestattet.

Um das hufeisenförmige Gebäude schließt sich ein fünfgeschossiger Bürokomplex, an den wiederum die Stadthalle mit ihren Zugängen grenzt. Das Ensemble wird durch eine hohe Galerie mit einem tonnenförmigen Glasdach gekrönt und zusammengehalten. Der extensive Einsatz von Glas mag sich Stirlings Bewunderung für Joseph Paxton verdanken.

Derby Civic Centre
Limited competition project
James Stirling with Leon Krier
Derby
1970

This competition design was made with the collaboration of Leon Krier, and marks the beginning of Stirling's keen interest in civic architecture.

The building shapes itself to a horseshoe footprint which makes both a public square and an informal theatre, an arena for outdoor activities. At the stage end the acoustic shield where the band plays carries on its back the facade of a historic building salvaged from war damage, tilted however to avoid any accusation of being over-serious. The square is further furnished by a monumental group of telephone kiosks which mark the presence below of the public lavatories. These notes contributed to Stirling's growing reputation as an ironist.

Wrapping around the horseshoe building are five floors of offices, and beyond, the public hall and its entrances. The ensemble is tied together by a tall galleria, the whole height of the building, capped by a barrel-vaulted glazed roof. The extensive use of glazed surfaces may derive from his admiration for Paxton.

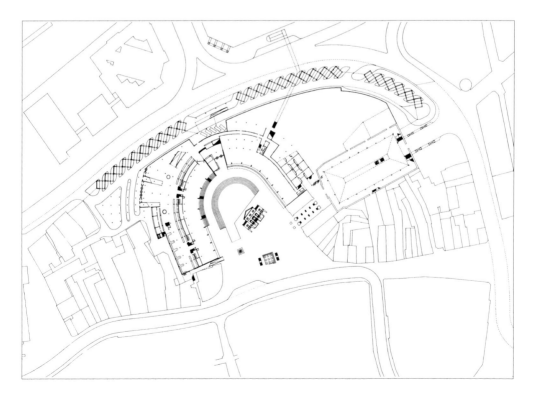

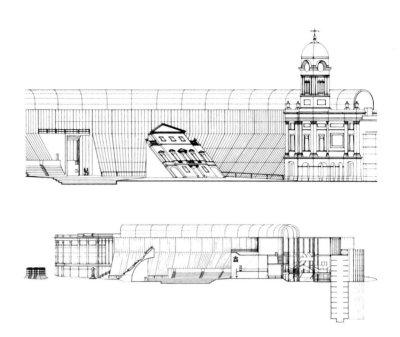

Grundriß Erdgeschoß
Schnittansicht von der Platzseite
Ansicht mit Konzertbühne
Umlaufende Erschließungsgalerie

Ground floor plan
Section elevation from square
Elevation with theatre
Circulation galleria

Olivetti Firmensitz

Projekt
James Stirling and Partner
Milton Keynes, Buckinghamshire
1971

Der Sitz von Olivetti liegt in einem großzügigen Landschaftspark mit einem bereits vorhandenen See. Die Verwaltungsbüros sind dem See am nächsten, die Lager- und Produktionsstätten, die den Komplex von der nahen Schnellstraße abschirmen, befinden sich dahinter. Das Parkhaus ist im Kellergeschoß versteckt.

Die Produktionsbereiche werden von den Büros durch einen durchlaufenden verglasten Hallengang getrennt, von dem aus die beiden oberen Bürogeschosse durch Galerien erschlossen sind. Durch die Krümmung des Gebäudes bleiben die Büros zum See hin orientiert, auf den man von durchlaufenden Galerien aus blickt. In der Gebäudekrümmung befindet sich ein Eingangsbereich, über dem Konferenzräume untergebracht sind. Am südlichen Ende des Bürotrakts schließt sich der Erholungsbereich mit Restaurant, Sportanlagen und Bootsclub an. Eine separate Zufahrt führt dorthin, die außerhalb der Bürozeiten am Wochenende benutzt werden kann.

Dieser Gebäudeteil in doppelter Geschoßhöhe wird von zylindrischen Säulen mit pilzförmigen Kapitellen getragen. Aus der perspektivischen Zeichnung wird erkennbar, wie Stirling hier sein klassizistisches Vokabular neu einsetzt.

Olivetti Headquarters

Project
James Stirling and Partner
Milton Keynes, Buckinghamshire
1971

The building is sited within an extensive park, close to an existing lake. The administrative centre is placed closest to the lake, with the warehousing and manufacturing areas behind, where their bulk screens the noise from a motorway. The car park is placed out of sight in the basement.

A glazed concourse separates the offices from the workshops, giving access to balconies which provide entry to the offices at two upper levels. The block bends around in a gentle curve to keep the offices close to the lake side, which they overlook from continuous balconies. At the point where the building curves the entrance is placed, with conference room directly above. At the southern end of the office building are the recreational facilities – restaurant, sports centre, and a boat club, with separate car access for convenience of use at the weekends, when the rest of the building is closed.

The social space is a double height volume contained by a sinuous glazed screen and supported by a grid of cylindrical columns with mushroom capitals. This space has been memorialised by the perspective which shows the architect apparently rearranging his neo-classical furniture for a special event.

Modellfoto
Schnitt
Blick in die Kantine
Isometrie
Grundriß

Model view
Section
View of the restaurant
Axonometric
Floor plan

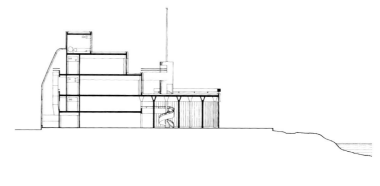

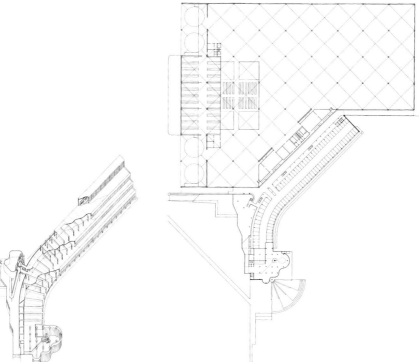

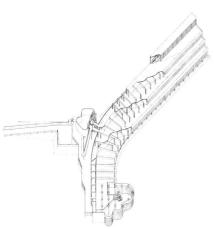

Kunstfakultät der St. Andrews Universität
Projekt
James Stirling and Partner
St. Andrews, Schottland
1971

Dies war Stirlings erster Entwurf einer Kunstgalerie, mit dem zugleich eine bestehende Villa im palladianischen Stil aufzuwerten war, die von der Scottish Fine Arts Commission unter Denkmalschutz gestellt worden war. Das Gebäude, das eine kleine Kunstgalerie, einen Theaterworkshop und einen Atelierbereich für Malerei und Bildhauerei umfaßt, mußte sich daher auf die Eckbebauung ihres Vorplatzes beschränken.

Der Theaterworkshop wurde so entworfen, daß er sich in Größe und Funktion durch bewegliche Trennwände verändern läßt, die sich nach oben ins Dachgebälk ziehen lassen, ähnlich wie beim Trainingszentrum von Olivetti.

Die einzelnen Teile der Komposition werden von einer verglasten Galerie zusammengehalten, die der palladianischen Komposition der Villa Badoer neues Leben einhaucht.

Arts Centre for St. Andrews University
Project
James Stirling and Partner
St. Andrews, Scotland
1971

This was Stirling's first project for an art gallery, and it involved rehabilitating an existing Palladian villa protected by the Scottish Fine Arts Commission, a circumstance which restricted new accommodation to just the corners of its forecourt. This comprises a small art gallery, a theatre workshop, and studio space for painting and sculpture.

The theatre workshop is designed to vary in size and function by means of moveable partitions, which withdraw upwards into roof housings, in a manner reminiscent of the variable space in the Olivetti Training School. The parts of the composition are tied together by a glazed gallery that re-animates the Palladian composition at the Villa Badoer.

Modellfoto von oben   Aerial view of model
Isometrie   Axonometric

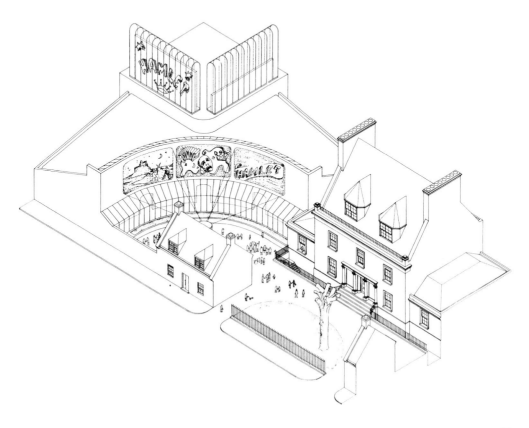

Wallraf-Richartz Museum

Projekt für eingeladenen Wettbewerb
James Stirling and Partner
Köln
1975

Die Lage des Grundstücks war problematisch, nicht zuletzt aufgrund der sich auftürmenden Masse des Kölner Doms und seiner seltsamen Ausrichtung auf die wuchtige Eisenbahnbrücke und die dazwischen liegenden Bahngleise. Die Architekten begegneten dieser Situation mit einem urbanen Entwurf, der sich auf beide Seiten der Bahnlinie ausdehnte und das Ende der Eisenbahnbrücke durch zwei «Torgebäude» auf jeder Seite markierte.

Eins davon wurde dann ein Teil des neuen Museums mit einem Theater auf dem oberen Niveau. Dorthin gelangt man mit einer Rolltreppe von der Eingangshalle, die von einem Säulengang umgeben ist. Unter dem Theater verteilen sich die Flächen auf mehrere Geschosse um ein kreisförmiges Foyer. Galerien umschließen den Vorhof, und den Eingang von der Tiefgarage bildet ein abgesenkter Hof, der in seiner Anlage an die Grundrißform einer Kirche mit Apsis erinnert.

Wallraf-Richartz Museum

Invited competition project
James Stirling and Partner
Cologne
1975

The site here presented many difficulties, not least the towering bulk of Cologne Cathedral and its strange alignment with the massive railway bridge and the intervening plateau of rail tracks. The architects faced up to this situation by suggesting an urban strategy that would extend on both sides of the rail tracks, and mark the end of the rail bridge by two «gateway» buildings placed one on either side.

One of these then became a part of the new museum, with a theatre on the upper level approached by an escalator tube from a peristyled entrance hall at lower level. Below the theatre, accommodation is organised at several levels around a circular foyer. The galleries enclose the forecourt, and the entrance from the underground car park is through a sunken court which takes the plan footprint of an apsidal church.

Lageplan

Schnittisometrie

Site plan

Cutaway axonometric

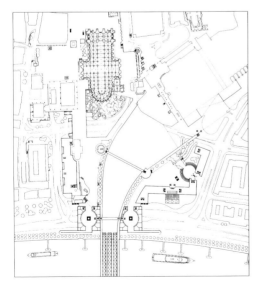

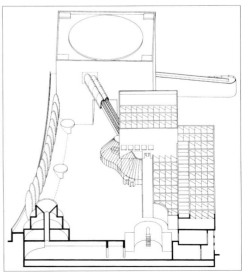

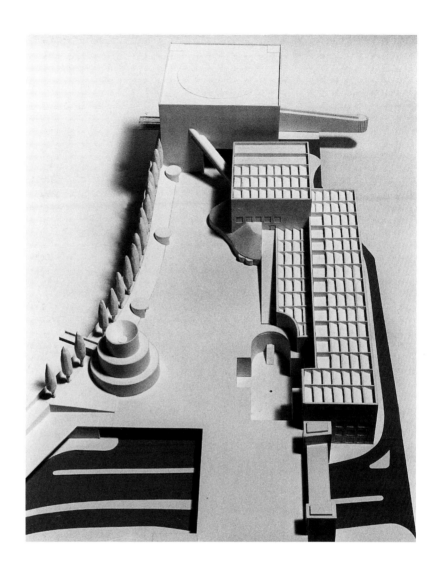

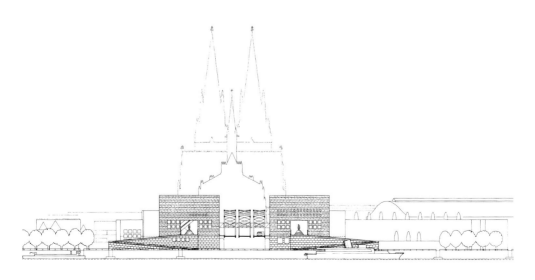

Kunstsammlung Nordrhein-Westfalen
Projekt für eingeladenen Wettbewerb
James Stirling and Partner
Düsseldorf
1975

Museum for Northrhine Westphalia
Invited competition project
James Stirling and Partner
Düsseldorf
1975

Dieser Entwurf weicht von der damals üblichen Methode ab, das Grundstück zunächst vollständig abzuräumen, um dann eine strahlende neue Schachtel darauf zu setzen. Er versucht im Gegenteil so viel wie möglich von der vorhandenen Bebauung zu erhalten und ihr durch die baulichen Eingriffe eine neue Bedeutung zu verleihen.

Die Gebäudemasse ist weit nach hinten gerückt, und eine Art Portikus, der Aufmerksamkeit erregt und den Eingang markiert, ist auf den vorderen Grundstücksteil gesetzt. Das Museum liegt auf einer Linie mit den Gebäuden und der Straße unmittelbar an seiner Nordseite und bildet auf diese Weise einen Winkel mit den dahinter liegenden Volumina. Eine gewundene Eingangshalle führt die Besucher zu den Einrichtungen, darunter ein Kino, das von einer runden Galerie überragt wird, sowie eine Reihe von Ausstellungsräumen, die sich um einen runden Hof verteilen.

Dieser Entwurf entstand kurz nachdem James Stirling Michael Wilford zu seinem Partner machte und markiert einen Wendepunkt in der Entwicklung des Architekturbüros. Von nun an wird bei der Entwurfsarbeit die Einbeziehung des Kontextes eine ebenso große Rolle spielen wie die funktionale Analyse.

This project departs from the conventional view of the time, which looked to clear the site and erect a shining new box like a machine. It works, on the contrary, to retrieve as much of the existing environment as possible, and make sense of it by the new additions.

The mass of the building is set well back, and a porch drawn forward to make a pavilion for publicity and mark the entrance point. This aligns itself with the buildings and street immediately to the north, and so appears at an angle with the volumes behind it. A sinuous entrance hall leads visitors back to the facilities, which include a cinema surmounted by a circular gallery, as well as the suite of galleries disposed around a circular court.

This design was conceived soon after Michael Wilford joined James Stirling as his sole partner, and marks a turning point in the evolution of the firm. From now on, we find that environmental context plays an equal part with functional analysis in the generation of design.

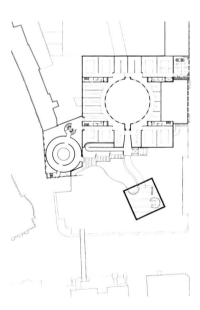

Grundriß Erdgeschoß

Ground floor plan

Grundriß Obergeschoß

Upper level plan

Modellfoto
Isometrie

Model view
Axonometric

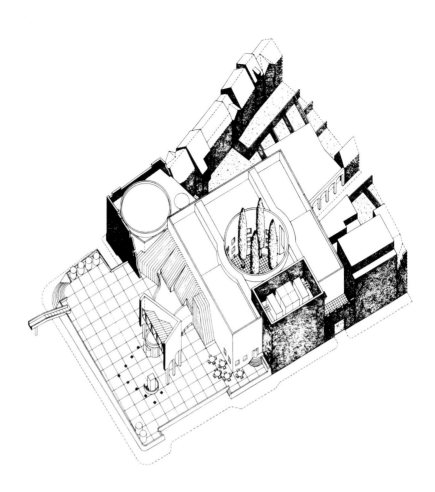

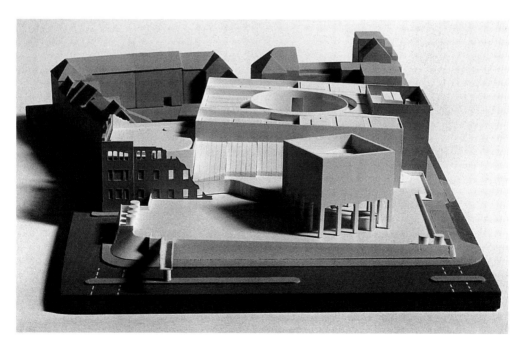

Hotel Meinekestraße
Projekt
James Stirling and Partner
Berlin
1976

Hotel Meinekestrasse
Project
James Stirling and Partner
Berlin
1976

Bei diesem Projekt handelt es sich um eine Etüde in Stadterneuerung von jener Art, für die der Brüsseler Architekt und Lehrer Maurice Culot mit seinem «Atelier de Recherche et d'Action Urbaine» seit 1968 eintrat. Wo eine umfassende Sanierung nicht möglich ist, bleibt doch immer die Möglichkeit, störende Gebäude wie hier durch schmale Baukörper zu verdecken. In diesem Fall ist es eine Tankstelle, die durch ein kleines Hotel abgeschirmt wird, ohne sie zu beseitigen.

Der Hotelbau, der um einige Wohnungen und Maisonettes erweitert ist und im Erdgeschoß Geschäfte beherbergt, ist als Band aus zwei zusammenhängenden Fassaden gestaltet, die einem aufgeschlagenen Buch ähneln und an der Straßenecke ihr «Scharnier» haben.

This is a little exercise in urban renewal, of a kind similar to that advocated in Brussels by the architect and teacher Maurice Culot and his «Atelier de Recherche et d'Action Urbaine». Where massive reconstruction is not possible, it may still be possible to transform the scene by screening objectionable buildings with a shallow building. In this case, the accommodation provided for a small hotel allows a petrol station to be hidden without removing it. The hotel, amplified by the addition of some flats and maisonettes, with shops at ground level, is treated as a band of two adjoining facades, treated like a book back, «hinged» at the corner.

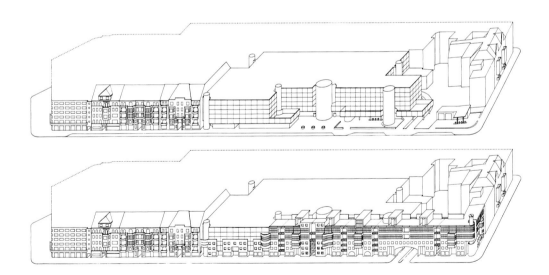

Isometrie:
oben bestehende Bebauung,
unten mit vorgesetztem Neubau

Axonometric:
top existing building,
below shallow new building

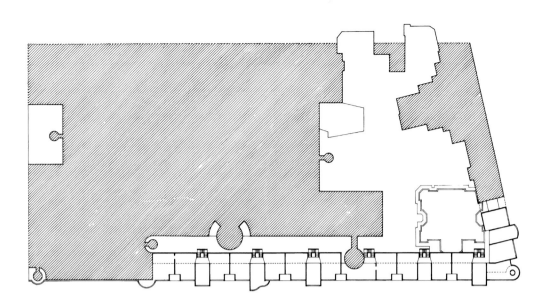

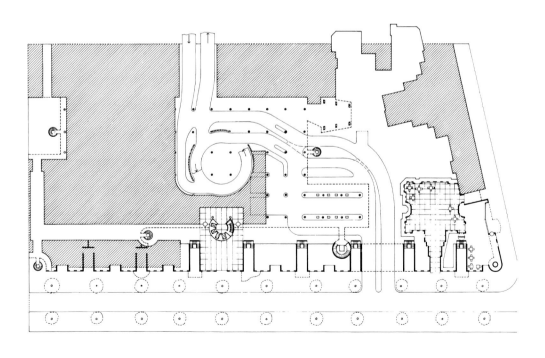

Grundrisse
Erdgeschoß (unten) und
Obergeschoß (oben)

Plans
of ground (bottom) and
upper floor (top)

Dresdner Bank
Projekt
James Stirling and Partner
Marburg
1977

Eine Straßenkurve ließ gerade genug Platz, um dieses Bankgebäude neben eine alte Mühle mit einer historischen Giebelwand zu setzen, wo es einen pseudo-historischen Bau aus der Nachkriegszeit ersetzt.

Mit einer Querachse, auf der die Nebeneingänge liegen, wird das Grundstück in zwei Teile geteilt. Die Achse wird von einer Bogenöffnung durchbrochen, die einen Fußgängerweg markiert, der durch den Komplex führt. Zu beiden Seiten dieses Durchbruchs verläuft der Fußgängerweg in Schlangenlinie und ist von einer Säulenreihe flankiert, die zur Hälfte eine Kolonnade, zur anderen eine verglaste Wand zur Bank und den Büros bildet. Es gibt auch einen Laden und einen Zeitungskiosk sowie Platz für eine Bushaltestelle.

Diese Architektur bringt die losen Enden der Stadt wieder zusammen, schafft einen öffentlichen Raum und einen lebendigen Raumeindruck. Sie ist weit entfernt von dem Stilmischmasch, der oft als postmodern durchgeht.

Dresdner Bank
Project
James Stirling and Partner
Marburg
1977

A bend in the road gave just enough space to insert this bank building alongside an old mill, to which a historic gable is still attached. The new building takes the place of a pseudo-old building erected just after the war.

A cross axis is established, with service entrances, which breaks the site in two, and is penetrated by an arched opening that marks the position of a pedestrian footpath traversing the site. On each side of this break, the line of the footpath becomes a sinuous curve, flanked by a line of columns, in one half forming a colonnade, in the other forming a new glazed wall to the bank and offices. There is also a shop and a newspaper kiosk, and space for a bus stop.

This is architecture that sews the city together again, makes public space, and creates spatial sensation. It is far removed from the sort of pastiche that often passes for post-modern style.

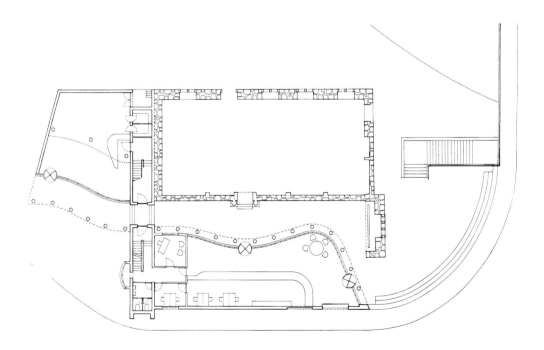

Grundriß Erdgeschoß

Ground floor plan

Isometrie   Axonometric

Neue Staatsgalerie

Beschränkter Wettbewerb
James Stirling and Partner
Stuttgart
1977 – 1984

Dieser Bau ist eine Erweiterung des alten klassizistischen Museums und folgt der ursprünglichen Anlage mit einem erhöhten U-förmigen Hof, der größer als die Vorlage ist und in seinem Zentrum eine Haltestelle für Taxis statt einer Statue hat. Das Hofmotiv wiederholt sich auf einer höheren Geschoßebene als intimer Raum zur Ausstellung von Plastiken. Dieser Hof hat in seiner Mitte eine kreisrunde Trommel, deren Form als Echo des mit einer Kuppel bekrönten Zentrums etwa bei Schinkels Altem Museum in Berlin oder beim Britischen Museum in London erscheint. Diese Trommel erweist sich jedoch als hohl und nach oben hin offen und ist tatsächlich ein Skulpturengarten. Noch offener wird die Komposition durch einen öffentlichen Fußweg, der auf einer Rampe um den Hof herumführt und ein öffentliches Wegerecht durch das Herz des Museums sicherstellt. Die Kombination hierarchisch gegliederter Räume und informeller Nutzungen ist typisch für Stirlings Ansatz, dem es hier gelingt, sowohl den Ordnungssinn als auch das liberale Streben des neuen demokratischen Deutschlands anzusprechen.

Die Anlage der Ausstellungsräume verschiedener Größe, die hintereinander aufgereiht sind, ist konventionell. Weniger konventionell ist die Eingangshalle zur linken Seite auf dem unteren Sockel mit ihrer markanten ziehharmonikaförmigen Glaswand mit belebenden, grünen Fensterprofilen. Im Inneren der Eingangshalle wird jedoch die Ordnung durch eine runde Garderobe sofort wieder hergestellt, die, von einem Säulenring geschützt, von oben erleuchtet wird und trutzig-entschlossen wirkt. Hinter dieser Garderobentheke fährt der Lift in seiner gläsernen High-Tech-Hülle nach oben – ein optimistisches, zukunftsfrohes Zeichen.

Vielleicht den bemerkenswertesten Eindruck in diesem bemerkenswerten Gebäude hinterlassen die Stellen, wo die zentrale Trommel den Wänden der angrenzenden Ausstellungsräume nahe kommen. Die Galerien blicken mit der Anmut eines aristokratischen Herrenhauses auf den Skulpturenhof und schließen oben mit einem emphatischen, gewölbten ägyptischen Gesims ab. Wo die Trommel sich nähert, machen sie dann mitsamt ihres Gesimses Platz. Hat Stirling hier improvisiert? Wenn ja, dann geschah es mit Genialität.

New State Gallery

Limited competition
James Stirling and Partner
Stuttgart
1977 – 1984

This is an extension of the original neo-classical museum, and it follows the original configuration with a U-shaped courtyard, wider than the original, and with a taxi set-down point at the centre instead of a statue. Further, the raised courtyard is repeated at an upper level as a private space for the display of statuary. It is occupied at its centre by a circular drum, whose enclosure appears to echo the traditional domed centre that one finds in Schinkel's Altes Museum in Berlin, or at the British Museum in London. However, this drum turns out to be hollow and roofless, and it is in fact a courtyard sculpture garden. A further loss of exclusivity is registered by the appearance of a public footpath, which circumambulates the court on a ramp, ensuring a public right of way through the heart of the museum. The combination of hierarchic spaces and informal uses typifies the Stirling approach, and allows this building to appeal both to the sense of order and to the liberal aspirations of the new democratic Germany.

The galleries themselves are conventional in layout, with a series of rooms of different sizes laid out en suite. Less conventional is the entrance hall, set to the left on the lower podium, and marked by an accordian-shaped glass wall in vivid green metal. Yet, inside the entrance hall, order is immediately restored by a circular counter guarded by a ring of columns and lit from above, almost Charlemagnian in its dedication. Beyond the cloakroom counter, the glass elevator rises in its high-tech cage, expressing a zest in the promise of the future.

Perhaps the most remarkable sensation in a remarkable building occurs where the outer surface of the central drum comes close to the walls of the adjoining galleries. The galleries face on to their sculpture courtyard with the grace of a patrician mansion, and are crowned by an emphatic Egyptian coved cornice. At the point where the drum impinges, the galleries are forced to withdraw, cornice and all, to allow enough room. The tight slot of space thus formed seems taut with energy. Is this improvisation? If so, it is done with genius.

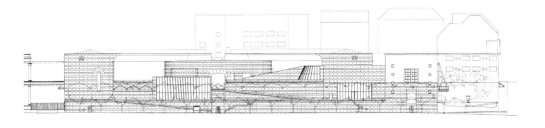

Ansicht von Westen   West elevation

Lageplan   Site plan

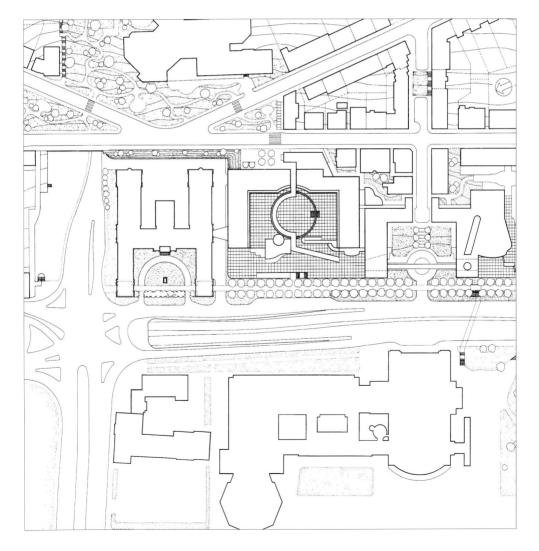

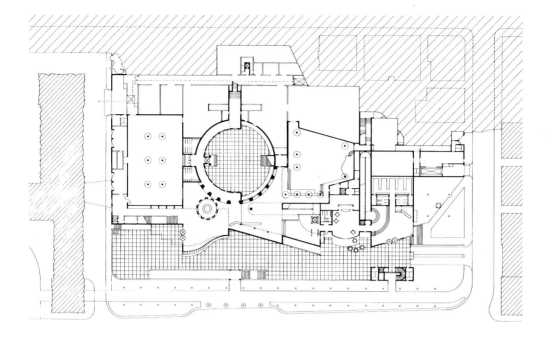

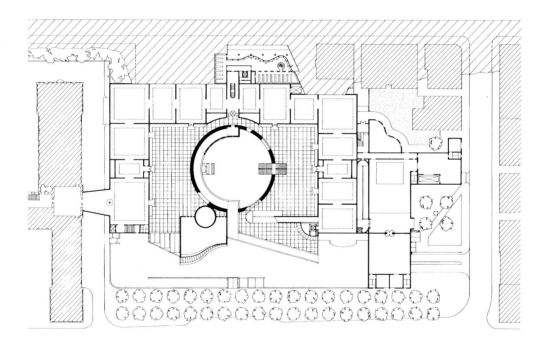

Grundrisse Erd- und Obergeschoß

Plans of ground and upper floor

Eingangsbereich und Rampe
Blick in den Skulpturenhof

Entrance and public ramp
View of sculpture courtyard

Fassadenausschnitt
Verwaltungstrakt

Facade detail
Administration wing

Blick in die Eingangshalle
Blick in einen Ausstellungsraum

Interior view of entrance hall
Interior view of a gallery

Bayer Pflanzenschutz-Zentrum
Projekt für beschränkten Wettbewerb
James Stirling and Partner
Monheim, Rhein
1978

Der große Pharmakonzern spielte hier die Rolle eines Bauherren des 18. Jahrhunderts: Statt eine streng zweckhafte Fabrik zu bauen, wurde er gebeten, eine Art Schloß zu entwerfen, das mit seinen Nebengebäuden ein aristokratisches Verhältnis zur Gartenlandschaft der Umgebung sucht. Trotz der strengen klassizistischen Untertöne bietet dieses Werk eine ideale Umgebung für Gespräche und Forschung.

Stirling schafft hier die gewünschte idyllische Atmosphäre, indem er die Labors für Forschung und Entwicklung im Pflanzenschutz hinter eine baumgesäumte Promenade zurücksetzt, die einen Halbkreis um das Verwaltungszentrum beschreibt. Hinter dieser natürlichen Schutzwand können sie sich in verschiedenen Formen frei entfalten und sich nach Bedarf ausdehnen.

Das zentrale U-förmige Gebäude mit Parkplatz am Eingang enthält unten ein Konferenzzentrum, an das sich weitere Einrichtungen anschließen. Der ganze Komplex ist außerdem auch außen von einem Baumgürtel umgeben.

Bayer Research Centre
Limited competition project
James Stirling and Partner
Monheim, Rhein
1978

This large pharmaceutical company has been forced into the role of an eighteenth century patron: instead of a utilitarian factory it was asked to build a kind of university, in which a *schloss* with its outbuildings would engage in a patrician relationship with its garden setting. In spite of the neo-classical overtones, the environment produced here is very conducive to conversation and research.

The arcadian ambiance is achieved by setting the laboratories for herbicidal research and development back behind a tree-lined promenade, which describes a hemicycle around the administrative centre. Behind this screen they are free to adopt different configurations and to expand as need dictates. The central U-shaped building faces the car court at the entrance, and contains a conference centre at its base, with other facilities adjoining. The whole complex is surrounded by a further swathe of trees.

Grundriß Erdgeschoß
Modellfoto

Ground floor plan
Model view

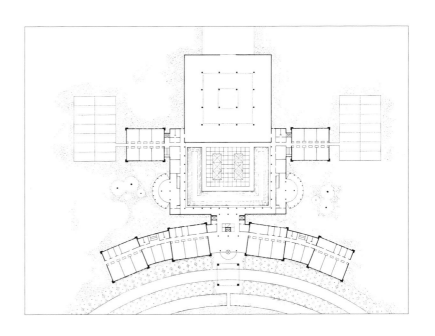

Manhattan Stadthäuser
Projekt für beschränkten Wettbewerb
James Stirling and Partner
New York
1978

Der Auftraggeber dieses Projekts war ein Architekt, der mit den elf Häusern in der East 67th Street Luxuswohnraum schaffen wollte – nur wenige in Manhattan können es sich leisten, in einem *Haus* zu wohnen. Eine Tiefgarage mit der erforderlichen Tragfähigkeit für fünf Geschosse war bereits vorhanden, allerdings mußte die Breite der Häuser wegen der existierenden Querschotten auf fünfeinhalb Meter beschränkt bleiben. Die Architekten schlugen jedoch einige Häuser mit doppelter Breite vor und schufen mit drei Hausformen typologische Abwechslung. So entstanden Fassaden von alternierender Breite, bei denen die schmalen Häuserfronten vorstehen. Zurückspringende Balkone über zwei Geschosse und Erkerfenster an den breiten Hausfassaden ergänzen dieses Wechselspiel.
Der Auftraggeber erwartete Luxus bei den sanitären Anlagen und der Ausstattung, großzügige Raumaufteilung und charaktervolle Gestaltung. Das Ergebnis ist eigenwillig und paßt sich doch in den traditionellen Kontext der Sandsteinfassaden in diesem Teil New Yorks ein.

Manhattan Townhouses
Limited competition projekt
James Stirling and Partner
New York
1978

The client for this project was an architect, who wanted the eleven houses at East 67th Street to appeal to a luxury market – few in Manhattan can afford to live in a *house*. There was an existing basement garage with sufficient structure to support five storeys of additional construction, but the structural bay dictated an eighteen foot limit to the width of each house. However the architects were able to suggest that some houses could take in a double frontage, giving more variety of dwelling type, in effect three variations. This translated into a terrace in which wide and narrow bays alternate, with the narrow bays protruding, allowing a play of double height recessed balconies and projecting bay windows that cross the double unit.
The client expected luxury standards in the provision of plumbing and services, generous space standards, the appearance of character. The result is both idiosyncratic, and conforms to the traditional brownstone vocabulary dominant in this part of New York.

Entwurfszeichnung
Grundriß Obergeschoß
Grundriß Erdgeschoß
Schnittisometrie

Design sketch
Upper floor plan
Ground floor plan
Cutaway axonometric

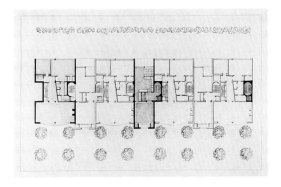

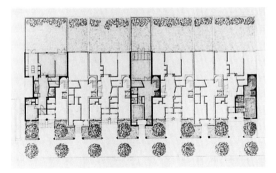

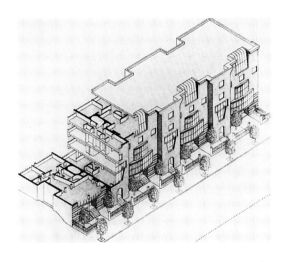

**Erweiterung der
Architekturfakultät der Rice University**
Beschränkter Wettbewerb
James Stirling and Partner
Houston, Texas
1979 – 1981

**Rice School of
Architecture Extension**
Limited competition
James Stirling and Partner
Houston, Texas
1979 – 1981

Der Anbau, der zusätzliche Atelierräume für den Architekturunterricht schafft, ist mit dem Altbau verzahnt und bildet mit einer bereits vorhandenen Kolonnade einen dreiseitig gefaßten, südwestlich ausgerichteten Hof mit gutem *feng shui*. Mit seinen Backsteinfassaden paßt der Neubau in Material und Größe zum bestehenden Gebäude, und die Fassadenbehandlung zeigt eine verhaltene Ähnlichkeit, ohne zur bloßen Nachahmung zu verkommen. Das Gebäude paßt auf den Campus, als stünde es dort schon seit 100 Jahren.

Es gibt jedoch zwei Merkmale, die typisch für Stirling sind: Die Querachse, an der sich die Erschließung orientiert, wird auf dem Dach an jedem Ende von einem Glaskegel markiert und verleiht dem Gebäude eine Art nautischen Zug; und der Eingang am Ende des Blocks, der von einer einzelnen Säule mit einem Backsteinbogen darüber zweigeteilt wird und dessen Einheit sich durch die runde Lünette direkt unter der Kämpferlinie wiedergestellt. Sie liegt nicht, wie man erwarten könnte, direkt im Zentrum, sondern ist zur Seite hin versetzt.

The new addition, which provides additional studio space for architectural classes, interlocks with an existing building, and with an existing colonnade beyond, forms a three-sided courtyard facing southwest, exemplifying an excellent *feng shui*. Its brick facades match the existing building in material and scale, and the elevational treatment is quietly sympathetic, without being a pastiche. The building fits into the campus as if it had been there for a hundred years.

There are two Stirlingesque touches, nevertheless: the cross axis which binds the circulation together is marked on the roofline by a glass cone at either end, imparting a nautical touch; and the entrance at the end of the block, divided into two by a single column, expanded by a tall brick arch, has its unity restored by a circular lunette set just below the springing; not bang on centre, as might be expected, but off to one side.

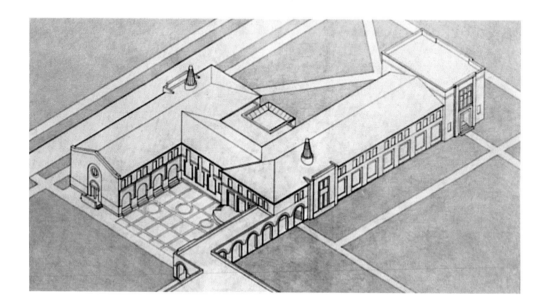

Perspektivische Zeichnung des Alt- und Neubaus

Perspective of extension and existing building

Grundriß Erdgeschoß
Innenhof

Ground floor plan
Courtyard

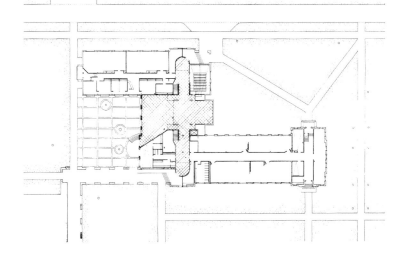

Wissenschaftszentrum
Beschränkter Wettbewerb
James Stirling and Partner
Berlin
1979 – 1987

Das Wissenschaftszentrum ist ein Institut für Sozialforschung. Das alte Gebäude aus dem 19. Jahrhundert, dessen Rückfassade sich zum Garten öffnet, blieb erhalten und wird als Sekretariat und für Konferenzen genutzt. Die neuen Gebäude gruppieren sich lose um den Garten und schaffen eine dem Institut angemessene, gesprächsfördernde Campus-Atmosphäre.

Das nicht gerade exotische Programm für das übrige Gebäude sah jedoch nur Büroflächen vor, und die konventionelle Lösung eines einzelnen Büroblocks hätte eine ganz andere Atmosphäre geschaffen und zudem den Altbau erdrückt. Stirling und Wilford begegneten diesem Problem beherzt, indem sie die Büroflächen auf vier neue Gebäude aufteilten, die vier Studienbereichen entsprechen, und schufen im Garten eine Kolonnade unter freiem Himmel. Schockierend fanden einige, daß die separaten Gebäude absichtlich und scheinbar willkürlich als Blöcke gestaltet sind, die Elemente der Architekturgeschichte Revue passieren lassen: Turmaufsatz, Halbrotunde, sechseckiger Turm, Kreuzkirche, griechische Kolonnade – all dies läßt sich hier finden. Die Elemente unterscheiden sich dabei in ihrer Form, nicht aber in der Fassadengestaltung, die einheitlich ist. Die Architekten hatten eingestandenermaßen ironische Absichten – die Fenster etwa sollten wie eine Art «Tapete» wirken, die um die Volumina «gewickelt» ist.

Ein geistreicher Entwurf, der vielleicht auch witzig erscheinen mag. Aber ein Besuch im Wissenschaftszentrum ruft einen ganz anderen Eindruck hervor: Dies ist ein Ort des Arbeitens. Die Stahlkonstruktion der Kolonnade und der Laterne des halbrunden Hofes sprechen vom rastlosen modernen Leben und wirken alles andere als zusammengewürfelt und kitschig. Für die Nutzer steht nicht die Ironie im Vordergrund, sondern die angenehme Arbeitsatmosphäre.

Science Research Centre
Limited competition
James Stirling and Partner
Berlin
1979 – 1987

The Wissenschaftzentrum is a social research institute. The original nineteenth century building has been retained and used for secretariat and conference facilities, and its rear porch opens on to the garden. The new buildings are grouped loosely around the garden to produce a campus-like setting suitable for exchanging greetings and conversations.

But the requirement for the rest of the accommodation was for nothing more exciting than offices, and the conventional solution employing a single office block would have produced a rather different atmosphere, and in addition would have cruelly overwhelmed the old palace. Stirling-Wilford have seized this problem head-on, by dividing up the offices among four new buildings, corresponding to four departments of studies, plus an open-air colonnade to back the garden. What has shocked many susceptibilities is the deliberate shaping of the separate buildings into apparently arbitrary blocks that replay a history of architecture: turreted tower, hemi-cycle, hexagonal tower, cruciform church, Greek stoa, are all to be found, distinguished by shape but not by elevational treatment, which is uniform. The architects agree that their intention here was ironical – the windows are meant to be a kind of wrap-around «wallpaper».

The concept is jokey, and even suggests a one-liner. But a visit to the Centre conveys a very different impression: this is a place of work. The steel structure of the colonnade and of the lantern to the semicircular courtyard of the hemi-cycle speak of the strenuous modern life, and there is no feeling of pastiche or kitsch at all. For those who use it, there is no joke, just a sympathetic environment.

Modellfoto; im Vordergrund der Altbau
Grundriß Erdgeschoß

Model view; the existing building is in the foreground
Ground floor plan

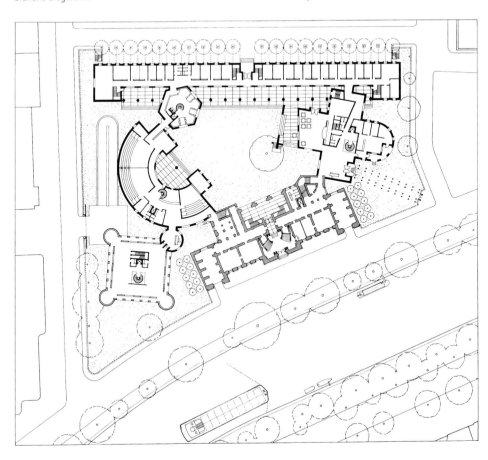

Schutzdach des halbkreisförmigen Gebäudes
Blick in den Garten und auf den Bibliotheksturm
Kolonnade zum Garten

Canopy of hemi-cycle building
View of the garden and the library tower
Garden colonnade

Sackler Galerie

James Stirling and Partner
Cambridge, Massachusetts
1979 – 1984

Die Galerie nimmt ein L-förmiges Grundstück nahe dem Fogg Museum der Harvard Universität ein, ist jedoch durch eine vielbefahrene städtische Durchgangsstraße von ihm getrennt. Die Architekten mußten also an eine Fußgängerbrücke zum Fogg Museum denken, oder, falls diese nicht gebaut würde, an ein Gebäude, daß aus sich selbst heraus Bestand hätte.

Dieses Dilemma lösten sie, indem sie die Front der neuen Galerie auf das Fogg Museum ausrichteten, so daß eine künftige Brücke direkt über den Eingang führen würde. In der Zwischenzeit werden die Pfeiler für das eine Ende der Brücke, die wie Luftschächte wirken, als Wachposten zu beiden Seiten des Eingangs stehen. Die Steinverkleidung und übrige Gestaltung der Front geben der künftigen Bedeutung des Gebäudes Ausdruck, während der Rest des Gebäudes an den angrenzenden Straßen liegt und bescheidene Ziegelsteinfassaden zeigt.

Diese Seitenfassaden mit der gestreiften Uniformität ihrer farblich alternierenden Backsteinverkleidung und den scheinbar willkürlich gesetzten, an der Raumverteilung orientierten Fensteröffnungen stießen nicht auf einhellige Zustimmung. Aber die Anordnung ist durchaus nicht so willkürlich: Die Südfassade wirkt von der angrenzenden Gund Hall aus gesehen ruhig und elegant.

Im Inneren weitet sich die Eingangshalle seitlich zu Treppenaufgängen, die von monumentalen Säulen abgeschirmt werden, während sich die Haupttreppe geradeaus in einem schmalen Tunnel nach oben zieht. Auch sie wirkt monumental, weil sie in einer geraden Linie, nur unterbrochen von den dazwischen liegenden Geschossen, ansteigt, um an ihrem Endpunkt das Niveau des Hauptausstellungsraums zu erreichen, von dem aus man die selbst als Ausstellungsgang genutzte zukünftige Brücke betreten wird.

Die neuen Ausstellungsräume werden diskret durch Oberlichter erhellt und wirken ruhig und elegant. Ihre Größe ist auf die meist kleinen Skulpturen zugeschnitten, die dort ausgestellt sind – ideal zum Studium der Werke. Nur an einem Punkt wird dieser Rhythmus durch ein Fenster zum Hof unterbrochen, von dem aus der Blick auf das alte Museum fällt.

Sackler Gallery

James Stirling and Partner
Cambridge, Massachusetts
1979 – 1984

The gallery occupies an L-shaped site next to the Fogg Museum at Harvard University, but separated from it by a busy cross-town road. The architects had to envisage it being linked to the Fogg by a bridge across this road, or, if the bridge was not built, to be capable of acting on its own.

This dilemma was resolved by having the new gallery face the Fogg, so that a future bridge would connect directly above the entrance. In the meantime, the piers that will carry one end of the bridge, disguised as ventilators, stand as sentinels on either side of the door. The stone facings and trim on this facade speak of future responsibilities, while the rest of the building fronts the adjoining streets with a modest brick facade.

Controversy surrounded this frontage, with its alternating colours of brick giving it a striped uniformity, while the windows are disposed in an apparently random order corresponding to room allocation. Yet, not altogether random: the view of the south face from the adjacent Gund Hall is quiet and elegant.

Inside, the entrance hall expands sideways to stairs shielded by monumental columns, while the main staircase proceeds straight ahead in a narrow funnel, monumental too because it continues in one straight line, with mere pauses at the intervening floors. When it stops, it is at the main gallery level, the level of a future bridge, which will be another gallery in itself. The new galleries have discreet top light and are quiet and elegant, well scaled to the generally small works of sculpture displayed, very suitable for study. At just one point, the rhythm is broken by a little window into the courtyard, from which the parent gallery can be glimpsed.

Ansicht
Museumsinnenraum
Ausgang
Treppe

Elevation
Interior view of the gallery
Exit
Staircase

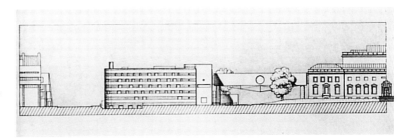

Chemiefakultät der Columbia Universität
Projekt
James Stirling, Michael Wilford and Associates
New York
1980

Dieses Gebäude mußte für ein schmales Grundstück an der Südwestecke des Campus der Columbia Universität zugeschnitten werden, deren Haupteingang am Broadway liegt. Die Höhe war beschränkt und mußte sich an den angrenzenden Gebäuden orientieren. Die Lösung der Architekten bestand darin, eine vorhandene Turnhalle zu überbrücken und eine Stahlgitterkonstruktion, die nur eine einzige freistehende Stütze hat, zum übrigen Gebäude zu führen. Ein Gebäudeflügel schwebt daher über dem Boden und gibt dem Eingang durch seine Auskragung Schutz.

Der restliche Baukörper, dessen Ende auf den Broadway stößt, ist konventionell und wirkt wie ein normales New Yorker Gebäude, mit einem regelmäßigen Muster kleiner Fenster und einem demonstrativ geschwungenen Gesims. Das Volumen ist an einem Punkt aufgebrochen. Ein zurückspringender Balkon markiert hier den Lese- und Versammlungssaal, wo Empfänge stattfinden können.

Chemistry Building for Columbia University
Project
James Stirling, Michael Wilford and Associates
New York
1980

This building had to be eased into a narrow site at the south-west corner of the Columbia Campus, with its main entrance on Broadway. The height was restricted by the heights of adjoining buildings. The solution was to bridge an existing gymnasium by placing a single column on clear ground, and leading a steel lattice structure back to the rest of the building. This means that one wing is carried clear of the ground, and its overhang shelters the entrance.

The remainder of the accommodation is put into a conventional building, the end of which reaches to Broadway. This has the look of a New York building, with a regular pattern of small windows and a demonstrative coved cornice. The volume is perforated at one point where a recessed balcony marks the presence of a reading and meeting room for receptions.

Modellfoto

Model view

Lageplan
Isometrie
Perspektivische Ansicht vom Broadway

Site plan
Axonometric
Perspective from Broadway

 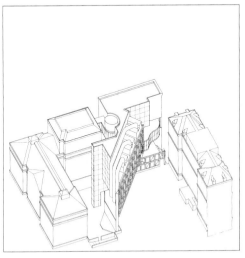

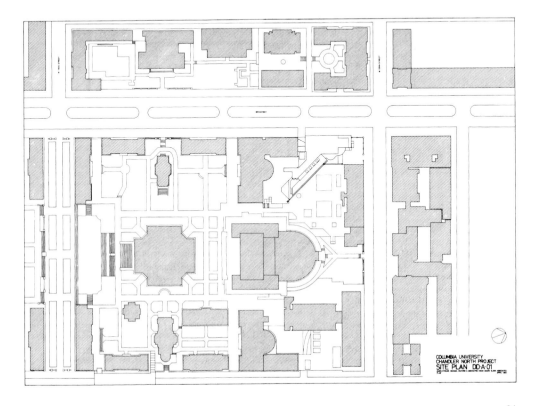

Clore Galerie

James Stirling, Michael Wilford and Associates
London
1980 – 1986

Die Clore Galerie ist eine Erweiterung des Tate Museums für Moderne Kunst für eine umfangreiche Sammlung von Gemälden William Turners. Sie liegt zwischen der Tate Gallery und dem vorhandenen Gartenhaus, auf das sie sich mit ihrer Gesimslinie und ihren Paneelwänden bezieht, während sie zum Museum respektvollen Abstand bewahrt. Der Eingang zum Clore-Flügel blickt jedoch auf den Portikus der Tate Gallery, ist mit Stein gerahmt und zeigt außerdem eine Giebelöffnung (als sei ein klassischer Tempel hierhin versetzt worden, so der Kommentar von Sir John Summerson) mit einem Halbrund darüber, das an George Dance oder Claude-Nicolas Ledoux erinnert, so daß das Gebäude Verspieltheit und Gelehrsamkeit zugleich zur Schau trägt. Dem Eingang nähert man sich durch einen Garten und gepflasterten Hof mit einem Wasserbassin und einer Pergola, welche die Besucher zur Tür führt.

Im Inneren strebt hinter der Rezeption eine Treppe in gerader Flucht noch oben, gegenläufig zu den Ausstellungsräumen. Oben angekommen, muß sich der Besucher neu orientieren, nicht durch den Bogen gehen, sondern sich wieder in die Gegenrichtung bewegen, um zu den zenital beleuchteten Ausstellungsräumen zu gelangen. Sie sind schnörkellos und zurückhaltend, aber sehr wirkungsvoll gestaltet. Wo die Eingangssequenz mit Richtungswechseln sowie Farben arbeitet, um die Besucher zu überwältigen, vertrauen die Ausstellungssäle ganz auf die Wirkung Turners.

Clore Gallery

James Stirling, Michael Wilford and Associates
London
1980 – 1986

The Clore is an extension of the Tate Gallery of Modern Art, and houses the extensive collection of paintings by J. W. Turner. It is situated between the Tate and the existing Lodge, and with its cornice line and panelled walls it ties in to the latter and shows deference to the Tate. Its entrance looks back at the Tate portico and is lined with stone, and in addition is marked by a large pedimental opening (as if a classical temple had been removed, said Sir John Summerson) with a half-round lunette above that reminds us of Dance or Ledoux, so the building evinces a combination of the playful and the scholarly. The entrance is approached by a garden and paved court, with a pool and a pergola to help turn the visitor towards the door.

Inside, beyond the reception desk, the staircase rises in a straight flight pointing away from the galleries, and the visitor has to pause at the top, re-orient, turn, and proceed in the opposite direction to enter the top-lit galleries, not pass through the arch. The galleries are managed without further rhetoric in a subdued but effective way. Where the entrance sequence employed turns and colours to dazzle the visitor, the galleries leave it all to Turner.

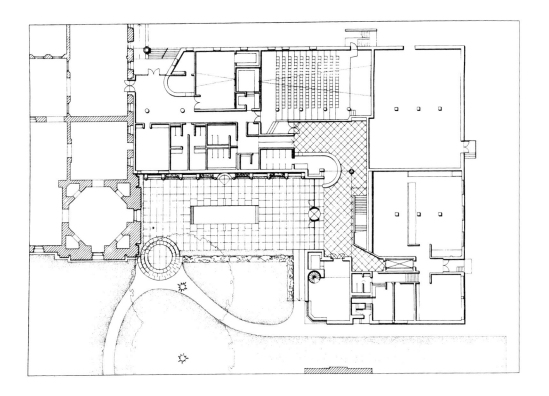

Grundriß Erdgeschoß
Blick auf den Eingang

Ground floor plan
View of entrance

Musikakademie

James Stirling, Michael Wilford and Associates
Stuttgart
1980 – 1994

Die Musikakademie blickt an ihrer Nordseite auf die Urbanstraße, wo eine Reihe von Gebäuden stehen, die nicht der Staatsgalerie weichen mußten. Die neue Fassade setzt die Dimensionen und den Charakter dieser Gebäude fort und stellt so die bauliche Kontinuität in dieser Straße sicher. Der Haupteingang präsentiert sich lediglich mit dem kontrollierten Nachdruck farbiger Stahl- und Glasvordächer, wie er für frühe Bauhausstudien kennzeichnend ist. An der Ecke ist die Mensa durch Zieharmonikaverglasung hervorgehoben, die einige Säulen erkennen läßt und zur Straße hin das soziale Innenleben sichtbar werden läßt.

Anders die Südseite, wo eine neue Piazza über einem Parkhaus den Fokus einer urbanen Gestaltung bildet: Zusammen mit den Bäumen, die den Rand der Konrad-Adenauer-Straße säumen, und einem Gebäude, das ursprünglich als Theaterhochschule geplant war und dessen Fertigstellung noch aussteht, wird hier mit dem berühmte Galathea-Brunnen, der versetzt wird, ein städtischer Platz direkt gegenüber dem Staatstheater entstehen. Auf dieser Seite schafft das Gebäude Räume, die sich in den Kontext der Nordecke des großen Stadtparks fügen und in städtischen Dimensionen zugeschnitten sind. Mit seiner sorgfältigen Berücksichtigung der Straße auf der einen und des Parks auf der anderen Seite ist dies ein Entwurf, der uns eine Idee von wirklicher *Stadtplanung* gibt.

Die Musikschule erstreckt sich über neun Geschosse mit Lehr- und Übungsräumen, die in dem linearen Gebäude entlang der Urbanstraße untergebracht sind. Diese Straßenfront ist in eine Reihe von Elementen aufgegliedert, die sich in ihrer Größe auf die benachbarten Gebäude beziehen. Der Turm dagegen hebt sich davon ab und bezieht sich auf die Stadt als ganze. Er beherbergt unten einen Konzertsaal, die Bibliothek darüber und auf seinem Dach eine Terrasse mit Panoramablick über das Stadtzentrum. Der Turm selbst ist von der Stadt aus sichtbar und gibt der Musikschule eine einzigartige Präsenz in der Stuttgarter Skyline. Seine vertikalen Fenster und sein geschwungenes Gesims verweisen auf Teile der Staatsgalerie. Die ausgehöhlt wirkenden oberen Öffnungen tragen zu einem heroischen, bedeutungsschwangeren Eindruck bei, der an Piranesi erinnert.

In das Gebäude gelangt man entweder von der Urbanstraße oder vom Platz aus, von wo aus auch ein Fußgängerweg über eine Brücke in den Stadtpark führt. Von beiden Seiten gelangt man in das große mehrgeschossige Foyer, an das sich in einer Ecke die Mensa anschließt. Der

Music Academy

James Stirling, Michael Wilford and Associates
Stuttgart
1980 – 1994

The Music School on its north side faces on to Urbanstrasse, where the Staatsgalerie left standing a number of buildings. The new facade continues with the scale and character of these buildings, thus ensuring the continuity of the street. The main entrance breaks into the street only with the controlled emphasis of one of those coloured steel and glass canopies that reminds us of early Bauhaus studies. At the corner the refectory is revealed by means of concertina glazing, exposing a few columns, and creating a social presence on the street.

On the south side, towards the park, there is a different story. A new raised plaza over a parking garage becomes a focus of the urban composition, with trees lining the edge to Konrad-Adenauer Strasse, and the eventual completion of the accomodation originally intended for the Theatre Academy will define a civic plaza directly opposite the State Theatre, where the famous Galathea fountain will be re-sited. On this side the building creates spaces that contribute to the north edge of the main city park and are pitched at city scale. With careful attention to street on one side and park on the other, this is a building that brings alive the idea of *urban design.*

The Music School comprises nine floors of teaching and practice rooms, accomodated in the linear building fronting Urbanstrasse. This is sub-divided into a series of building elements relating in scale to adjacent buildings, against which the tower stands out as an element that refers to the city as a whole. This contains the concert hall below, the library above, and on top a roof terrace with a panoramic view of the city centre. The tower itself is visible from the city, giving the Music School a unique presence on the city skyline. Its vertical windows and coved cornice make reference to parts of the Staatsgalerie, and the emptiness of the upper openings contributes to the heroic sense of Piranesian destiny established there.

The building can be entered either from Urbanstrasse or from the plaza, where a pedestrian route leads via a footbridge to the city park. Both approaches lead into a grand multi-level foyer that connects to the refectory at the corner. The public entrance to the concert hall is directly from the plaza.

The Music School mirrors the Staatsgalerie by continuing the sandstone, travertine, and stucco wall finishes, as well as by its informal use of the formal composition. The combination of axial planning and diagonal movement produces a dynamic balance between the circular court of the Staatsgalerie rotunda and the Music School tower.

öffentliche Zugang zur Konzerthalle liegt direkt an der Piazza.

Die Musikhochschule spiegelt mit ihrer Sandstein-, Travertin- und Putzverkleidung sowie mit dem informellen Einsatz formaler Kompositionselemente die Gestaltung der Staatsgalerie wider. Die Kombination von Axialität und diagonaler Bewegung schafft eine Balance zwischen dem runden Freilichthof der Rotunde der Staatsgalerie und dem Turm der Musikhochschule.

Lageplan

Site plan

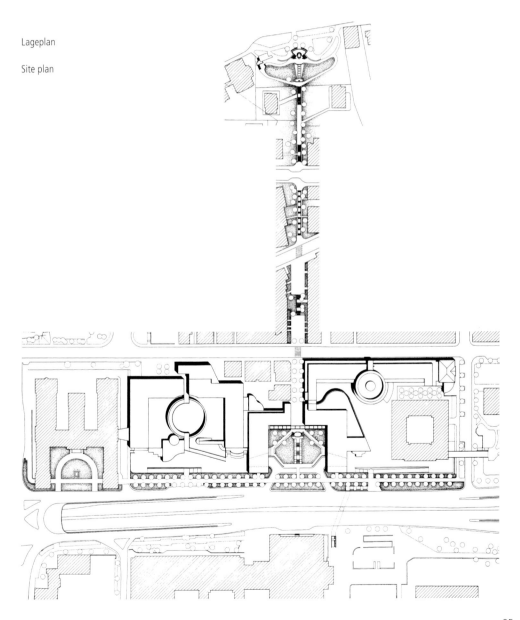

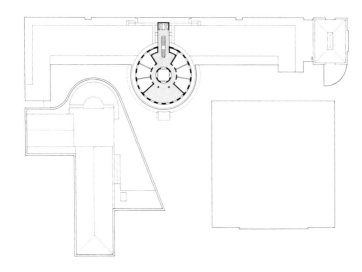

Grundrisse Erdgeschoß,
1. und 3. Obergeschoß

Plans of ground,
first and third floor

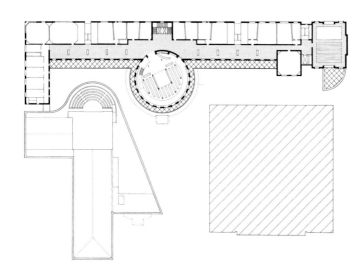

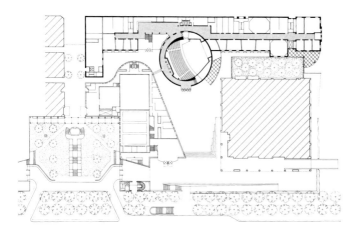

Gesamtansicht   Overall view
Eingang   Entrance

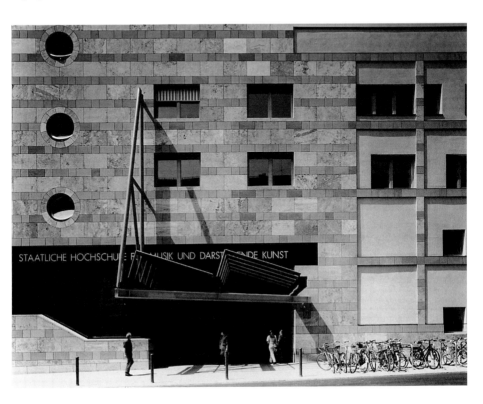

Konzertsaal   Concert hall

Blick auf den Turm durch den gerahmten Ausschnitt in der steinverkleideten Wand

View of tower through a framed opening in the stone veneered wall

Turm mit Terrasse   Tower with roof terrace

Fakultät für Darstellende Künste der Cornell Universität

James Stirling, Michael Wilford and Associates
Ithaca, New York
1983 – 1988

Das Grundstück gegenüber der Cascadilla Schlucht liegt am Stadtrand und blickt auf den Universitätscampus, der das Hochplateau auf der anderen Seite einnimmt. Das Gebäude gliedert sich um eine Kolonnade gegenüber der Schlucht, die an einem Ende zur Hauptstraße, auf der anderen Seite zum Parkplatz führt.

An der Seite zur Straße ist der Eingang zur Arkade durch ein achteckiges Gebäude hervorgehoben, das als Bushaltestelle, Informations- und Fahrkahrtenschalter dient. Es markiert außerdem die Brücke über die Schlucht und gehört zu den Elementen, die einen kleinen städtischen Platz definieren, auf den die Masse des Volumens blickt. Die großen Fenster im ersten Stock sind Teil des großen Tanzstudios. Der Fahrstuhlturm hat gewisse Ähnlichkeit mit einem Glockenturm. Man könnte fast meinen, daß man sich in der Toskana befindet, und Stirling erzählte, daß er zufällig die Bemerkung eines Besuchers hörte, es handle sich um «eine Art Beutezug durch Florenz».

Die Architekten entwarfen das Gebäude für eine beeindruckende Zahl von Einrichtungen und nutzten die vorhandene Fläche dabei geschickt aus. Es verfügt über eine Rahmenbühne mit 450 Sitzen, eine Raumbühne, wo bis zu 170 Personen Platz finden, ein Tanzstudio mit herausnehmbaren Sitzen für 130 Zuschauer und im unteren Bereich eine Studiobühne für 100 Besucher. Insgesamt gibt es zehn Aufführungsräume, aber auch einen Lesesaal, Räume für die Schauspieler, Verwaltungsbüros und Fakultätsräume, Räume für Proben und Requisiten.

Das Foyer im Zentrum ist durch die Unterbringung derart vieler Nutzungen nicht so großzügig ausgefallen. Dafür gelangt man von hier aus in den Pausen der Aufführungen auf die Loggia. Der Entwurf ist kompakt, funktional und gleichzeitig offen und urban. Die Kombination formeller Figuren und informeller Nutzungen zeigt Stirling von seiner besten Seite.

Performing Arts Center for Cornell University

James Stirling, Michael Wilford and Associates
Ithaca, New York
1983 – 1988

The site facing Cascadilla Gorge marks the edge of town and looks out towards the university campus, which occupies the high plateau on the other side. The building is organised around a colonnade that faces the gorge, and at one end connects to an important street, at the other gives access from the car park.

At the street end, the entrance to the end of the arcade is marked by an octagonal building that acts as a bus stop and contains information and booking facilities. It also serves to mark the bridge over the gorge, and helps to define a little urban square to which the mass of the building fronts, the large windows at first floor level being part of the principal dance studio. The elevator tower has something of the look of a campanile. There is some suggestion that we are in Tuscany, and Stirling relates how he overheard a visitor say «it's some sort of Florentine rip-off».

The building is packed full of facilities, in what amounts to an ingenious use of a small site. There is a proscenium theatre with 450 seats, a flexible theatre that can accommodate up to 175 people, a dance performance studio with removable seating for 130 people, and at low level a laboratory or black-box studio for 100 people. Altogether there are ten performance spaces, but also a reading room, greenrooms, administration and faculty offices, rehearsal rooms, and scenery props and costume shops.

The general foyer, at the centre, is somewhat restricted by the pressure of all this accommodation, but it can overflow into the loggia at the intervals. The design is compact, functional, and at the same time public and civic. This combination of formal shapes and informal uses shows Stirling at his best.

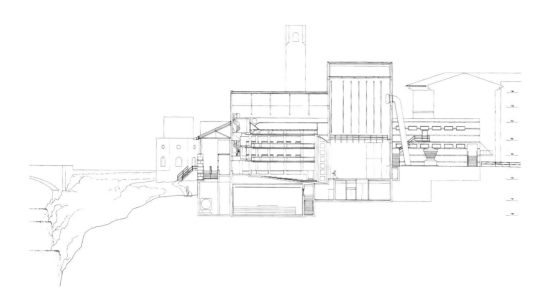

Querschnitt
Grundriß Erdgeschoß

Cross section
Ground floor plan

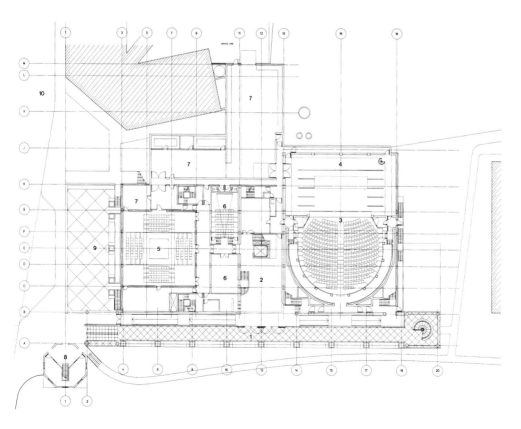

Vorplatz mit achteckigem Pavillon
Blick auf die Kolonnade

Square with octagonal information booth
View of the colonnade

Straßenansicht   Street facade

Innenansicht des Theaters

Interior view of theatre

Sitz der British Telecom
Projekt für beschränkten Wettbewerb
James Stirling, Michael Wilford and Associates
Milton Keynes, Buckinghamshire
1983

British Telecom Headquarters
Limited competition project
James Stirling, Michael Wilford and Associates
Milton Keynes, Buckinghamshire
1983

Der auffälligste Aspekt bei diesem Sitz des privatisierten Telekommunikationskonzerns ist der Gemeinschaftsbereich in der Mitte der Anlage. Dieser Bereich enthält verschiedene einzelne Gebäude, die sich zu einem campusähnlichen informellen Arrangement gruppieren. Dies entsteht aber durch eine absichtliche Brechung des Campus-Konzepts, wie sie schon beim Wissenschaftszentrum in Berlin vorlag. Hier gilt das gleiche Prinzip, es wird die gleiche Lösung vorgeschlagen. Und daher ergibt sich hier wieder eine Revue historischer architektonischer Typologien.

In Milton Keynes gab es aber nicht das Problem, daß ein existierendes Gebäude aus dem 19. Jahrhundert nicht durch einen großen Büroneubau erdrückt werden sollte. Daher ist das Entwurfskonzept noch offenkundiger und wirkt als *jeu d'esprit*. Aber die Lösung ist auch praktisch überzeugend, denn die campusähnliche Organisation sorgt für eine gute Arbeits- und Forschungsatmosphäre und schafft an diesem etwas isoliert gelegenen Industriestandort eine Form, die an die Stadt und ihre Annehmlichkeiten erinnert.

The notable aspect of this headquarters for a privatised company responsible for national communications is the treatment of the social area in the centre of the layout. Not only has this been broken up into a number of separate buildings arranged informally to make a kind of research campus, but the way of doing this is by a deliberate reworking of the idea already proposed for the Wissenschaftszentrum in Berlin. The same principle holds good, so the same solution is proposed. So we again find a sort of historical review of architectural typologies.

In this case, however, there is not the same need to avoid over-shadowing an existing nineteenth century building with a bulky office block, so the effect is more evidently arbitrary, and a *jeu d'esprit*. Yet the solution is perfectly valid, since the campus-like arrangement not only provides a good research environment in itself, but brings to this isolated industrial site a compensating reminder of city form and its social rewards.

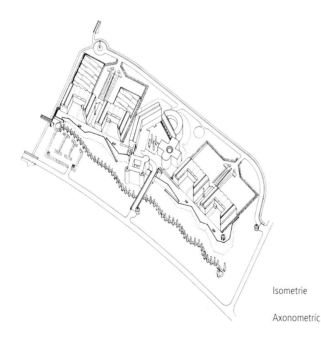

Isometrie

Axonometric

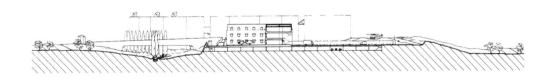

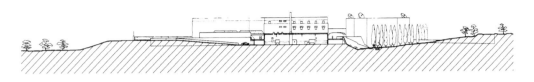

Ansichten

Elevations

Modellfoto

Model view

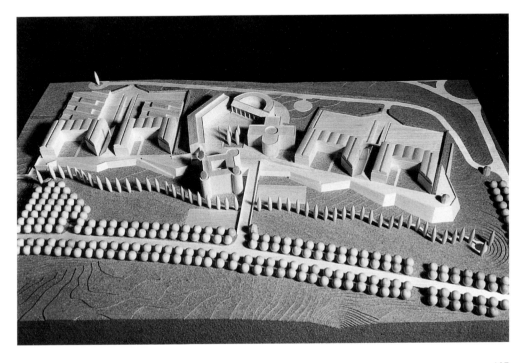

Stadtbücherei von Latina
Projekt
James Stirling, Michael Wilford and Associates
Latina, Italien
1983

Die Stadt Latina in Italien wurde unter Mussolini gegründet, und so fehlt ihr eine eigene Geschichte. Die neue Bücherei sollte ebensosehr Kulturzentrum wie Bibliothek sein und Raum für bis zu 500 Menschen sowie Stellflächen für 200 000 Bücher bieten.

Das Gebäude verbindet zwei Straßen und blickt auf einen Garten, der nach dem Entwurf auf dem Grundstück einer alten Villa entstehen sollte, die heute als Nebengebäude eines Krankenhauses dient. Dieser Garten wird von einer Loggia eingefaßt und ist von der Bibliothek aus über eine Rampe auf der Gebäudeachse zugänglich. Die Loggia hat die für Stirling typische Form, eine Abfolge von Rasterfeldern unter einem durchlaufenden Schrägdach, das in diesem Fall verglast ist. Die Endfelder knicken rechtwinklig ab, so daß ihre Konstruktion sichtbar wird. Man betritt das Gebäude von beiden Seiten der Loggia, eine Erschließung, die an die Fakultät für Darstellende Künste der Cornell Universität erinnert.

Eine genaue Analyse der künftigen Nutzung ergab zwei Nutzergruppen, denen mit zwei getrennten Lesesälen entsprochen wird. Beide sind in Zylindern untergebracht, die das Volumen des Gebäudes durchstoßen und etwa auf Firsthöhe enden. Einer der Säle dient als Ausleihbibliothek und ist durch Regale gekennzeichnet, die zur Raummitte hin höher werden und dort einen geschützten Bereich schaffen, der durch ein Dachfenster zenital erhellt wird. Der andere Lesesaal ist eine wissenschaftliche Handbibliothek, deren Regale von einem zentralen Pult zu den Umfassungsmauern hin höher werden. Gemahnt diese Form an die Grenzen der Wissenschaft, so bringt der andere Saal den privaten, introspektiven Charakter der individuellen Leseerfahrung zum Ausdruck.

Dieses Gebäude hat viel Charakter und Finesse. Die Zylinder der Lesesäle sind vom Klassizismus inspiriert, aber die übrige Dachform entstammt der lokalen Bautradition. Keines dieser unterschiedlichen Elemente dominiert das andere, vielmehr fügen sie sich zu einer harmonischen Form. Die Architekten beziehen sich bewußt auf Kultur und Geschichte der Architektur, setzen aber formale Kompositionselemente informell ein, wie es unserer heutigen informelleren Zeit angemessen ist.

Die Trommeln und die Loggia sind eine großartige, aber nicht pompöse Geste, und das ganze Gebäude ist mit eindrucksvoller Anmut auf den Garten bezogen. Auf dem Niveau des Gartens schaffen die Kinderbücherei und das Café, die zur Sonne und zur Gartenterrasse ausgerichtet

Public Library
Project
James Stirling, Michael Wilford and Associates
Latina, Italy
1983

The town of Latina was created under Mussolini, and lacks a history. The new library was to act as much as a cultural centre as a library, offering facilities for up to 500 people at a time, and accommodating some 200,000 books. The building connects two streets and faces a public garden made from the grounds of an old villa, now used as a hospital adjunct. This garden can be approached from the library by way of a ramp on the axis, and it is embraced by the loggia that runs the entire length of the building. This has the classic Stirling shape of a number of bays under a single pitched roof – glazed in this case – the end bays of which are turned to reveal their structure. The building is entered via the loggia from either end, in a way that reminds us of the similar arrangement at the Cornell Center for the Performing Arts.

Research led to the identification of two bands of users, and to the adoption of two reading rooms: both are placed in cylinders that rise through the building volume and terminate at the level of its roof ridge. One is the lending library, marked by tiers that rise progressively towards the centre, creating a snug space below, lit by a central well. The other is the reference library, and has tiers that rise from the central desk progressively towards the outer walls. One form seems appropriate for private introspection, the other geared to the frontiers of science. This is a building of great character and finesse. The cylinders of the reading rooms are neo-classical in inspiration, but the roof form is vernacular. One does not dominate the other, they are united in a smooth form. The architects are aware of the history and culture of architecture, but they are happy that their formal organization is used informally, as befits a casual age.

The drums and the loggia constitute a grand gesture, but there is no pomposity. There is a singular grace about the way the building relates to its garden. At garden level, it is the children's library and the café-bar which face the sun and the garden terrace, setting up an intimate ambiance on either side of the division made by the ramp that leads down from the loggia above, more an exit than an entrance.

sind, eine intime Atmosphäre zu beiden Seiten der sie trennenden Rampe, die von der darüber liegenden Loggia nach unten führt und eher einen Ausgang als einen Zugang bildet.

Lageisometrie

Site axonometric

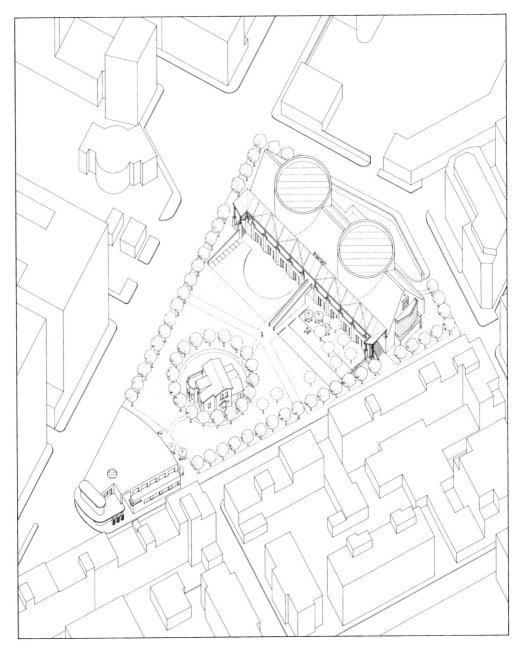

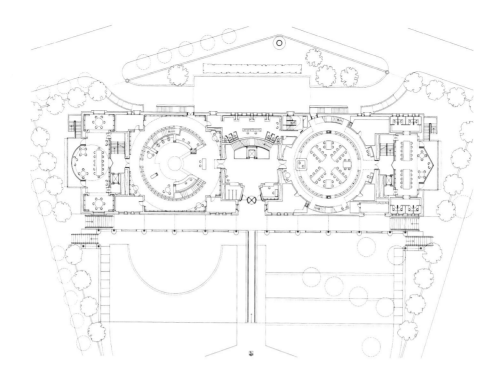

Grundriß Erdgeschoß
Entwurfsskizzen

Ground floor plan
Design sketches

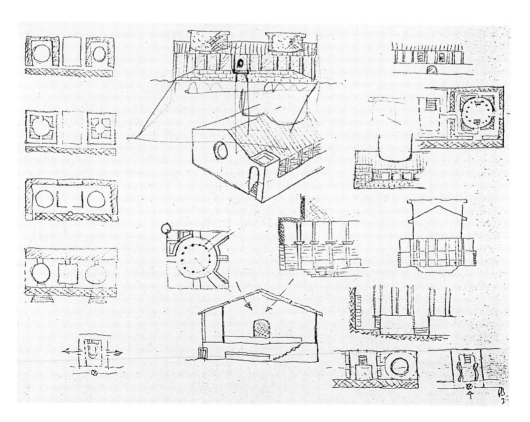

Querschnitt
Eingangsfassade
Rückfassade
Modellfoto

Cross section
Entry facade
Rear facade
Model view

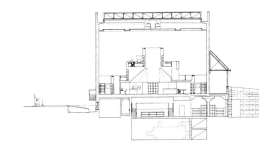

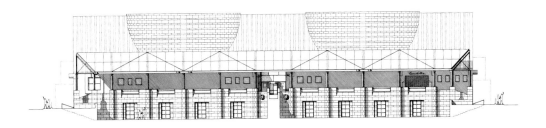

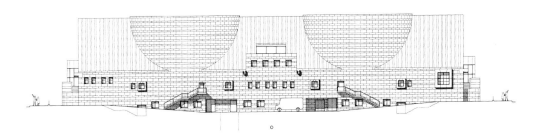

Erweiterung der Nationalgalerie

Projekt für beschränkten Wettbewerb
James Stirling, Michael Wilford and Associates
London
1985

Dieser Entwurf war ein Wettbewerbsbeitrag für den neuen Sainsbury-Flügel in der Nähe des Trafalgar Square und hätte im Fall seiner Realisierung eine bedeutende Wirkung im besonders stark von Touristen besuchten Londoner Westend entfaltet. Der individuelle Charakter des Projektes zeigt sich besonders an der Südfassade mit ihren majestätischen Fenstern unter dem gewölbten Gesims, die zweifellos jene Qualität von *Präsenz* schafft, nach der Stirling strebte.

Die Ausstellungsräume liegen auf der Ebene der Brücke, die zur Beletage des Hauptgebäudes des Architekten William Wilkens von 1838 führt. Die Räume werden durchgehend von oben beleuchtet, und selbst in dem schmalen dreigeschossigen Einschnitt direkt hinter der Hauptfassade wird zenitales Licht bis nach unten geführt, vor allem durch ein rundes Auge über dem Eingangsfoyer. Die Ausstellungsräume haben unterschiedliche Größen, passend für die vor allem religiösen Renaissancebilder, für die sie entworfen wurden. Sie gliedern sich nach einer zentralen Achse, die von der Vorder- zur Rückseite verläuft, und auf die man vom Erdgeschoß aus über eine zentrale barocke Treppe stößt. Der Eingang von der Straße zum Foyer liegt jedoch rechtwinklig zu dieser Achse, wodurch ein scharfes Abknicken der Treppe notwendig wird. Durch diesen Kunstgriff blickt der Eingang auf den Portikus des Hauptgebäudes, so daß der Erweiterungsbau ähnlich wie bei der Clore Galerie auf das «Muttergebäude» bezogen wird. Gleichzeitig schafft Stirling auf diese Weise eine urbane Geste über die National Gallery hinaus in Richtung auf den Portikus von St. Martin-in-the-Fields an der Ostecke des Trafalgar Square.

Diese Verbeugung wird von dem gewölbten Gesims noch betont, das dem Gesims der Staatsgalerie in Stuttgart ähnelt und auf die Vorderseite beschränkt bleibt. Dieser Gebäudeteil ist völlig mit Stein verkleidet, während die hinteren Teile, die enge Straßen säumen, Putz mit Steinbändern zeigen.

National Gallery Extension

Limited competition project
James Stirling, Michael Wilford and Associates
London
1985

This design was a competition entry for the new Sainsbury wing close to Trafalgar Square, and if selected would have had a major impact on the west end of London seen particularly by the tourists. The individual character of the project is evident in the south elevation, with its majestic windows under a coved cornice, and would have clearly had that quality that Stirling called *presence*.

The galleries are arranged on the level of the bridge connecting to the *piano nobile* in the main building of 1838, by the architect William Wilkins. Top lighting is used throughout, and even on a shallow three-storey section immediately behind the main front, top lighting has been brought down to the lower levels, in particular by a circular eye above the entrance foyer. The galleries make up a series of rooms of different sizes, suitable for the display of mainly religious painting of the Renaissance. They are organised by a central axis running from front to back, approached by a central baroque staircase from the ground floor foyer. The entry to the foyer from the street, however, is arranged at right angles, requiring a sharp turn on to this axis, this turn being incorporated in the narrower spaces of the staircase. This slight of hand enables the entrance to face towards the main portico, so inflecting the building towards its «parent», as at the Clore Gallery, while also making an urban gesture across the National Gallery towards the portico of St. Martin-in-the-Fields, at the east corner of Trafalgar Square.

This genuflection is emphasized by the coved cornice, similar to that used at the Staatsgalerie, which is applied to only the front section of the building. This part is entirely dressed in stone, while the rear portions, which line narrow streets, are covered with stucco rendering, with stone bands.

Ansicht von Pall Mall
Ansicht von Trafalgar Square
Untersicht von Pall Mall
Untersicht von Trafalgar Square

Elevation to Pall Mall
Elevation to Trafalgar Square
View up from Pall Mall
View up from Trafalgar Square

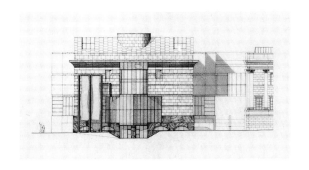

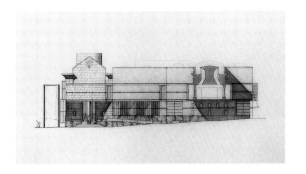

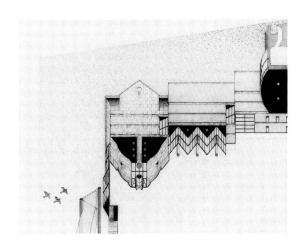

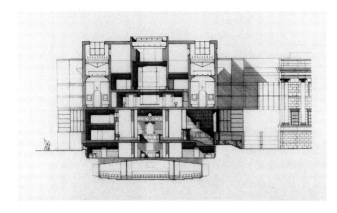

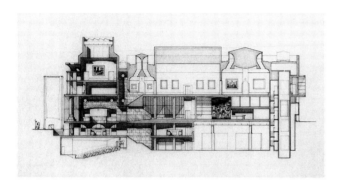

Querschnitt
Längsschnitt
Grundriß Erdgeschoß

Cross section
Longitudinal section
Ground floor plan

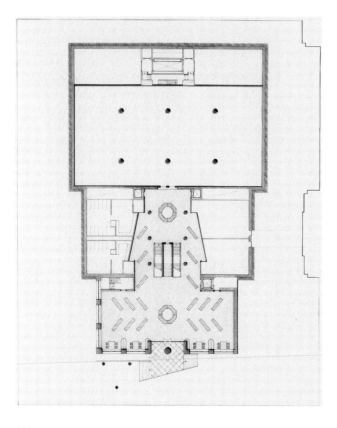

Poultry Nr. 1

James Stirling, Michael Wilford and Associates
London
1986 – 1998

Dieses Gebäude im Herzen der Finanzmeile der Londoner City verdankt sich dem Mäzen und Entwickler Peter Palumbo, der vorher versucht hatte, auf einem größeren Grundstück am selben Ort ein von Mies van der Rohe entworfenes Gebäude zu errichten. Die Baugenehmigung für diesen Entwurf wurde verweigert, und 1986 trat Lord Palumbo an James Stirling und Michael Wilford heran und gab ihnen den Auftrag. Hatte Mies einen rechteckigen Turm ohne Konzessionen an die übrigen Straßenfassaden und Höhenbegrenzungen vorgeschlagen, gingen Stirling und Wilford von der Idee eines gegenüber seinem Kontext sensiblen Gebäudes aus, das neben den hervorragenden Gebäuden von John Soane, Edwin Lutyens, George Dance und Nicolas Hawksmoor bestehen könnte.

Die Architekten fertigten zwei Entwürfe an: Einer sah die Erhaltung, der andere die vollständige Beseitigung des bestehenden Eckgebäudes vor. Der zweite Entwurf wurde ausgewählt, weil er mit einer geringeren Höhe auskam und mit den angrenzenden Traufhöhen übereinstimmte.

Das Gebäude enthält Geschäfte im Keller- und Erdgeschoß, bietet fünf Bürogeschosse darüber und schließt mit einer Dachterrasse mit Restaurant ab. Eine Fußgängerpassage führt durch das Erdgeschoß, verbindet einen offenen, runden Hof im Zentrum mit Einkaufskolonnaden an der Poultry und Queen Victoria Street und ist mit der Bank Station der Londoner U-Bahn verbunden. Der Hof ist im Parterre und im ersten Geschoß rund und gewinnt auf der Höhe der oberen Bürogeschosse eine dreieckige Form.

Allgemein zugänglich sind die Büros vom Hof aus, während an der Gebäudespitze der Eingang für Empfänge und ähnliche Anlässe liegt, wo eine prachtvolle Treppe zum Balkon im ersten Stock führt, der um den zentralen Hof läuft. Fahrstühle erschließen die öffentlichen und privaten Ebenen des Hofes, die Büros und das Dachgartenrestaurant. Das Zentrum des Dachgartens wird von einer runden Wand mit Pergola umschlossen. Die Verkleidung besteht aus Sandstein und Granit mit bronzenen Metallelementen. Die gestreifte Fassade erinnert an die Staatsgalerie und die Fakultät für Darstellende Künste der Cornell Universität. Nach langwierigen Verzögerungen wurde das Gebäude 1998 fertiggestellt.

No. 1 Poultry

James Stirling, Michael Wilford and Associates
London
1986 – 1998

This building in the heart of the City of London's financial district owes its inception to patron and developer Peter Palumbo, who had earlier attempted to erect a building designed by Mies van der Rohe on a larger site in the same location. Planning permission for that design was refused, and in 1986 Lord Palumbo approached James Stirling Michael Wilford and commissioned them directly to make a design. Where Mies had proposed a rectangular tower making no concessions to the street frontages and height limits, Stirling and Wilford started from the idea of a contextually sensitive building that would take its place among distinguished buildings by Soane, Lutyens, Dance, Hawksmoor.

The architects prepared two schemes, one retaining part of an existing building on the corner, and one replacing it entirely. The second design was preferred because it required less height, and ennabled the building to conform to adjoining parapet heights.

The building contains shops at basement and ground floor levels, and provides five floors of offices above, with a roof garden and restaurant. A pedestrian passage traverses the ground floor, linking an open circular court in the centre to shopping colonnades on frontages to Poultry and Queen Victoria Street, with a link down to the Bank station on the London Underground system. The court is circular at ground and first floor levels, and interlocks with a triangular plan for the upper office floors.

Public access to the offices is from the court, with a ceremonial entrance at the apex of the building, where there is a grand stair connecting to the first floor balcony that encircles the central court. Lifts connect the public and private levels of the court, the offices, and the rooftop garden restaurant. The centre of the roof garden is enclosed by a circular wall and pergola. The building is faced in sandstone and granite, with exposed metalwork in bronze. The striped effect is reminiscent of the Staatsgalerie and the Performing Arts Center at Cornell University. After a twelve year delay, the building opened in 1998.

Grundrisse Erdgeschoß,
1. und 3. Obergeschoß

Plans of ground,
first and third floor

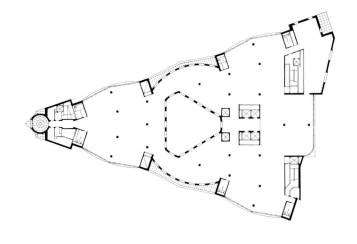

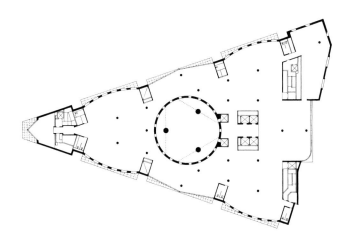

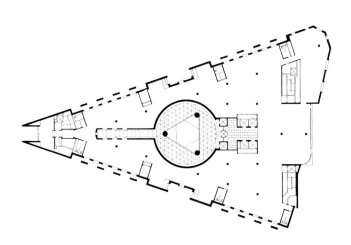

Blick auf den Turm

View of tower

Folgende Seiten:
Turm an der Gebäudespitze
Aufzugsbereich
Dachgarten
Straßenansicht

Following pages:
Tower at the building apex
Elevator lobby
Roof garden
Street facade

Braun Werksanlagen

Beschränkter Wettbewerb
James Stirling, Michael Wilford and Associates
mit Walter Nägeli
Melsungen
1986 – 1992

Dieses Gebäude ist eine Fabrik und ein Auslieferungszentrum für medizinische Produkte. Obwohl es sich um ein Industriegebäude handelt, wollte der Auftraggeber Georg Braun für seine Firma ein weithin sichtbares Aushängeschild, ein Werk wirklicher Architektur.

Die Architekten verfolgten dieses Ziel auf sehr praktische Weise. Sie unterschieden zwischen den technischen Produktionsanlagen auf dem hinteren Teil des Grundstücks und den öffentlich sichtbaren Gebäudeteilen. Diese Trennung vollzogen sie durch eine hohe, doppelte Betonschirmwand mit Treppen in ihrem Inneren, die das mehrgeschossige Parkhaus dahinter erschließen. Das Parkhaus ist aus Kostengründen eine Standardlösung und wird von der Wand wirkungsvoll verdeckt. Gleichzeitig befreit es das Gelände von den üblichen ebenerdigen Parkplätzen, ein Umstand, der der optischen Wirkung des Komplexes sehr zugute kommt.

Arbeiter, die das Parkhaus verlassen, gehen die imposante Brücke aus Holz und Glas hinunter, die beide Enden des Grundstücks – die Verwaltung auf der einen und die Produktionsstätten und Kantinen auf der anderen Seite – verbindet. Die Form dieser Loggia mit ihren schrägen Holzpfeilern, die an der Wand dahinter «lehnen», ist monumental und informell zugleich. Sie neigt und verengt sich leicht zum Zentrum hin, das direkt über jener Stelle liegt, von der aus Wasser in den künstlichen See fließt. So macht sie die umliegende Landschaft bewußt und bringt gleichzeitig die Begegnung von Natur und Kultur zum Ausdruck.

Die übrige Landschaftsgestaltung mit Baumgruppen und einem gewundenen Kanal, der den Parkhauszugang vom Besuchereingang trennt, wirkt in seiner Eindringlichkeit parodistisch. Die Besucher kommen eine vorspringende Brücke hinauf, die sie unter die Auskragung des geschwungenen Verwaltungsgebäudes führt. Die Eingangshalle wird von zwei massiven kegelförmigen Gebilden direkt vor ihrer Glaswand beherrscht: Es handelt sich um die entlang der Gebäudemitte in einer einzigen Linie aufgereihten konischen Stützen, auf denen das Gebäude ruht.

Die Farben, die Behandlung der Wände und die Beleuchtung dieses Bereichs schärfen in ihrer sorgsamen Gestaltung die visuelle Wahrnehmung der Besucher und führen ihnen zu Bewußtsein, daß ein Fabrikgebäude auch ein Kunstwerk sein kann.

Braun Headquarters

Limited competition
James Stirling, Michael Wilford and Associates
with Walter Nägeli
Melsungen
1986 – 1992

This is a factory and distribution centre for plastic medical products. Although an industrial building, it was commissioned by Georg Braun with the aim of making his company highly visible, to be a true work of architecture. The architects have dealt with this intention in a highly practical way, making a distinction between the production and technical plant towards the rear of the site, and the parts seen by the public. The division is made by a high concrete double wall, containing staircases, which afford access from a multi-storey car park behind it. The car park building is a standard product, for economy, and the wall conceals it. At the same time, the use of a parking building frees the site from ground level car parking, a measure that greatly enhances the visual appeal of the complex.

Workers leaving the car park descend into a grand covered way built of timber and glass, which connects both ends of the site, with administration at one end and production and canteens at the other. The form of this loggia, with its raked timber supports «leaning» on the wall behind, is monumental and informal at the same time. It dips and narrows gently towards the centre, which is directly over the point where water flows into the ornamental lake, so making one aware of the landscape and situating the factory simultaneously in an interface between Nature and Culture.

The rest of the landscaping, with clumps of trees, and a sinuous canal that separates the car park approach from the visitors' entrance, is parodic in its intensity. The visitors mount to a cantilevered bridge that delivers them under the overhang of the curved administration building. The entrance hall is dominated by the presence of massive conical structures just outside the glass: these are the conical caps that support the office floors above, forming a single line of columns along the centre of the building. The colours, wall surfaces, and lighting have all been given attention in such a way as to heighten the visitors' visual awareness, convincing evidence that a factory can aspire to be a work of art.

Längsschnitt
Grundriß Erdgeschoß

Longitudinal section
Ground floor plan

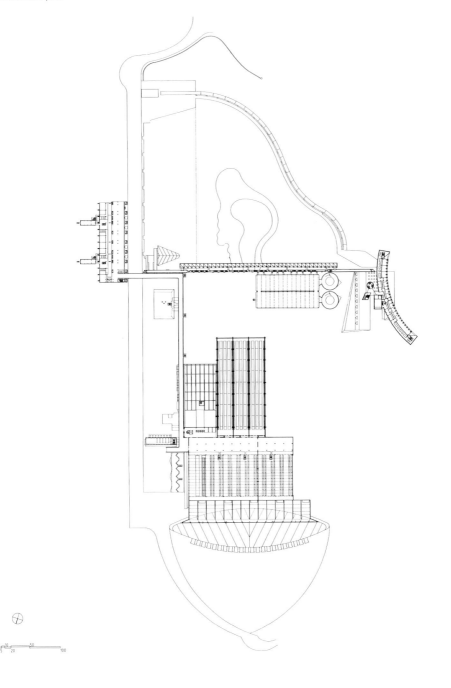

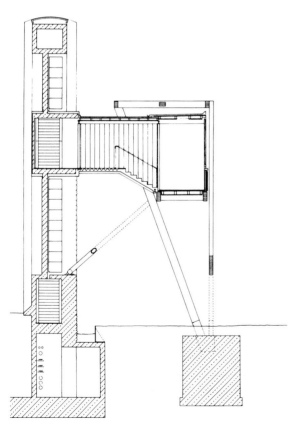

Verglaste Brücke mit schrägen Holzstützen
Schnitt durch die verglaste Brücke

Glazed bridge with canted timber piers
Section of glazed bridge

Fassadenansicht
Zufahrt

View of facade
Access road

Untersicht des Verwaltungsgebäudes mit den konischen Stützen
Verwaltungsgebäude mit Zugangsbrücke

Overhang of administration building with conical columns
View of administration building with access bridge

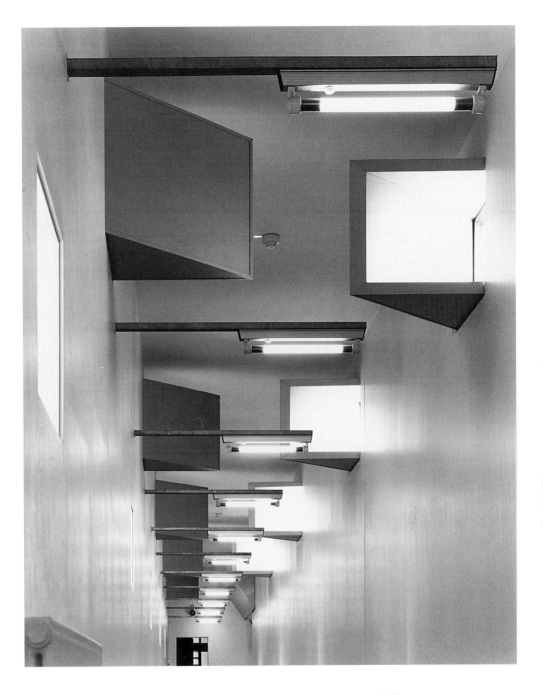

Flur im Verwaltungsgebäude

Corridor in administration building

Sammlung Thyssen-Bornemisza

Projekt für beschränkten Wettbewerb
James Stirling, Michael Wilford and Associates
Lugano
1986

Thyssen-Bornemisza Gallery

Limited competition project
James Stirling, Michael Wilford and Associates
Lugano
1986

Durch die ständige Vergrößerung der Privatsammlung von Baron Thyssen in seiner Villa im schweizerischen Lugano war eine Erweiterung erforderlich, die in das Ensemble vorhandener Gebäude integriert werden mußte. Der Entwurf von Stirling und Wilford hätte die ursprüngliche Villa als Kernstück der Komposition erhalten, mit einer neuen Ausstellungsfläche, die ein Gegengewicht zum existierenden Ausstellungsbereich bildet, und hätte auch eine vorhandene Pergola in das Projekt einbezogen. Besucher folgen der Pergola zu einem Eingang, der in ein rundes Foyer führt, wo man die Eintrittskarten bekommt, im Laden einkaufen und die Garderobe abgeben kann. Von hier aus gelangen sie auch in einen Raum für audiovisuelle Vorführungen und zum Café und Restaurant, von dem aus man den Garten überblickt.

Die neue Treppe erschließt alle Ausstellungsräume einschließlich der Säle der Villa und der Verwaltungsbüros in einem Halbgeschoß. Der neue Ausstellungssaal im Zentrum des Blocks ist zenital beleuchtet und eignet sich für wechselnde Ausstellungen. Er wird von Ausstellungsräumen geringerer Größe flankiert, in denen kleinere Werke ausgestellt werden können. Auf der Seeseite wird das Volumen durch Kreuzbogenöffnungen gegliedert, von denen man über die darunter liegende Loggia des Altbaus hinweg auf den See blickt.

With the continued expansion of the private collection of Baron Thyssen at his villa in Lugano in Switzerland, it was necessary to integrate any expansion with the collection of existing buildings. The Stirling-Wilford proposal would keep the original villa as the centrepiece of the composition, adding a new gallery to balance the first, and incorporating an existing pergola into the project. Visitors follow the pergola to an entrance leading to a circular foyer, where they can purchase tickets, call at shop and cloakroom, access an audio-visual room, and use the café-restaurant overlooking the garden.

A new staircase provides access to all the galleries, including the rooms of the villa, as well as to the administrative offices at a half level. The new gallery along the centre of the block has top lighting, and is suitable for temporary exhibitions. It is flanked by smaller galleries, suitable for the display of smaller works. On the side towards the lake it is articulated by sections with cross vaulted openings, looking out to the lake across the old loggia below.

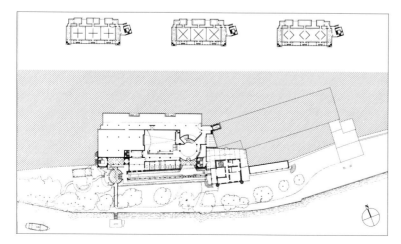

Grundriß Erdgeschoß

Ground floor plan

Westseite der Seefassade
mit Eingang
Innenansicht der Galerie
Blick von der Loggia über
den Luganer See

Western part of lake
elevation with entrance
Gallery interior
View from the loggia over
Lake Lugano

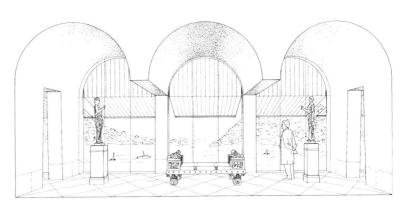

Kunstsammlung Palazzo Citterio

Projekt
James Stirling, Michael Wilford and Associates
Mailand
1987

Da nur Fragmente vom ursprünglichen Palazzo erhalten sind, waren hier alte Fassaden und neue Einrichtungen miteinander in Einklang zu bringen. Das Gebäude, eine Erweiterung des Brera Museums, gliedert sich um drei Räume: Der ursprüngliche Hof mit seinen klassizistischen Fassaden bleibt erhalten, wird aber mit einem neuen Glasdach abgedeckt, das von einer einzelnen massiven Säule in der Hofmitte getragen wird, ein Eingriff, der den Vorteil hat, ein altes, schlecht proportioniertes Dachgeschoß zu verdecken, das nicht beseitigt werden konnte. Von diesem Hof gelangt man zur Kasse, Informationsstand, Buchladen, zur Garderobe und, mit dem Fahrstuhl oder über die Treppe, zu den übrigen Geschossen.

Der zweite Hof bildet das Dach der Einrichtungen im Kellergeschoß, die einen Vortragssaal und ein Foyer einschließen und über eine Rampe vom Vestibül erreichbar sind. Hier befindet sich auch ein großzügiger quadratischer Ausstellungssaal, der sich für wechselnde Ausstellungen eignet und über zwei gleichgestaltete Treppenabgänge zugänglich ist. Das neue Dach dieses Raumes ist als Garten gestaltet, und die Besucher können sich an einer Seite in einer eleganten neuen Bar erfrischen. Der dritte Hof ist ebenfalls ein Garten mit einem halbrunden Amphitheater, das hinten von einer Pergola umschlossen ist.

Die neuen Teile sind in einem schlichten Stil gehalten, der klassizistisch-erhaben wirkt, ohne aufdringlich zu sein, auch wenn sich der Betrachter der beeindruckenden räumlichen Effekte schwerlich entziehen kann, die durch die Vervollständigung der alten Fassaden mit den baulichen Eingriffen der Architekten entstehen.

Palazzo Citterio Art Gallery

Project
James Stirling, Michael Wilford and Associates
Milan
1987

Only fragments remain of the original palazzo, so it was necessary to sew together old facades and new facilities. The building, which is an extension of the Brera Museum, is organised around three spaces: the original courtyard with its classical facades is retained, but capped with a new glazed roof supported on a single massive column at the centre, a measure which has the advantage of hiding an old attic storey of dubious proportions that could not be removed. From this courtyard there is access to ticketing, information, bookshop, and cloakrooms, and by stair and lift to the remaining levels.

The second courtyard forms the roof to basement facilities which include lecture theatre and foyer, accessible by a ramp from the vestibule, and a spacious square exhibition gallery suitable for changing shows, accessible by a pair of matching stairs. The new roof of this space is paved as a garden, and is served by a stylish new bar from one side. The third courtyard beyond is designed as a garden containing a classical open-air amphitheatre of semi-circular form, backed by a pergola.

The new parts are designed in a simplified manner that suggests neo-classical grandeur without being obtrusive: except that the spatial effects employed in complementing old faces with new structure are fairly stunning.

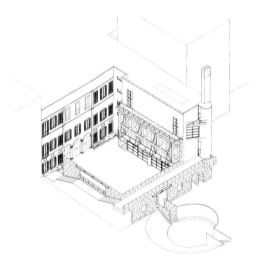

Isometrie

Axonometric

128

Perspektivzeichnung des alten Innenhofs

Perspective of existing courtyard

Oper Glyndebourne

Projekt für beschränkten Wettbewerb
James Stirling, Michael Wilford and Associates
Glyndebourne, Sussex
1988

Glyndebourne Opera House

Limited competition project
James Stirling, Michael Wilford and Associates
Glyndebourne, Sussex
1988

Ein Ausflug zur Oper Glyndebourne, um einen Abend mit guter Musik mit einem Picknick im Garten eines alten Herrenhauses zu verbinden, ist fester Bestandteil der englischen Saison. Obwohl das vorhandene Opernhaus eine hervorragende Akustik hatte, war es notwendig, sich neuen Erfordernissen anzupassen und ein größeres Publikum anzusprechen.

Der Vorschlag von Stirling und Wilford sah vor, die Gebäude mit dem Opernsaal und seiner Bühne zu erhalten, in ihnen ein Restaurant und Bars einzurichten und ihre Nähe zum Herrenhaus mit seiner Gartenanlage vom Beginn des Jahrhunderts zu nutzen. Eine neue Loggia hätte dann als Promenade – im Winter verglast, im Sommer zum Garten hin offen – den Zugang zum neuen Auditorium gebildet und zu den Parkplätzen geführt. Ein großer Vorteil dieses Plans war, den Neubau weit vom alten Haus abzurücken und dessen Auditorium während der Bauarbeiten weiterhin so lange wie möglich zu nutzen.

Der neue Opernsaal bietet 1150 Sitzplätze auf drei Niveaus gegenüber der Bühne und den Seitenlogen. Er verbindet eine intime Atmosphäre mit zuschauerfreundlicher Gestaltung. Der rechteckige Grundriß, die abfallende Decke und Holzpaneelierung dienen zur Verbesserung der Akustik. Außen verschleiert das Auditorium seine Masse durch ein Schrägdach, und das Volumen der Bühne erreicht kaum die Höhe des Altbaus, so daß die Wirkung seiner traditionellen Formensprache weitgehend erhalten bleibt.

The outing to the Glyndebourne Opera to combine an evening of good music with a picnic supper in the grounds of an old manor house has become one of the institutions of the English season. A larger auditorium was necessary to attract larger audiences.

The Stirling-Wilford proposal would retain the buildings containing the auditorium and its stage, converting this section to use for restaurants and bars, and exploiting its position close to the manor house and its Edwardian garden. A new loggia would then provide a main promenade, glazed in winter, open in summer to the gardens, giving
access to the new auditorium behind and on to the car parking areas. A great advantage of this scheme was that it kept the new construction well away from the house, and permitted the first auditorium to be retained in use for as long as possible during the construction phase.

The new auditorium provides 1,150 seats on three levels facing the stage, with flanking boxes, combining an intimate atmosphere with a good sense of the audience. The rectangular plan, sloped ceiling, and timber panelling were all chosen to enhance the acoustic performance.

Externally, the auditorium dissimulates its mass with its pitched roof, and the stage house rises barely to the height of the original one, so that the disruption to the vernacular setting is minimal.

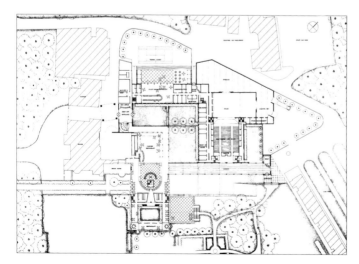

Lageplan
Site plan

Gartenansicht
Längsschnitt
Schnittisometrie

Garden elevation
Longitudinal section
Cutaway axonometric

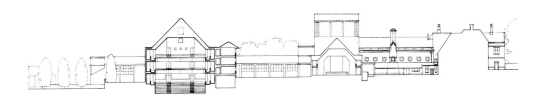

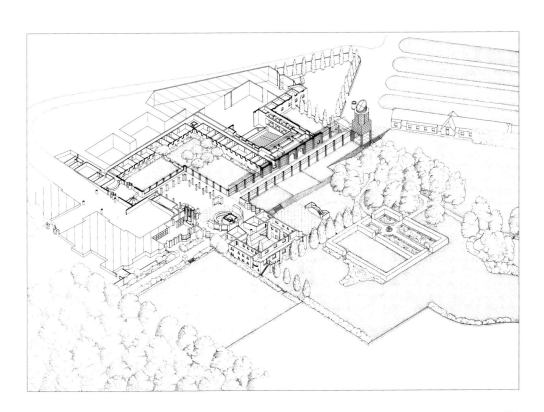

Wohnanlage
Canary Wharf
Projekt für beschränkten Wettbewerb
James Stirling, Michael Wilford and Associates
London
1988

Mit diesem Entwurf schlagen die Architekten einen großen Wohnpark am Themse-Ufer zwischen einer linearen Gebäudefolge mit Büros, Geschäften und einem Hotel vor. Terrassen fallen mit alternierenden Gras- und Kiesflächen sanft zum Ufer hin ab. Das Ufer wird von einer Kette von Wohntürmen gesäumt, die zum Fluß hin keinen ununterbrochenen Wall bilden und so nicht nur vielfältige Ausblicke bieten, sondern den Blick auch zwischen sich hindurchlassen. Ein Park führt zum wichtigsten Bürokomplex an der Canary Wharf, der vom Hochhausturm Canada Square dominiert wird. Im Vergleich dazu sind die Ausmaße der Wohntürme klein und bescheiden und erlauben mit ihren unterschiedlichen Volumina eine ansprechende Vielfalt von Wohnungszuschnitten und Ausblicken.

Die Geometrie ihrer individuellen Formen setzt sich aus aufeinander getürmten Baukörpern zusammen: dreieckige oder rechteckige Sockel tragen runde oder achteckige Aufsätze, die überwiegend von zylindrischen oder halbrunden Volumina gekrönt werden und in fünfgeschossigen Stufen nach oben streben. Die Fassaden bestehen hauptsächlich aus Glas und greifen auf das makellose, von Mies van der Rohe bei seinen Lakeshore Drive Apartments eingesetzte Modul zurück. Die Stufung der Gebäude schafft ein abwechslungsreiches Bild mit Lichtspiegelungen, die sich jeden Moment verändern. Mit den zwischen die Blöcke gepflanzten Pappeln und Zypressen entsteht ein einladende, idyllische Atmosphäre. Die Idee, verschiedene Volumina übereinander zu setzen, erinnert an sarazenische Kirchen, die sich in den Hafenstädtchen an der italienischen Südwestküste finden. Nach Westen auf die Londoner City blickend, schaffen sie eine ideale visuelle Verbindung zum touristischen Zentrum der Stadt.

Canary Wharf
Residential Development
Limited competition project
James Stirling, Michael Wilford and Associates
London
1988

This design proposed a large riverside park enclosed by a linear building containing offices, shops and a hotel. Terraces descend gently to the waterside, with alternating bands of grass and gravel. The front to the river is lined with a necklace of residential towers, which do not form a continuous barrier to the river, and allow views out and in between them. The park leads through to the main office complex at Canary wharf, dominated by the high-rise Canada Square. By comparison, these residential towers are mini-towers, modest in scale, and with their varied massing allowing a pleasing variety of flat types and outlooks.

The geometry of their individual outlines makes use of superimposed volumes: triangular or rectangular bases bearing circular or octagonal stages, capped generally by cylindrical or semi-cylindrical stages, progressing upward in five-storey steps. The facades are mainly of glass, in a module derived from the immaculate unit used in Mies van der Rohe's Lakeshore Drive Apartments. The stepping creates a varied appearance, which would reflect light at any one moment in a diverse way. With the intervening planting using cypress or poplar trees, the result has a pleasing arcadian quality. The idea of superimposing different volumes is reminiscent of the «Saracen» churches that are found in Italian ports arount the south western coasts to the Mediterranean. Facing west to the City of London, they provide an ideal visual link to the centre of touristic London.

Lageplan
Perspektivzeichnung

Site plan
Perspective drawing

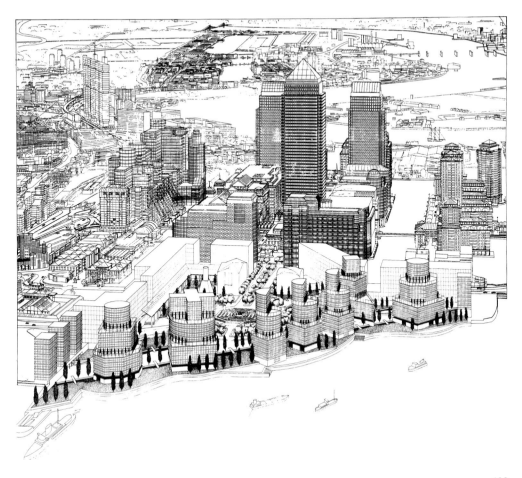

Disney Philharmonie

Projekt für beschränkten Wettbewerb
James Stirling, Michael Wilford and Associates
Los Angeles
1988

Auf dem Grundstück in einem Stadtteil, der für Los Angeles überraschend urban und verdichtet ist, mußte eine große Konzerthalle für sehr unterschiedliche Musikveranstaltungen mit allen dafür erforderlichen Einrichtungen Platz finden. Die Architekten erreichen dies, indem sie das Hauptauditorium erhöhen und das Foyer direkt darunter setzen. Vom zentralen Foyer führt ein Ring von doppelten Rolltreppen nach oben zu den äußeren Vorräumen, von denen man zu den Sitzrängen gelangt. Die oberen Reihen ziehen sich ganz um den Saal und ermöglichen so, hinter der Bühne im «Chor» zu sitzen. Das Hauptfoyer mit den Rolltreppen ist der zentrale Begegnungsraum des Gebäudes. An einer Seite hat es eine informelle Bühne für kleine Aufführungen. Das zentrale Foyer öffnet sich nach allen Seiten zu den anderen Bereichen: zwei kleinere Auditorien und ein separater Baukörper mit verschiedenen technischen und betrieblichen Einrichtungen.

Außen ist die zentrale Trommel, die das Hauptauditorium enthält, auf drei Seiten von einem Ring kleinerer Körper mit unterschiedlichen geometrischen Formen umgeben, die zusammen einen städtischen Häuserblock definieren. Das rechteckige Gebäude mit den Betriebseinrichtungen und die kleineren Auditorien für Kammermusik ziehen sich an den Straßen entlang. Der Hof des Betriebsgebäudes hat ein Gartenrestaurant, von dem man in Richtung Innenstadt blickt, während am anderen Ende drei kleinere Baukörper mit Geschenkladen, Theaterkasse und Kino sowie die große Treppe zwischen ihnen den nördlichen Eingangsbereich charakterisieren.

Die kraftvolle Geometrie der ergänzenden Bauten betont den sozialen Charakter eines Veranstaltungsortes, der eher ein Club und Erholungszentrum als eine traditionelle städtische Konzerthalle ist. Von der Ebene der obersten Galerien des Hauptkonzertsaals gelangt man auf eine Dachterrasse mit Bars und Restaurants, wo sich Entspannung und Vergnügen mit dem anregenden Blick über Los Angeles und die Hügel von Hollywood verbinden.

Disney Philharmonic Hall

Limited competition project
James Stirling, Michael Wilford and Associates
Los Angeles
1988

In a part of the city which is, for Los Angeles, surprisingly urban and dense, the problem was to fit on to the site a large concert hall for a diversity of musical performances, together with all the subsidiary facilities. This is achieved by raising the main auditorium up, and placing the foyer directly below it. From the central foyer a ring of double escalators rises up into the peripheral lobbies, from which the tiered seating can be reached. The upper tiers extend right around the space, allowing audience or choir seating behind the performance platform. The main foyer with its escalators is a centre of social activity, and contains at one side an informal performance space. The central foyer opens out on all sides to take in the other activities: two smaller

auditoria, and a special building for varied support facilities.

Externally, the central drum containing the main auditorium is surrounded on three sides by a ring of smaller volumes of varied geometry, that together define a city block. The rectangular masses of the Support Facilities Building and the smaller auditorium for chamber music carry on the street lines. The courtyard in the Support building contains a garden restaurant which looks downtown, while at the other end three smaller volumes containing gift shop, box office and cinema, and grand staircase between them define the northern entrances.

The vigourous geometry of the subsidiary elements emphasizes the social aspects of a facility which is more of a club and recreational centre than the traditional civic concert hall. The top balcony level of the main auditorium has access to a roof terrace with bars and restaurants, from where views of Los Angeles and the Hollywood Hills can build up an atmosphere of relaxation and enjoyment.

Außenansicht
Grundriß Erdgeschoß
Foyer
Modellfoto

Exterior view
Ground floor plan
Lobby
Model view

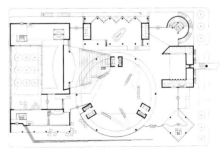

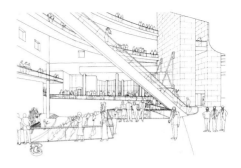

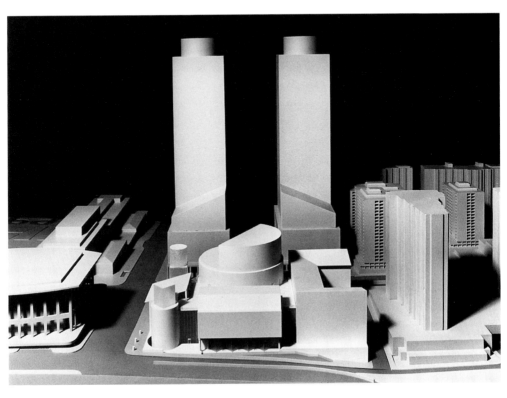

Biologiebibliothek der Universität von Kalifornien in Irvine

James Stirling, Michael Wilford and Associates
Irvine, Kalifornien
1988 – 1993

Der Campus der Universität von Kalifornien in Irvine liegt inmitten der wogenden Hügel und Canyons der ehemaligen Vieh-Ranch Irvine fünf Kilometer vom Meer entfernt und 65 Kilometer südlich von Los Angeles. Er ist um einen runden Park angelegt, von dem sechs getrennte viereckige Blöcke strahlenförmig nach außen führen. Das Quadrat der Biologieabteilung verbindet auch die Medizinfakultät mit dem Zentrum des Campus, so daß die Bibliothek sowohl von den Medizin- wie von den Biologiestudenten genutzt werden kann. Wahrscheinlich werden in einer späteren Erweiterung in diesem Bereich Forschungslabors hinzukommen, und die Bibliothek wird hier das einzige Gebäude ohne Labors bleiben.

Das Gebäude, Herzstück seines Blocks, ist ein Wahrzeichen des Campus und von allen Seiten sichtbar. Seine einzigartige Form entspricht dem funktionalen Programm, das eine kohärente Gliederung, direkte Verbindungen zwischen den Fachbereichen und natürliche Belichtung aller Lesesäle und Räumlichkeiten für den Lehrkörper forderte. Seine konzentrierte Form schafft eine ansprechende Raumerfahrung und vermittelt den Eindruck urbaner und räumlicher Identität.

Der zentrale Hof erlaubt es, den Eingang ins Herz des Gebäudes zu verlegen und den Innenraum mit Tageslicht zu erhellen. Seiner Form entsprechen zwei differenzierte Fassaden: der fokussierte Eingang am Ende, der auf den zentralen Park blickt, sowie eine ausladende, zur Medizinfakultät hin offene Fassade.

Durch das Gebäude verläuft ein Fußgängerweg, der über den ganzen Campus führt und sich unter dieser schattigen Überbauung zu einer Abfolge von Räumen weitet und verengt. Der Lichteinfall durch die großzügige Verglasung entlang dieses Weges wird von elektronisch gesteuerten Sonnenblenden kontrolliert. Die so geschützten großen Fenster kontrastieren mit dem Tüpfelmuster der kleinen Fenster nach draußen, mit dem die Architekten das Schwergewicht auf die Kommunikation innerhalb des Gebäudes legen. Die Verglasung des dreieckigen oberen Hofes ist opak, um die Bücher zu schonen. Die Konstruktion besteht aus einem Stahlrahmen, der mit verputzten Paneelen verkleidet ist. Ein Sockel und eine Lage aus rotem Sandstein machen den dreigliedrigen Aufbau des Volumens ablesbar. Auch der Hof ist mit rotem Sandstein gepflastert.

Es gibt keinen traditionellen großen Lesesaal (wie bei der Geschichtsfakultät in Cambridge). Statt dessen verteilen

Biological Sciences Library for University of California at Irvine

James Stirling, Michael Wilford and Associates
Irvine, California
1988 – 1993

The Irvine Campus of the University of California is situated amongst the rolling hills and canyons of the former Irvine cattle ranch, three miles from the sea and 40 miles south of Los Angeles. It is arranged around a circular park, from which six separate quadrangles radiate outwards. The Biological Sciences quadrant also connects the Medical School to the centre of the campus, so the Library is used both by Medical and Biological Sciences students. Future expansion of this sector will probably be in research laboratories, and the Library is likely to be the only non-laboratory building.

The building is a campus landmark, visible from all approaches, and the centre piece of its own quadrangle. Its unique form corresponds to the functional brief which called for a coherent organisation, direct connections between departments, and provision of daylight to all reader and staff spaces. Its concentrated form provides a sense of urban and spatial identity, along with a variety of pedestrian experience. The central courtyard enables the entrance to be located at the heart of the building as well as providing daylight to the interior. Its shape differentiates the two faces: a focussed entrance at the end facing the central park, and a spreading, open facade towards the Medical School.

The building bridges the pedestrian route through the campus, providing shade and enclosure, and a sequence of swelling and narrowing spaces. The generous glazing facing this route is controlled by electrically operated sun blinds. The protected large windows are in contrast with the dotted pattern of small windows facing outward, and this emphasizes the inward social contact. The glazing to the triangular upper courtyard is translucent, in order to reduce the exposure of the books. Construction is of steel frame, faced with stuccoed panels, and a red sandstone base and string course together make legible the tri-partite organisation of the volume. The courtyard is also surfaced with red sandstone.

Unlike the traditional model, there is no central grand reading room (as at the Cambridge History Faculty). Instead, reader spaces are distributed throughout the building, offering a choice of location and ambience, and a variety of views, from centres of high activity to absolute seclusion. Entry is from the courtyard at ground level, with reference periodicals and circulation services situated immediately above, technical support services next above, and reader spaces with stack access in the re-

sich die Leseräume über das Gebäude und bieten eine je unterschiedliche Atmosphäre, eine Vielzahl von Ausblicken, geschäftige und absolut abgeschiedene Bereiche. Der Eingang liegt im Erdgeschoß im Hof. Die Zeitschriften- und Periodikaabteilung befinden sich direkt darüber. Es folgt ein Geschoß für die technischen Einrichtungen. Die übrigen drei Geschosse beherbergen die Leseräume mit Zugang zum Magazin. Eine dramatisch wirkende Treppe steigt von der Eingangshalle zur Buchausleihe an, wo auch die Eingangskontrolle untergebracht ist. Die doppelte Geschoßhöhe belebt den größeren Lesesaal, der den Hof sowie die Leseräume an den Gebäudeenden umschließt.

maining three levels. A dramatic staircase rises from the entrance hall to the loan desk which controls public access. Double height enlivens the larger reading room which encircles the courtyard and the terminal reading rooms that are located at the extremities.

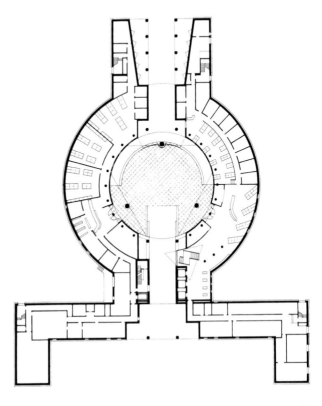

Grundriß Erdgeschoß

Ground floor plan

Gesamtansicht Overall view

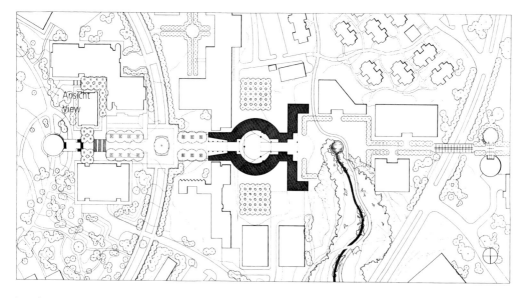

Lageplan Site plan

Ansicht   View

Blick in den zentralen Hof   View of central courtyard

Apartmenthaus Carlton Gardens 5 – 7
Beschränkter Wettbewerb
James Stirling, Michael Wilford and Associates
London
1988 –

Dieser kleine Apartmentblock liegt hinter Pall Mall in einem sehr feinen Teil von St. James, London an einer ruhigen Straße, die an jedem Ende mit Platanen-Gärten abschließt. In diesem Bezirk gibt es viele berühmte Clubs wie das Athenaeum, und die Architektur der italienischen Palazzi, die ihnen als Modell diente, nahmen auch Stirling und Wilford als Vorlage.

Der achtgeschossige Block – zweiachsig und auf jeder Achse symmetrisch angelegt – wirkt nach außen wie ein Gebäude von sechs Geschossen zur Straße und vier Geschossen zur Gartenseite und reflektiert damit die Traufhöhen der umliegenden Gebäude. Unten befinden sich Büros mit Zugang von der Straße und einer Garage im Kellergeschoß. Darüber liegen Luxuswohnungen, zu denen man durch Vestibüle an jedem Ende gelangt: Das eine führt von Carlton Gardens an einer Portiersloge vorbei ins Gebäude, vom anderen gelangt man in den Privatgarten. Die Vestibüle sind durch einen offenen Hof im Zentrum des Apartmenthauses verbunden.

Besonders ansprechend wirkt die *gravitas* der Giebelseiten mit ihren schweren zentralen Säulen, Erkerfenstern und kegelförmigen Säulenschäften in den Ecken. Dieser Entwurf schafft im Bereich des Wohnbaus eine Urbanität, wie sie beim Bürokomplex Poultry Nr. 1 von Stirling und Wilford bereits Triumphe feierte. Die unterschiedliche Größe der Fensteröffnungen, die auf die Vierergruppen der oberen Geschosse abgestimmt sind, knüpft an die italienische Palazzi der dreißiger Jahre ebenso wie an jene der Renaissance an.

5 – 7 Carlton Gardens Apartments
Limited competition
James Stirling, Michael Wilford and Associates
London
1988 –

This small apartment block is situated behind Pall Mall in a very select part of London, St. James, facing a quiet street, with gardens filled with plane trees at either end. This area is studded with famous clubs, such as the Athenaeum, and the Italian Palazzo – which served as their model – is in turn adopted as the model here.

What is effectively an eight-storey block appears as six storeys facing the street, and four storeys facing the gardens, reflecting the heights of the adjacent buildings. It is bi-axial and symmetrical on both axes. Below are offices, with a basement garage, and access from the street. Above are luxury apartments, approached through vestibules at either end, one leading from Carlton Gardens, with a porter station, the other leading out into the private gardens. The vestibules are joined by an open court at the centre of the building.

Particularly to be enjoyed in this design is the *gravitas* of the end elevations, with their weighty central column, projecting bay windows, and conical trees at the corners. This is a domestic version of the urban architecture to be found triumphantly displayed at Number One Poultry. The varied scale of the window openings, keyed to the foursomes of the upper storeys, ties back to the Italian palazzi of the thirties as much as to those of the Renaissance.

Grundriß Erdgeschoß mit
Wohn- und Büroeingängen
Grundriß 1. und 2. Obergeschoß
mit Büros
Grundriß 4. Obergeschoß mit
Luxuswohnungen

Ground floor plan with
residential and office entrances
Plan of first and second floor
with offices
Plan of fourth floor with
luxury apartments

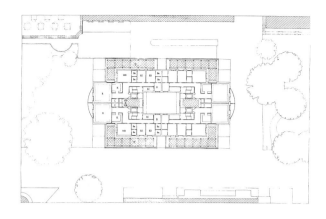

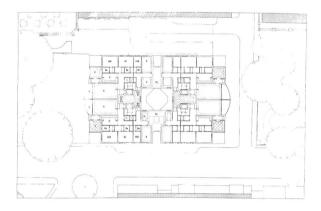

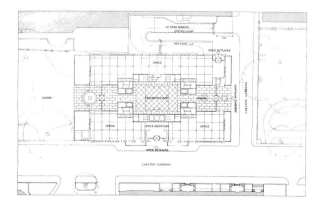

Modellfotos   Model views

Stadionkomplex

Projekt
James Stirling, Michael Wilford and Associates
Sevilla
1988

Dieses Projekt mußte ein vorhandenes Sportstadion integrieren, das regelmäßig von Scharen lärmender Fans besucht wird. Um mit dieser Situation umzugehen, schufen die Architekten einen traditionellen Sockel als öffentliches Forum, auf dem sich die Gebäude in relativer Ruhe erheben, während die Menschenmengen darunter über einen tieferliegenden beeindruckenden runden Platz geschleust werden.

Unter diesem Platz befindet sich ein zweigeschossiges Kaufhaus mit eigenem Parkhaus auf zwei weiteren Ebenen. Der Eingang zum Kaufhaus und den beiden Büroblöcken wird durch umgekehrte Kegelstümpfe markiert, die als Lichtschächte für die sechseckigen Foyergebäude dienen, von denen Rolltreppen nach unten führen.

Zu beiden Seiten des Sockels stehen zwei zwölfgeschossige Büroblöcke, deren Vorhangfassaden fast durchgehend aus metallenen Sonnenblenden bestehen. Auf etwa halber Höhe gliedert ein zurückspringendes, mit Fliesen verkleidetes Geschoß die Gebäudemasse und stellt so eine Beziehung zur Höhe des Stadions auf der einen Seite und der nahen städtischen Blockbebauung auf der anderen Seite her.

An einer Ecke des Sockels steht ein Hotel, dessen Eingänge an den Ecken liegen. Die 280 Zimmer haben je einen Balkon mit individuell verstellbaren Sonnenblenden. Die Masse des Hotelvolumens vermindert sich nach oben hin in drei Stufen, ähnlich wie bei den Baukörpern des Wohnparks Canary Wharf.

Stadium Development

Project
James Stirling, Michael Wilford and Associates
Seville
1988

This project had to deal with the life of an existing stadium, where sports fans make noisy and frequent descents. These conditions were dealt with by creating a more or less traditional podium, making a public forum from which the buildings arise in relative peace, while below the crowds are channelled through an impressive circular plaza leading through to the stadium.

Underneath the plaza there is a two-storey department store, with its own parking on two further levels. Entrances to the department store and to the two office blocks are marked by truncated cones, light funnels in fact, inverted above hexagonal halls, into which the escalators rise.

On either side of the podium stand two twelve-storey office blocks. These have curtain walls shaded by metal sunscreens on the edges, and by the escape stairs at the ends. About halfway up a recessed storey, clad in tiling, articulates the mass and relates to the height of the stadium on one side and the nearer city blocks on the other. At one corner of the podium there is a hotel, with its entrance on the corner, containing 280 rooms, each with a shaded balcony with adjustable lattice sunscreens. The bulk of the hotel is reduced by cutting back the plan profile in three stages, reminiscent of the residential towers proposed for the Canary Wharf development.

Situationsisometrie
Grundriß

Site axonometric
Site plan

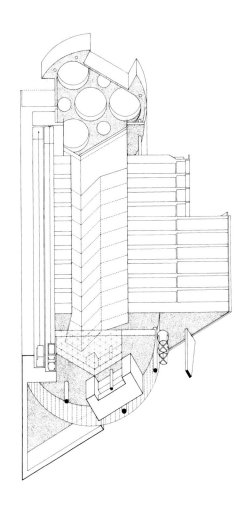

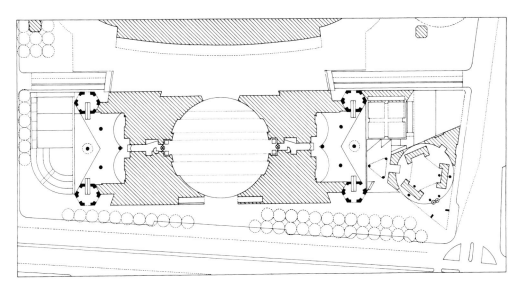

Bibliothèque de France
Projekt für beschränkten Wettbewerb
James Stirling, Michael Wilford and Associates
Paris
1989

Ins Blickfeld der Öffentlichkeit rückte der Ort, wo die französische Nationalbibliothek steht, durch den minimalistischen Entwurf des Architekten, der den Wettbewerb gewann. Statt Perraults vier getrennten, aber identischen Eckkörpern, die symbolisch «offene Bücher» darstellen sollen, schufen Stirling und Wilford eine lebhafte Komposition aus abwechslungsreichen und kontrastierenden Elementen, die sich um einen Garten gruppieren. Sie sollen nichts symbolisieren, sondern bieten eine Fülle architektonischer Verweise sowohl auf moderne wie historische Vorläufer, mit einer gewissen Betonung der klassizistischen Anspielungen, die an den großen Claude-Nicolas Ledoux erinnern. Die Gestaltung sollte jedoch nicht schwerfällig, sondern spielerisch wirken: Die Sockelgeschosse sind steinverkleidet, die höheren Geschosse in Glas und Stahl gehalten.

Der zentrale Garten führt in gestuften Terrassen zur Front an der Seine hinunter. Der Kuppelbau beherbergt die Bibliothek mit Neuerwerbungen, während in dem tonnenförmigen Volumen die Handbibliothek untergebracht ist. Der Gesamtkatalog befindet sich im kegelförmigen Baukörper, die Forschungsbibliothek im achteckigen Pavillon nebenan. Magazin, Dokumentenstelle und technische Dienste befinden sich alle im Keller, geschützt von der schädlichen Einwirkung des Sonnenlichts. Eine Passage mit abwechslungsreichem Profil umgürtet den zentralen Garten, erschließt alle Abteilungen und kommuniziert zugleich mit dem grünen Außenraum. Der Haupteingang liegt auf der zentralen Achse an der Straßenseite. Zwei öffentliche Fußwege durchqueren das Gebäude, geben stellenweise das Innenleben der Bibliothek preis, ohne die Sicherheit zu gefährden, und führen zu den Service-Einrichtungen.

Diese Offenheit sollte die Öffentlichkeit mit der Bibliothek vertrauter machen und zu ihrer Nutzung ermuntern. Daher sieht der Entwurf auch Geschäfte, Restaurants, Buchläden, Cafés, Galerien und ein Konferenzzentrum vor.

Bibliothèque de France
Limited competition project
James Stirling, Michael Wilford and Associates
Paris
1989

The site occupied by the Bibliothèque de France has been brought to public notice through the minimalist aesthetic adopted by the architect who won the competition. In place of Perrault's four separate but identical corner masses, designated as «symbolic» open books, Stirling-Wilford offered a lively composition made up of varied and contrasting elements grouped around a garden, not symbolic of anything, but full of architectural references to both modern and ancient precedents, with a certain emphasis on a sort of neo-classicism reminiscent of the great Ledoux. Yet it was not to be ponderous, but playful, with the lower levels cased in stone, the higher floors in steel and glass.

The central garden rises in stepped terraces from the frontage to the River Seine. The domed space houses the Recent Acquisitions Library, the vaulted rectangle houses the Reference Library. The general catalogue is in the cone, and the Research Library is in the octagonal pavilion adjoining. Book storage, document processing, and technical services are all housed in the basement, away from the hazards of daylight. A concourse of varied profile surrounds the central garden and gives access to all departments, while engaging with the central garden. The main entrance is located on the main axis, facing the street. Two public footways traverse the building, screened in places so as to expose the workings to public view without compromising the requirements of security, and connecting to social facilities.

This openness to scrutiny was intended to familiarize the general public and encourage them to use the building. The social side was to be further extended by providing shops, restaurants, bookstores, cafés, exhibition galleries, and a conference centre.

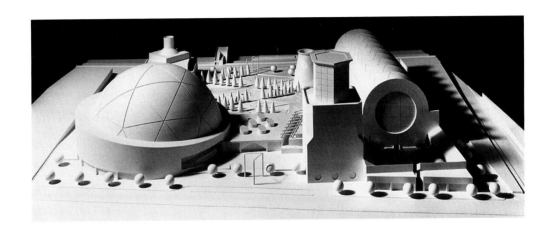

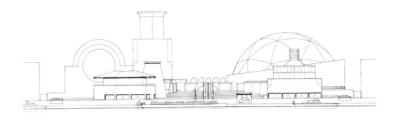

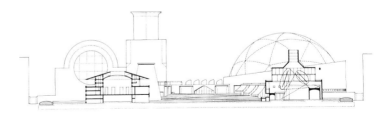

Modellfoto
Schnitte

Model view
Sections

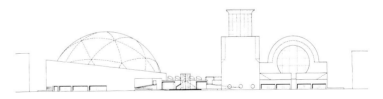

147

Tokyo International Forum

Projekt für beschränkten Wettbewerb
James Stirling, Michael Wilford and Associates
Tokio
1989

Das Forum, das in einem Blockgrundstück am Rand eines Bezirks von Tokio mit Straßenraster liegt und an eine Bahntrasse mit einem wichtigen oberirdischen Bahnhof grenzt, stellt einen bedeutenden baulichen Eingriff in dieser dichtbevölkerten Stadt dar. Es weist eine Vielzahl von Einrichtungen auf: Konferenzzentren, Konzerthallen, Versammlungssäle, Restaurants.

Ein halbkreisförmiges Gebäude, dessen Durchmesser sich über die ganze Länge einer der Grundstücksseiten erstreckt, hat geschlossene Wände zur Straßenseite und Glasfassaden nach innen zum zentralen Platz. Es beherbergt eine große Halle mit 5000 Plätzen. Ein ähnlicher, quadratischer Baukörper mit zwei Hallen für 1500 bzw. 200 Menschen liegt ihm auf der anderen Seite gegenüber. Diese beiden Volumina werden durch eine große Passage getrennt, die öffentlich zugänglich ist und Verbindung zu zwei U-Bahnlinien und einen Busbahnhof hat. Sie ist Treffpunkt für Konferenzteilnehmer, verfügt über Fahrkarten- und Informationsschalter und ist auf eine zylindrische, offene Piazza zentriert, die sich für Freilichtkonzerte oder andere Aufführungen zeitweise mit Stühlen ausstatten läßt oder für die informelle Nutzung frei bleiben kann.

Die Passage geht bruchlos in das große Eingangsfoyer des dritten Gebäudes über, ein Turm auf dem hinteren Teil des Grundstücks mit Büros, Versammlungs- und Konferenzräumen, einem Festsaal für Bankette, einem Empfangssaal und einem Luxusrestaurant. Dieser Turm mit seiner stark verglasten Fassade stuft sich von einem halbkreisförmigen Körper über einen kreisförmigen zu einem sechseckigen ab. Nach unten stellen Rolltreppen die Verbindung zu den Ausstellungssälen her, die sich über die ganze Länge des Grundstücks erstrecken. Sie führen auch zur Tiefgarage, zum unterirdischen Busbahnhof und den Service-Bereichen. Der Zugang für Autos vom Straßenniveau ist auf der Rückseite in der Nähe des Turmsockels, so daß die übrige Grundstücksfläche Fußgängern vorbehalten bleibt.

Der gesamte Komplex ist erdbebensicher und so entworfen, daß er in kürzester Zeit evakuiert werden kann. Die unteren Geschosse und der runde, offene Platz sind mit Stein, die restlichen Fassaden mit Spezialglas verkleidet.

Tokyo International Forum

Limited competition
James Stirling, Michael Wilford and Associates
Tokyo
1989

Situated on a city block on the edge of a gridded sector of Tokyo, and adjacent to a railway embankment and important surface station, the Forum is a major intervention in a crowded city. It has many facilities: conference centres, concert halls, meeting rooms, restaurants.

A semicircular building whose diameter defines one edge of the site has solid walls to the street and glass walls facing inward to a central plaza. It contains a large hall for 5000 people. A similar building, square in volume, faces it from the other side, containing halls for 1500 and for 200 people. These two volumes are separated by a large concourse open to the general public, and connecting to two subway lines, and a bus station. It is a meeting place for conference delegates and ticket registration, and for general information. It is centred on a plaza of cylindrical form, open to the sky, which can be partially filled with temporary seating for open-air concerts and other performance events, or can be left clear for informal use.

The concourse flows smoothly into a large entrance foyer serving the third major structure – a tower at the back of the site containing offices, meeting and conference rooms, a banqueting suite, a reception suite and a luxury restaurant. This tower has highly glazed facades, and steps up in a sequence of hexagonal, circular, and semicircular volumes. Downward, escalators connect to the exhibition halls, which extend across the whole length of the site, underground parking, an underground bus station, and service areas. Vehicle access from street level is concentrated at the rear, close to the base of the tower, so that the rest of the site is free for pedestrian movement.

The whole structure is earth-quake resistant, and designed for immediate evacuation. Stone facing is used in the lower levels, and in the circular open-air plaza. Otherwise the buildings are clad in special glass.

Grundrisse Erdgeschoß
und Obergeschosse

Plans of ground
and upper floors

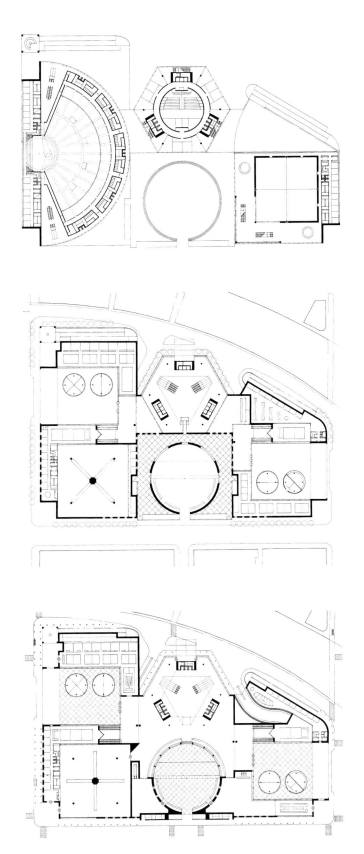

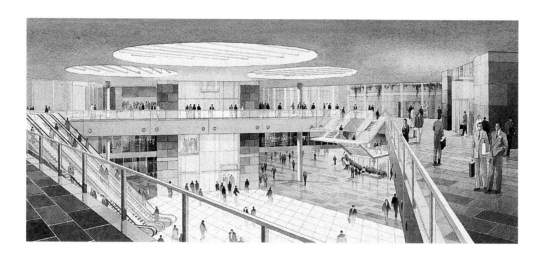

Passage   Concourse

Innenansicht und Blick in den zentralen Innenhof   View of interior and central plaza

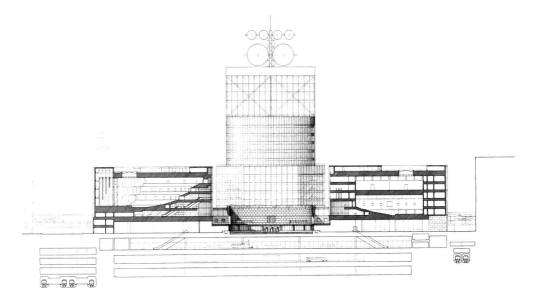

Ansicht   Elevation

Modellfoto   Model view

Oper Compton Verney

Projekt für beschränkten Wettbewerb
James Stirling, Michael Wilford and Associates
Compton Verney, Warwickshire
1989

Dieses ehrgeizige Unterfangen, das vom Erfolg der Oper in Glyndebourne angeregt wurde, betrifft das Grundstück einer palladianischen Villa, wo man in ländlicher Umgebung Musik genießen kann. Der Entwurf zielt darauf ab, diese ländliche Umgebung zur Geltung kommen zu lassen, indem die verschiedenen Elemente der Komposition zu einem informellen Ensemble gruppiert werden, wobei der Bühnenturm nach hinten gerückt wurde, wo seine Auswirkung auf die Landschaft am unauffälligsten ist, ein Tribut an die traditionelle englische Kunst malerischer Landschaftsgestaltung.

Die Oper wird von der Villa durch einen künstlichen Teich getrennt, den eine Brücke von Robert Adam überspannt. Der Pfad über die Brücke führt zu einem formellen, quadratisch abgezirkelten Rasen, an dessen einer Seite sich die Loggia befindet. Sie hat die klassische Stirling-Form mit einem Schrägdach und rechtwinklig abknickenden Endfeldern, die so den Vorplatz einfassen und die Struktur des Daches zu erkennen geben. Aus der Achse gerückt, überbrückt auf einer Seite das Restaurant das Ende des Teiches und neigt seine Fassade zum Wasser und zum Haus.

Hinter der Loggia führt ein dreieckiges Foyer zum Konzertsaal auf der einen und zum Bürogebäude auf der anderen Seite. Die Büros umschließen einen quadratischen Hof mit eigener Loggia, und sie sind nach außen gerichtet, um die zurückhaltende Atmosphäre dieses Hofs zu erhalten. Im Zentrum stützt eine einzige Säule das Glasdach des Foyers. Der Konzertsaal liegt in einer ruhigen Abfolge rechtwinkliger Volumina. Das geneigte Dach reduziert die Wirkung des Baukörpers, und die Bepflanzung mit Bäumen trägt zusätzlich dazu bei, daß sich die Baukörper zu einem bauernhofähnlichen Ensemble fügen.

Opera House Compton Verney

Limited competition project
James Stirling, Michael Wilford and Associates
Compton Verney, Warwickshire
1989

This ambitious venture was inspired by the success of Glyndebourne Opera, where music may be enjoyed in a rural setting, in the grounds of a Palladian villa. The design aims to exploit the rural setting by dispersing the various elements into an informal grouping, with the stage tower placed well to the rear where it will impact least on the landscape, so that the traditional English art of picturesque landscape may be re-established.

The opera house is separated from the original house by an ornamental lake, crossed by a bridge designed by Robert Adam. The path across the bridge arrives at a formal lawn, square in plan for clear definition, one side of which is made by the entrance loggia. This is of classic Stirling vintage, with a single-pitch roof, and the ends returned by one whole bay to expose the roof structure and embrace the forecourt. Off axis, to one side and spanning the end of the lake as a bridge, is the restaurant, with its bowed face turned towards the lake and the house.

Behind the loggia, a triangular foyer leads to the auditorium on one face, and to the administration building on the other. The latter is formed around a square courtyard with its own loggia, and the offices look outward to preserve the low scale of the courtyard. At the centre, a single pillar supports the glazed roof of the foyer. The auditorium is contained in a quiet series of rectangular volumes. Its pitched roof reduces the impact of its volume, and tree planting further contributes to its general acquiesence in a farm-like collection of buildings.

Lageplan
Längsschnitt
Perspektivzeichnung
Ansicht

Site plan
Longitudinal section
Perspective view
Elevation

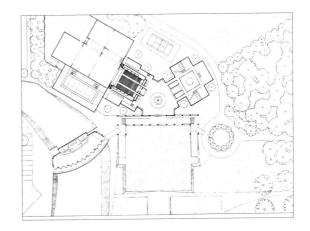

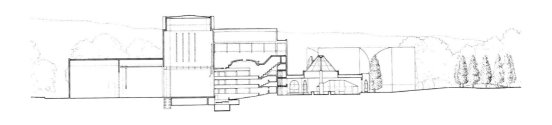

Biennale Buchladen

James Stirling, Michael Wilford and Associates
Venedig
1989–1991

Das Gebäude liegt an der Hauptstraße in der Nähe des Eingangs zum Biennale-Park in einer baumbestandenen Landschaft mit den Ausstellungspavillons von 25 Nationen, die hier ihre Kultur präsentieren. Der Baukörper hat die Form eines kleinen Pavillons, wie ein in die Länge gezogenes Boot. Er paßt sich an seinem Standort zwischen zwei Baumreihen ein, deren Stämme beinahe wie Säulen wirken, was den Seiten des Gebäudes etwas von einem griechischen Tempel verleiht. Wie es sich für ein Boot gehört, bildet das «Heck» eine sanfte Rundung, und der «Bug» richtet sich zu einem kleinen Turm auf, der von einem «Schornstein» gekrönt wird, aus dem ein einzelner Laserstrahl nachts in den Himmel leuchtet.

Im Inneren verstärken Fenster auf Augenhöhe, die sich ums ganze Gebäude ziehen, den Eindruck, in einem *vaporetto* zu sein, und tatsächlich kann man von hier aus den Bootsverkehr beobachten und die tatsächlichen *vaporetti* sehen, die am nahen Landesteg anlegen. Buchregale gibt es nur unterhalb der Fensterbänke. Das polierte Holz des Präsentationsregals korrespondiert mit der Holzverkleidung der Decke. Das Walmdach darüber ist mit Metall verkleidet und schließt mit einem durchlaufenden Lichtgaden ab. Die stählerne Dachkonstruktion mit ihren Drahtseilverstrebungen ist ein weiteres bootsähnliches Element. Der Grundriß ist klar und ebenfalls schiffsförmig: Ein kleines Foyer trennt die Toilette vom Laden ab, die Ladentheke schiebt sich leicht gekrümmt in den Raum. Das Licht wird durch die Bäume gefiltert, als würde es von Wellen reflektiert.

Schönheit, wie sie sich hier im kleinen offenbart, schafft, so hat es der englische Dichter Ben Jonson einmal formuliert, im Leben Momente der Vollkommenheit:
«In small proportions we just beauties see
And in short measures life may perfect be.»

Biennale Bookshop

James Stirling, Michael Wilford and Associates
Venice
1989–1991

The building is situated near to the public entrance to the Biennale garden and alongside the principal avenue, in a tree-dotted landscape containing some 25 exhibition pavilions representing national cultures. The building takes the form of a small pavilion, elongated like a boat, and it fits into a space contained by two rows of trees, whose trunks serve almost as columns defining the edges of the pavilion like a Greek temple. As befits a boat, its «stern» is a smooth curve, its «prow» rears up to a little tower capped by a «funnel» from which a single laser beam takes off vertically into the night sky.

Inside, eye-level windows all round reinforce the feeling of being in a *vaporetto*, and indeed views may be had of the boat traffic, including the *vaporetti* putting in at the adjacent landing stage. The books are restricted to continuous shelving underneath the window cill. The polished wood display shelf responds to the timber roof lining. Above, the hipped roof is clad in metal, like a hull, and capped by a continuous clear-storey window. The steel roof structure with its wire bracing is another boat-like feature. The plan is neat and ship-shape: a vestibule separates a toilet and store, the counter projects into the space with a gentle curve. The light is filtered through the trees as if it were reflected from waves. As the English poet Ben Jonson said:
«In small proportions we just beauties see
And in short measures life may perfect be.»

Vorderansicht   Entrance elevation   Querschnitt   Cross section

Rückansicht   View of rear facade

Dachuntersicht der
Gebäuderückseite
Grundriß

Roof overhang at rear
Floor plan

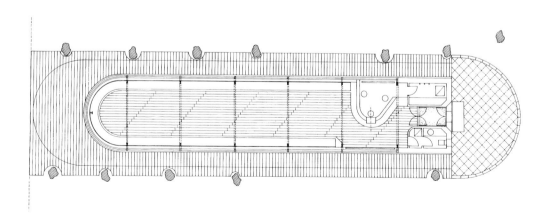

Innenansichten
Vorderansicht

Interior views
View of entrance facade

Filmpalast

Projekt für beschränkten Wettbewerb
James Stirling, Michael Wilford and Associates
mit Marlies Hentrup und Norbert Heyers
Venedig
1990

Das Filmfest in Venedig weckt periodisch die voyeuristische Neugier, wenn sich die Starlets unter die Badenden am Lido mischen und die Menge von der Erwartung bewegt wird, daß die Stars zu ihr hinabsteigen. Das Grundstück liegt am Strand und wird vom Excelsior Hotel und dem Kasino flankiert. Der Wunsch, diese Lage auszunutzen, beseelt den Entwurf. Die Verwaltung sowie die Service-Einrichtungen sind an einer Seite und im hinteren Gebäudeteil untergebracht, während die zwei Seiten vorne offen gestaltet sind und dem Blick freie Bahn lassen.

Der Hauptkinosaal für 3000 Menschen ist diagonal davor gesetzt. Er kann für ein kleineres Publikum durch eine doppelte Trennwand, die sich nach oben in den Dachstuhl ziehen läßt, zweigeteilt werden. Dahinter liegt ein kleinerer Saal und darüber eine Reihe von Vorführ- und Interviewräumen mit eigenem Foyer. Eine Rampe erschließt vom Foyer aus alle Ebenen und führt schließlich zu einer großen Dachterrasse mit Bar, die einen herrlichen Blick über die Adria bietet. Großzügige Treppenhäuser an jedem Ende der öffentlichen Bereiche tragen Turmaufsätze, von denen aus nachts Laserstrahlen die Ecken des Komplexes markieren, der überwiegend abends und bis spät in die Nacht genutzt wird.

Das Hauptfoyer, das groß genug ist, um Ausstellungen aufzunehmen, wird von zylindrischen Stützen auf quadratischem Raster strukturiert. Die ausdrucksstarke Zickzacklinie der Glasfront dringt in diesen geordneten Raum ein und läßt am Eingang sogar eine der Stützen als Wächter isoliert an der Außenseite des Gebäudes zurück. Das Erdgeschoß ist erhöht, um einen besseren Blick auf den Strand zu erlauben und wird über eine gekurvte Rampe erreicht. Ohne sich von der funktionalen Disziplin der konsolidierten Tradition der Moderne zu lösen, erreichen Stirling und Wilford mit diesem Ensemble eine spielerische Architektur.

Cinema Palace

Limited competition project
James Stirling, Michael Wilford and Associates
with Marlies Hentrup and Norbert Heyers
Venice
1990

The Venice Film Festival periodically forms the focus of paparazzi interest when the starlets mingle with the bathers on the Lido, and expectation of the descent of the stars animates the crowd. The site faces the beach, and is flanked by the Excelsior Hotel and the Casino. The wish to take advantage of this setting determined the layout, where one side and the back is occupied by administration and services, leaving two sides open to the views.

The main auditorium, for 3000 people, fits the resulting space on the diagonal. It can be divided into two for smaller audiences, by means of a double partition which can be retracted upward into a roof housing. At the back is a smaller hall, and above it a series of viewing rooms and interview rooms, with their own foyer. A ramp rises through the foyer connecting all the levels, and gives access finally to a large roof terrace and bar, with spectacular views across the Adriatic. Generous staircases at either end of the public spaces carry towers with laser beams marking the extent of the scene. Much of the activity occurs in the evenings and late into the night.

In the main foyer, which is large enough to mount exhibitions, the scene is regulated by a square grid of cylindrical columns. Through this orderly space the glazed wall dashes in an impetuous zig-zag, contriving to leave one column isolated on the outside to act as guardian at the entrance. The floor is raised to allow better views of the beach, so a snaking ramp defines the point of entry. The ensemble provides an architecture of play, without departing from a functional discipline that is canonic in its «modernity».

Perspektivische Ansicht
Grundrisse Erd- und Obergeschoß

Perspective view
Plans of ground and upper floor

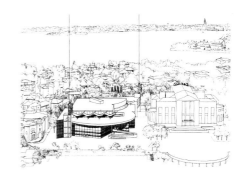

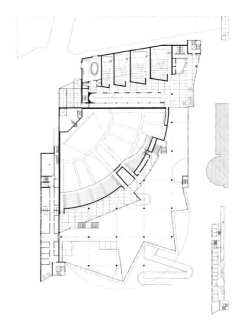

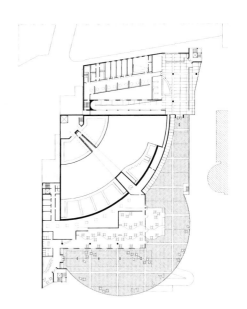

Sitz von Channel Four
Projekt für beschränkten Wettbewerb
James Stirling, Michael Wilford and Associates
London
1990

Der Block wird zum Teil von einer Gruppe von vier Wohngebäuden eingenommen, die zwei Seiten eines Platzes bilden. Gepflastert verwandelt er sich in einen öffentlichen Raum, dessen andere beiden Seiten der Fernsehsender Channel Four definiert. Die ganze Fläche ist für eine Tiefgarage unterkellert.

Das Eingangsfoyer auf dem Niveau des Platzes ist von einer geschwungenen Wand aus Glassegmenten umhüllt und bietet ungehinderten Zugang ins Gebäude. Der Großteil der Flächen ist in einem rechteckigen Block untergebracht, der auf einer Seite an den Platz, auf der anderen an eine Straße grenzt. Er ist tief genug, um Platz für zwei trichterförmige Lichtschächte zu lassen, von denen einer den Eingangspunkt markiert. Eine Kolonnade, die der geschwungenen Linie der Eingangshalle folgt, führt zu einem separaten Gebäude, das ein Fernsehstudio enthält — ein quadratischer Pavillon, der von einem achteckigen Körper mit der Klimaanlage gekrönt wird und an seiner Rückseite einen Ladebereich hat.

Das vordere Hauptgebäude hat drei normale Bürogeschosse, eine Eingangshalle in doppelter Geschoßhöhe und ein Restaurant im Halbgeschoß, von dem aus man die Halle überblickt. Der Fahrstuhlturm ist im zweiten Lichtschacht untergebracht, den die Architekten als «Lichtkegel»
bezeichnen. Die tragenden Teile sind an die Außenseite des Komplexes verlegt, so daß viel Spielraum bleibt, um die Innengliederung nach Bedarf zu verändern. Zusätzliche Treppen und Fahrstühle an den Gebäudeecken gewährleisten eine flexible Erschließung.

Channel Four Headquarters
Limited competition project
James Stirling, Michael Wilford and Associates
London
1990

The city block is partly occupied by a set of four apartment buildings, arranged so as to form two sides of a square. This square is confirmed by paving it so that it becomes a public place, with the Television Centre sited so as to define the remaining sides. This has not prevented the entire basement level being cleared to form an underground car park.

Entrance is by a foyer at plaza level, contained in a segmental curve that does not block the way through the building. Most of the accommodation is contained in a rectangular block defining the square and fronting a street on the other side. It is deep enough to warrant being perforated by two funnel-shaped light wells, one of which marks the entrance point. A colonnade following the curve of the entrance hall leads to a separate building containing a television studio – a square pavilion surmounted by an octagon housing the air-conditioning equipment, with a loading bay behind it.

In front, the main building contains three regular floors of offices, a double-height entrance hall with a restaurant overlooking it from a mezzanine. The lift core is placed in the second light well, referred to by the architects as a «light cone». Structure is confined to the outsides of the office building, allowing ample opportunity for changing the plan arrangement if required. Additional stairs and lifts placed at the corners contribute to the flexibility.

Grundrisse Erd- und Obergeschoß

Plans of ground and upper floor

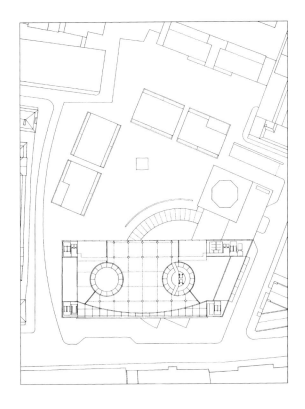

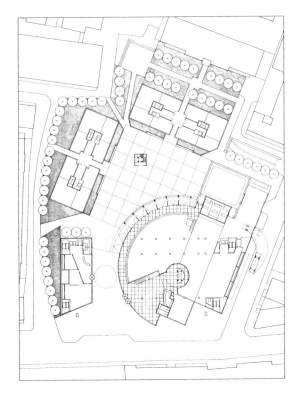

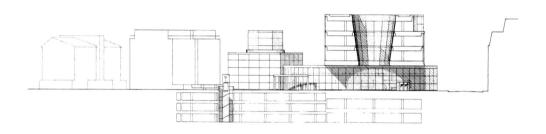

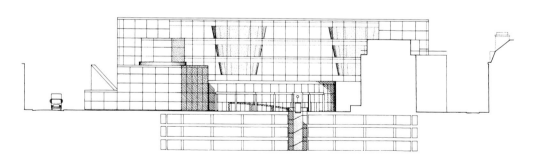

Perspektivische Ansicht
Querschnitt
Längsschnitt

Perspective view
Cross section
Longitudinal section

Isometrie
Innenansicht

Axonometric
Interior view

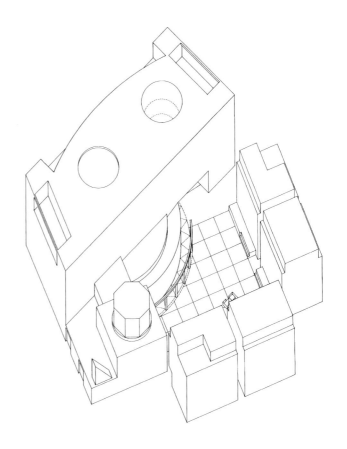

Kyoto Centre
Projekt für beschränkten Wettbewerb
James Stirling, Michael Wilford and Associates
Kioto
1991

Das Grundstück trennt einen bedeutenden Platz im Stadtzentrum von Kioto vom Bahnhof und seinen Gleisen. Die Architekten sahen diese Lage als Schwelle zwischen der traditionellen Stadt im Norden und der modernen zukünftigen Stadt, die im Süden Gestalt annimmt. Aus diesem Grund hat der Komplex an zwei Stellen Durchgänge, die zu Brücken über die Gleisanlagen führen. Diese Durchlässe werden zu Toren in beiderlei Richtung und vermindern so die trennende Wirkung der Bahnlinie an dieser Stelle. Eine der Brücken ist überdacht und dient als Teil des Bahnhofs vor allem den Fahrgästen. Die andere, offene Brücke ist von Läden gesäumt und über einen ovalen Platz zugänglich, der sich in die Reihe der neuen Gebäude fügt.

Diese umfassen ein großes Kaufhaus auf zehn Stockwerken und am anderen Ende des Komplexes ein Kulturzentrum mit einem Wintergarten und Ausstellungsflächen, darunter ein großer Ausstellungssaal. Dieser Raum enthält eine spektakuläre spiralförmige Rampe, die sich um eine geneigte Achse windet, sowie einen riesigen schwebenden großen Bildschirm, zwei dynamische Elemente, welche die zunehmende Bedeutung der Kommunikation im heutigen Leben versinnbildlichen. Weiterhin gehört zu den neuen Gebäuden ein Hotel, das eine ebenso kraftvolle Komposition kontrastierender Volumina bildet: ein Hexaeder, auf den ein Zylinder gesetzt ist, der wiederum von einem kreuzförmigen Turm mit abgeschrägten Fassaden gekrönt wird.

Der untergründige Symbolgehalt des Komplexes spricht sowohl den zeitgenössischen wie den traditionellen Geschmack an: eine Anordnung von Flaggenmasten am Eingang des Bahnhofs und ein sozusagen abgemagerter Bogengang, der durch den Platz zur Altstadt führt, aber ein erkennbar japanisches Profil bewahrt.

Kyoto Centre
Limited competition project
James Stirling, Michael Wilford and Associates
Kyoto
1991

The site separates a major city square in downtown Kyoto from the railway station and its tracks. The architects saw the site as a threshold between the traditional city to the north and the future modern city still taking shape to the south. For this reason the centre is perforated at two points leading to bridges across the railway tracks, becoming gateways in either direction, and reducing the division which the tracks make at this point. One is a covered bridge meant for train users, and forming part of the station. The other is open and lined with shops, and approached through an oval plaza contained in the line of new buildings.

These include a large department store on ten floors, and at the other end a cultural centre containing image facilities, a winter garden and a large area for exhibitions. This space contains a spectacular spiral ramp, circling an inclined spine, and a suspended projection box of great size, two dynamic features which comment on the expanding role of communications in modern life. At the other end of the range of new buildings is a hotel, another energetic series of contrasting volumes, with hexahedron surmounted by cylinder surmounted by a cruciform tower with canted facades.

There are symbolic overtones that speak both to the modern and the traditional citizen: an array of flag-posts at the entry to the station, and a somewhat emaciated archway leading through the plaza to the traditional town, which has nevertheless a distinctly Japanese profile.

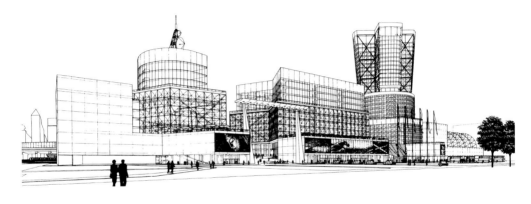

Außenansicht   Exterior view

Modellfoto   Model view

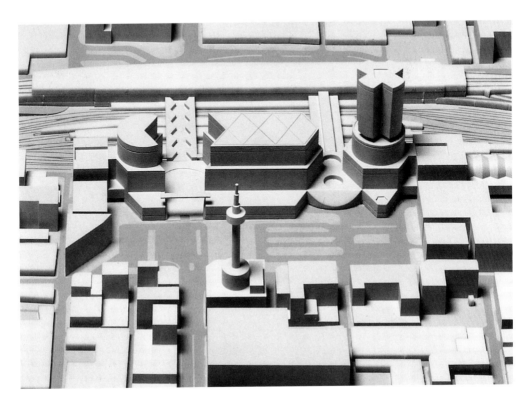

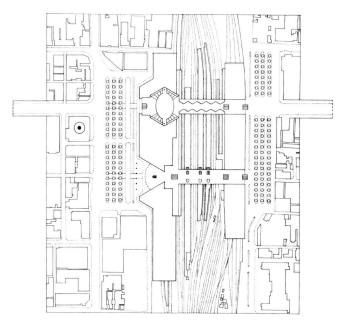

Lageplan
Blick in den Ausstellungsbereich

Site plan
Exhibition area

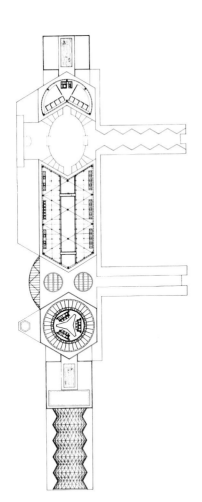

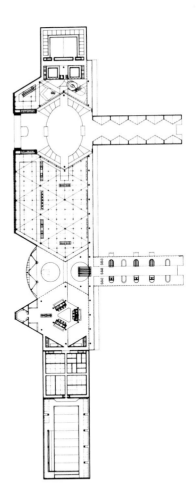

Grundriß Erd- und Obergeschoß
Modellfoto von oben

Plan of ground and upper floor
Model view from above

Temasek Polytechnikum

James Stirling, Michael Wilford and Associates
Singapur
1991 – 1996

Das Temasek Polytechnikum ist eine «Lernstadt» für 11 500 Studenten und 1500 Dozenten, die eine Schule für angewandte Wissenschaft, eine Technikhochschule, eine Wirtschaftsschule und eine Hochschule für Design umfaßt. Es liegt in einem 30 Hektar großen Landschaftspark am östlichen Ende der Insel.

Ein erhöhter Eingangsplatz ist der räumliche Brennpunkt des Campus, und seine urbane Intention wird sofort erkennbar, wenn man sich Stirlings Entwurf für das Stadtzentrum von Derby in Erinnerung ruft, das eine ähnliche Hufeisenform hat. Eine große Öffnung in der geschlossenen Wand der Gebäude schafft Ausblicke über den großen dreieckigen Garten zu einem Wasserreservoir. Diese dramatische Öffnung verstärkt noch den Eindruck von räumlicher Tiefe und verhindert zudem, daß der Bereich des Landschaftsgartens hinter dem Gebäude von der Gebäudefront abgeschnitten wird. Eine überdachte Fußgängerbrücke verbindet den Platz mit Bushaltestellen auf beiden Seite der Tampines Avenue.

Eine Promenade mit einer Bank, Geschäften und den Eingängen zu den Schulen auf dem unteren Niveau des Verwaltungsgebäudes läßt sich als zeitgenössische Version einer traditionellen chinesischen Geschäftsgasse lesen. Unter dem Platz befinden sich ein Auditorium und ein Mehrzwecktheater mit einem gemeinsamen, öffentlich zugänglichen Foyer, zu dem man von der Tampines Avenue gelangt.

Die vier Schulen gliedern sich entlang großzügiger Fußgängerpassagen, die von der Promenade abzweigen und von den oberen Geschossen der Gebäude geschützt werden. Bei der vertikalen und horizontalen Organisation achteten die Architekten auf eine möglichst effiziente Gestaltung des Zugangs zu den Gebäuden und der inneren Erschließung. Jede Schule hat eine eigene Cafeteria mit Blick auf den Park. Die Promenade bildet zusammen mit den Passagen und überdachten Wegen durch den Landschaftspark ein wettergeschütztes Erschließungsnetz, das alle Schul- und Erholungsbereiche miteinander verbindet. Die Straße, die um das Areal führt, verknüpft alle Gebäude und Parkplätze und ist an jedem Ende des Campus durch kontrollierte Eingangstore von der Tampines Avenue aus zugänglich.

Der Bibliotheksturm, der sich an das Verwaltungsgebäude anschließt, ist der höchste Baukörper auf dem Campus und signalisiert die Präsenz des Polytechnikums in der Skyline der Stadt. Das Studentenzentrum und die Mensa liegen im dreieckigen Garten in der Nähe der

Temasek Polytechnic

James Stirling, Michael Wilford and Associates
Singapore
1991 – 1996

Temasek Polytechnic is a «city of learning» for 11,500 students and 1500 staff, encompassing schools of applied science, technology, business, and design. It is situated in a landscaped park of 30 hectares at the eastern end of the island.

A raised entrance plaza is the focus of the campus, its urban intentions will be clear to those familiar with the project for Derby Civic Centre, as it has a similar «horseshoe» form. A large opening through the enclosing wall of building opens views across a large triangular garden towards the reservoir. This dramatic opening adds to the sense of deep space, and also prevents the landscaped area at the rear from feeling cut-off from the front. A covered footbridge connects the plaza to bus shelters on either side of Tampines Avenue.

A promenade with bank, shops, and school entrances, situated in the base of the administration building can be read as a contemporary version of the traditional Chinese shopping street («five foot way»). Beneath the plaza an auditorium and a multi-purpose theatre share a public foyer with an entrance from Tampines Avenue.

The four schools are organised along spacious pedestrian concourses radiating from the promenade and sheltered by the upper levels of the buildings. Access and distribution are taken into account in the organisation of vertical and horizontal movement. Each school has its own canteen overlooking the park. The promenade, concourses and covered ways through the landscaped park form a weather-protected network connecting all academic and recreational areas. A perimeter service road links all buildings and car parks, with controlled entry gates from Tampines Avenue at each end of the campus.

The library tower, attached to the main administration, is the highest building on campus, and signals the presence of the Polytechnic on the city skyline. The student centre and refectory are situated in the triangular garden, close to the sports hall and stadium. Residential towers for faculty are situated at the western end of the site. The landscaping has been varied to accord a sense of identity to the different parts, with a due formality concentrated at the triangular garden (reminiscent of the landscaping at the Bibliothèque de France).

Sporthalle und des Stadions, während die Wohnungen für Fakultätsangehörige an der Westseite des Grundstücks untergebracht sind. Die abwechslungsreiche Landschaftsgestaltung bringt die jeweils eigene Identität der verschiedenen Teile des Ensembles zum Ausdruck, mit einer angemessen formalen Anlage des dreieckigen Gartens (der an die Gartengestaltung des Projekts für die Bibliothèque de France erinnert).

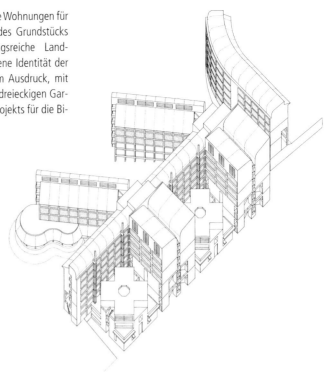

Isometrie
Gesamtansicht

Axonometric
Overall view

Blick auf den hufeisenförmigen Verwaltungstrakt

View of the «horse-shoe» administration building

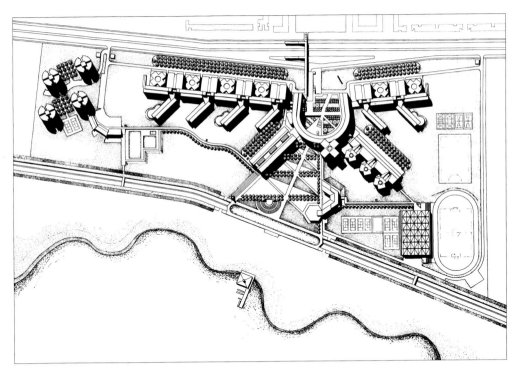

Lageplan
Blick auf den Eingangsplatz

Site plan
View of entrance plaza

Cafeteria

Cauteen

Lowry Centre, Salford Quays
James Stirling, Michael Wilford and Associates
Manchester
1992 –

Das Lowry Centre ist ein Kulturzentrum mit Einrichtungen für visuelle und darstellende Künste. In einem ungewöhnlichen, von sanierten Kanälen durchzogenen Areal gelegen, das sich für Erholungs- und Bildungseinrichtungen anbietet, wird es zu einem öffentlichen Wahrzeichen werden. Das dreieckige Grundstück ist auf zwei Seiten von Kanälen und auf der dritten von einem öffentlichen Platz begrenzt, so daß es im Schnittpunkt dreier verschiedener Zugänge liegt und zudem mit einer neuen U-Bahnstation verbunden sein wird. Ein geplantes Hotel und ein Parkhaus sollen die übrigen Grundstücksseiten abschließen.

Das Gebäude enthält eine Sprechbühne (1650 Plätze), eine Raumbühne (400 Plätze), Ausstellungsräume für temporäre Ausstellungen und die städtische Sammlung von Gemälden des Malers Laurence Stephen Lowry, eine Kindergalerie und Läden, Bars sowie ein Restaurant am Wasser. Ein zweigeschossiges Foyer erstreckt sich über die ganze Länge der Front zum Platz.

Das Sprechtheater ist das Herz des Gebäudes mit eigenen Treppenzugängen und Balkonen. Pavillons auf jeder Seite des Foyers bilden die Eingänge zur Kindergalerie und der Lowry Galerie darüber. Die Läden auf jeder Seite der Eingangstüren sind durch das Foyer oder über den Platz von außen zugänglich.

Die Raumbühne hat die Form eines Hofes und läßt sich auch als Rahmen-, Arena- und Rundumbühne einrichten. Sein geschwungenes Foyer bietet spektakuläre Ausblicke über den Schiffskanal von Manchester. Eine zenital beleuchtete Galerie verbindet die Theaterfoyers, und ein innerer Promenadengang um das Gebäude erschließt alle Bereiche der verschiedenen Aktivitäten des Komplexes.

Eine Bar, ein Café und ein Restaurant stehen den Besuchern beider Theater zur Verfügung, wo man bei gutem Wetter draußen auf Terrassen sitzen kann, die auf das Wasser blicken. Die Atmosphäre ist weniger die eines städtischen Theaters als eines Theaterworkshops und Gemeinschaftszentrums, das auch Proberäume, einen Künstlertreffpunkt und einen Dachgarten bietet. Der Verwaltungsturm ist oben von einer beleuchteten Anzeigetafel umschlossen, die das Weichbild belebt und auf laufende Aufführungen aufmerksam macht.

Lowry Centre, Salford Quays
James Stirling, Michael Wilford and Associates
Manchester
1992 –

The Lowry Centre is a cultural centre containing facilities for both visual and the performing arts. Located in an area of rehabilated canals, it will provide a public landmark in an unusual situation favourable for recreation and education. With canals on two sides of a triangular site, and a new public plaza on the third, it will be at the confluence of three approaches, and will be connected to a new metro terminus. A hotel and parking building are planned to enclose the remaining sides.

The building contains a Lyric Theatre (1,650 seats), a Flexible Theatre (400 seats) Art Galleries to display the City's collection of paintings by L. S. Lowry as well as temporary exhibitions, a Children's Gallery and shops, bars, and a waterfront restaurant. A two-storey foyer extends across the full width of the Plaza frontage. The Lyric Theatre forms the heart of the building, with its own system of stairs and balconies. Pavilions on either side of the foyer provide entrances to the Children's Gallery and the Lowry Gallery above. Shops on either side of the entrance doors can be entered from the foyer, or from the plaza outside. The Flexible Theatre has a courtyard form to accomodate proscenium traverse, thrust, and in-the-round performances. Its curved foyer has dramatic views across the Manchester Ship Canal. A roof-lit galleria connects the theatre foyers. An internal promenade around the building links all the activities. The bar, café and restaurant serve both theatres, and in fine weather can serve to outside terraces overlooking the water. The atmosphere is less that of a municipal theatre than of a theatre workshop and community centre, with access to rehearsal spaces and an artist's lounge and roof garden. The administration tower is crowned by an illuminated sign announcing current productions, and enlivening the skyline.

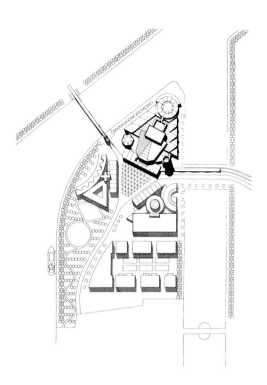

Lageplan
Modellansicht

Lageplan
Model view

Grundrisse Erd- und Obergeschoß
Modellansicht

Plans of ground and upper floor
Model view

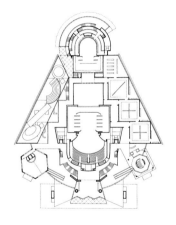

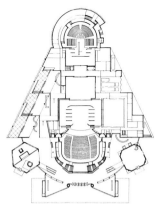

Modellansicht

Model view

Abando Umsteigebahnhof

Michael Wilford und Partners
Bilbao
1992–

Strategisch günstig gelegen, trennt der bestehende Abando Bahnhof mit seinen Bahngleisen die Stadtviertel aus dem Mittelalter und dem 19. Jahrhundert und stellt eine beträchtliche Barriere für den urbanen Verkehrsfluß und freien Austausch der Menschen in der Stadt dar. Der Entwurf zur Entwicklung dieses Areals versucht, diesen Nachteil durch die Schaffung neuer Verbindungen zwischen den Vierteln und die Ersetzung der gegenwärtigen Industrie- und Versorgungsanlagen durch neue Flächen für Geschäfte, kulturelle Nutzungen und Wohnungen auszugleichen, die dieser zentralen Stadtlage angemessener sind.

Der Entwurf schließt einen zentralen Busbahnhof und zwei neue Bahnhöfe ein. Diese Verkehrsbauten sind direkt mit der Metro und neuen «flankierenden» Straßen verbunden, um den Zugang für die Fahrgäste zu erleichtern und die Erschließung zu verbessern. Der Plan sieht neben Büroflächen, Wohnungen und einem Hotel zudem eine Ladenpassage, ein Welthandelszentrum und eine Postfiliale vor. Durch Beseitigung der bestehenden Bahnsteige, die ins Zentrum des Komplexes versetzt werden, entsteht ein neuer öffentlicher Platz, der mit dem vielfältigen Geschäftsleben der angrenzenden Straßen verbunden ist und so einen ganz neuen urbanen Bereich der Begegnung und des Austauschs schafft. Fußgänger können den neuen Bahnhofskomplex von allen Seiten und auf mehreren Ebenen betreten. Die neue Passage verbindet die flankierenden Straßen an vielen Stellen und bildet so ein Netz von Fußgängerwegen, die sowohl die beiden Seiten der Stadt verbinden als auch Zugang zu den Transportsystemen bieten.

Das Welthandelszentrum ist der Knotenpunkt für die Busfahrgäste und Autofahrer, die durch das San Francisco-Tor kommen, und bildet die Nordgrenze einer dreieckigen Grünanlage, die lineare Häuserfluchten im Osten und Westen begrenzen. Den Busbahnhof, eine große Halle auf der Ebene des Platzes mit Stadt- und Überlandlinien, erreicht man über Rampen von der Autobahnabfahrt. Fahrstühle und Rolltreppen in der mehrgeschossigen linearen Passage erschließen alle Ebenen, und Reisende finden großzügige Warteräume in der Nähe der jeweiligen Stationen, die durch angrenzende Läden, Cafés und Bars noch attraktiver werden.

Der neue Platz bildet den Vorhof des Bahnhofskomplexes und bietet bequeme Haltestellen für Taxis und Privatwagen. Mit seinem dramatisch gewölbten Dach wird er ein wesentlicher Teil des Stadtbildes werden und Einwohnern wie Besuchern gleichermaßen Orientierung geben.

Abando Passenger Interchange

Michael Wilford and Partners
Bilbao
1992–

Although strategically located, the existing Abando Station and its associated rail tracks separate the medieval and nineteenth century quarters of the city, and constitute a formidable barrier that reduces urban flow and social intercourse. The new Interchange aims to counteract these deficiencies, by opening up new connections between the quarters, and by replacing the current service and industrial facilities with new business, cultural and residential amenities more appropriate to the central location within the city.

The scheme includes a central bus station and two new railway stations. These transport facilities are linked directly to the metro, and to new «flanking» streets, in order to provide easy passenger access and improve connections. The scheme also contains a retail concourse, a world trade centre, and a post office, along with offices, residential accommodation and a hotel. By removing the existing station plateau, and placing the railway stations at the centre of the site, it is possible to construct a new public plaza linked to mixed uses in the adjoining streets, and so to open up a whole new zone of social interaction. The Interchange can be entered by pedestrians from all sides and at several levels. The new concourse connects the flanking streets at numerous locations, and so provides a network of pedestrian routes connecting the two sides of the city, as well as users of the transport systems.

The world trade centre is the focus of the Interchange for bus and car passengers arriving through the San Francisco gateway, and forms the northern side of the triangular garden. Linear housing encloses the east and west sides of this garden. The bus station is accessed by way of ramps from the motorway link, and accommodates intercity and suburban buses in one large hall at plaza level. Lifts and elevators in the multi-level linear concourse connect all levels, and spacious waiting areas close to the various stations are enlivened by their closeness to shops, cafés and lounges. The new plaza leads into the Passenger Interchange, with convenient car and taxi points. With the dramatic vaulted roof above, it will become an essential part of the city experience, providing orientation for citizens and visitors alike.

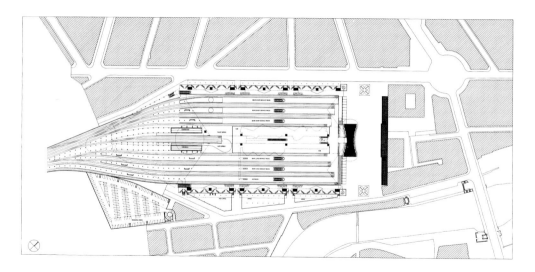

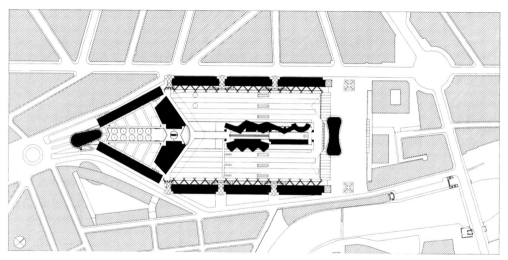

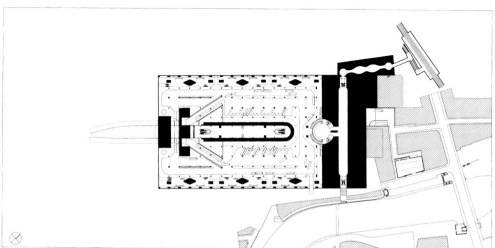

Grundrisse Fernbahnhof, Bahnhof mit Grünanlage und Busbahnhof (von oben nach unten)

Plans of RENFE railway station, railway station with park and bus station (top to bottom)

Ansicht Hauptfassade
Längsschnitt
Modellfoto

Plaza elevation
Longitudinal section
Model view

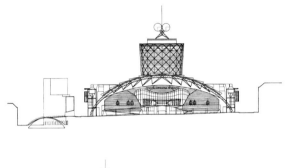

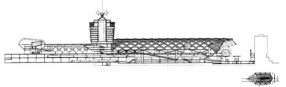

Architekturfakultät
Newcastle
Michael Wilford and Partners
mit Suters Architects Snell
Newcastle, Australien
1992

Zwei Pavillons stehen sich hier, getrennt durch einen gepflasterten, von einem Vordach geschützten Weg, gegenüber. Der eine ist ein Vorlesungs- und Ateliergebäude,
der andere beherbergt eine Reihe von Seminarräumen
mit Fakultätsbüros darüber. Indem Michael Wilford den
Atelierblock und auch das Foyer auf eine Ecke gedreht
hat, schafft er eine sanfte, die Gebäudegruppe belebende
Dynamik.
Eine weitere belebende, geradezu überschwengliche
Geste stellt die Stahlkonstruktion in knallroter Farbe dar,
die nicht nur bei der überdachten Passage, sondern auch
bei den Fensterblenden und in der Verkleidung mit ihrem
diagonalen Muster hervortritt. Das Gebäude entstand in
Zusammenarbeit mit dem örtlichen Architektenbüro Su-
ters Architects Snell, und Studenten der Schule hatten die
Möglichkeit, am Projekt mitzuarbeiten.

Architecture School
Newcastle
Michael Wilford and Partners
with Suters Architects Snell
Newcastle, Australia
1992

Two pavilions face each other across a paved concourse
protected by a canopy. One accommodates a studio-lec-
ture theatre. The other a pair of classrooms, with faculty
offices above. The layout is simple, but not ordinary. By
turning the studio block to an angle, that repeats in its
vestibule, Michael Wilford has introduced a gentle dynamic that enlivens the group.
Further enlivenment, indeed a joyful exuberance, is produced by the steel structure, finished in the reddest of
reds, evident not only in the canopy, but in the window
shades and the cladding with its diagonal pattern. The
building was constructed with the collaboration of the
local architects Suters Architects Snell, and students had
the opportunity to work on the project.

Grundrisse Erd- und Obergeschoß

Plans of ground and upper floor

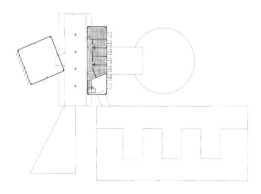

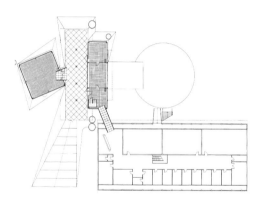

Pavillons mit Schirmdach
Pavillon mit Unterrichtsräumen

Pavilions and canopy
Classroom pavilion

Nationales Literaturzentrum und Stadtbibliothek
Beschränkter Wettbewerb
Michael Wilford and Partners
Swansea, Wales
1993

National Centre for Literature and City Library
Limited competition
Michael Wilford and Partners
Swansea, Wales
1993

Das Ty Llen Nationale Literaturzentrum liegt an einem Boulevard am westlichen Ende des Zentrums und soll zu einer bedeutenden Kultureinrichtung der Stadt werden. Ein umschlossener öffentlicher Platz, der zwei Hauptstraßen verbindet, schafft einen sozialen Begegnungsraum unter freiem Himmel. Die Eingänge zum Literaturzentrum und der Stadtbücherei an diesem Platz liegen einander gegenüber. Die Rotunde der von oben beleuchteten Ausstellungsräume ist an den Boulevard gesetzt, wo sie ihre größte Wirkung erreicht.

Im Inneren der Bibliothek sind der Haupteingang, der Ausstellungsbereich und die Kinderbücherei durch eine große Treppe mit der Musik-, Theater- und Ausleihbibliothek im ersten Stock verbunden. Die Handbibliothek darüber wird zenital beleuchtet. Der Sockel und die Seitenwände des Zentrums sind mit walisischem Schiefer verkleidet, während bei der Trommel und den Dachfensterprofilen patiniertes Kupfer eingesetzt wurde.

The Ty Llen National Centre for Literature is appropriately located on a boulevard at the western edge of the town centre, of which it will form a significant cultural element. An enclosed public square linking two major streets provides an outdoor communal space and social centre. Entrances to the Literature Centre and to the City Library face each other across the square. The rotunda form of the top-lit exhibition galleries fronts the boulevard, for maximum impact.

Within the library, the main entrance, exhibition area and children's library are linked by a grand staircase to the music, drama and lending libraries on the first floor. These share a central reading room which overlooks the square. The reference library above has the benefit of roof lighting. The base and flanking walls of the Centre are faced with Welsh slate, and the drum and gallery rooflights are clad in green pre-patinated copper.

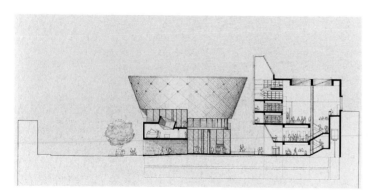

Schnittansicht
Modellfotos

Section elevation
Model views

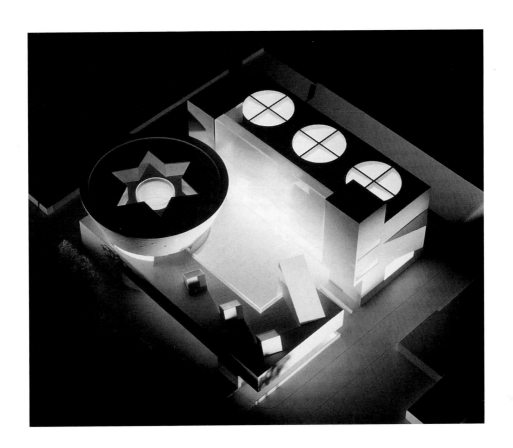

Campus-Masterplan für die Technische Universität Dresden

Wettbewerbsprojekt
Michael Wilford and Partners
Dresden
1994

Der Campus liegt am Ende einer der städtischen Hauptachsen im Süden der Stadt, wo vier verschiedene Stadtgrundrisse aufeinandertreffen. Er wird gegenwärtig von einer Hauptstraße durchschnitten und verfügt über keinen klaren Haupteingang.

Der neue Verwaltungsturm mit einer Reihe kreisförmig angeordneter Vorlesungssäle schafft ein zentrales Eingangsforum an der Hauptstraße und markiert den wichtigsten Fußgängerweg über den Campus. Der Turm signalisiert die Präsenz der Universität im Weichbild der Stadt.

Neue lineare Gebäude schaffen eine Reihe von verzahnten Hofgärten, die in einer durchlaufenden Abfolge vom Eingangsplatz wegführen. Bepflanzung mit Bäumen und andere Mittel der Landschaftsgestaltung verleihen jedem Hof ein individuelles Gesicht.

Die neuen Fakultätsgebäude respektieren in ihren Dimensionen und Materialien die bestehenden Gebäude auf dem Campus, während Turm und Vorlesungsblock durch ihre Metall- und Stahlflächen hervortreten.

Campus Masterplan for Dresden Technical University

Competition project
Michael Wilford and Partners
Dresden
1994

The campus is situated at the end of a major urban axis on the southern edge of the city, at the junction of four urban grids. It is currently divided by a major street, and has no clear main entrance.

A new administration tower with a circular cluster of lecture theatres defines a central entrance forum, fronting to a major street, and marking the main pedestrian spine of the campus. The tower signals the presence of the university on the city skyline.

New linear buildings establish a series of interlocking courtyard gardens, which together add up to form a continuous network leading away from the entrance plaza. Tree planting and other landscaping has been used to give individual character to each courtyard.

The new faculty buildings respect the scale and materials of the existing buildings on campus, while the tower and lecture theatre cluster stand out by their metal and glass surfaces.

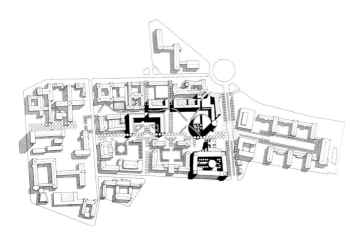

Lageisometrie
Modellfoto

Site axonometric
Model view

Sto AG
Werksanlagen
Michael Wilford and Partners
Weizen, Baden-Württemberg
1994 – 1997

Der Komplex im baden-württembergischen Weizen überblickt von einem Plateau aus das Wutach-Tal und wird an drei Seiten von steilen, baumbestandenen Hügeln überragt. Der Gesamtplan sieht in einem Entwicklungszeitraum von 15 Jahren die Schaffung von Gebäuden für den Verwaltungssitz, für Forschung, Marketing und Schulung sowie Erholungsbereiche für die Mitarbeiter und eine Fabrikanlage auf einem weitläufigen Gelände vor.

Das erste zu bauende Gebäude umfaßt drei Funktionen: einen viergeschossigen, linearen Büroflügel für die Marketing-Abteilung, einen zweigeschossigen quadratischen Sockel mit Schulungseinrichtungen und einen ovalen Eingangspavillon zu diesen beiden Bereichen. Der Baukörper fügt sich zwischen dem Hotel Sonne und dem Sto-Designstudio in eine leichte Senke und ist über eine Fußgängerbrücke mit dem ersten Abschnitt der erhöhten zentralen Gartenanlagen verbunden. Ein separater niedrigerer Eingang führt vom Parkplatz neben dem Hotel direkt in den Empfangsbereich der Schulungsstätte.

Der Büroflügel schiebt sich über den Bau mit den Trainingsräumen zum Haupteingangsbereich und bildet ein Tor für die gesamte zukünftige Anlage. Mit seiner fließenden Gestaltung paßt sich der Komplex in die Landschaft ein und sucht den Blick auf das Tal vom Garten aus so weit wie möglich freizuhalten.

Die Büros verteilen sich über vier Geschosse entlang der Seiten des linearen Gebäudes und bieten herrliche Ausblicke auf die Landschaft. Jedes Geschoß ist gegenüber dem darunter liegenden leicht nach vorne gezogen, so daß eine dynamische Silhouette entsteht. Die entsprechende Zurückstaffelung auf der anderen Seite schafft eine Verbindung zu den traditionellen Schrägdächern der vorhandenen Gebäude.

Der ovale Pavillon beherbergt den Eingang für Mitarbeiter und Besucher. Drei Seminarräume und ein großer Empfangs- und Ausstellungsbereich befinden sich im Erdgeschoß. Durchgehende Fenster erlauben hier den Blick auf die unterhalb liegenden Werkstätten für die praktische Ausbildung. Die Trennwände sind beweglich, so daß bei besonderen Anlässen die gesamte Fläche genutzt werden kann. Bei Veranstaltungen außerhalb der Bürozeiten gelangt man durch den unteren Eingang ins Gebäude.

Der Baukörper besteht hauptsächlich aus einer Stahlbetonkonstruktion und repräsentiert mit vielfältigen Putzverkleidungen in unterschiedlichen Farben auch die Produktpalette der Firma.

Sto AG
Headquarters
Michael Wilford and Partners
Weizen, Baden Wurttemburg
1994 – 1997

The plant is located in Weizen, Baden Wurttemburg in Germany, on a plateau overlooking the Wutach valley, and enclosed on three sides by steep tree-lined hills. The master plan provides locations for administration headquarters, research, marketing, and training facilities, together with staff amenities, as well as production. It provides for an extended campus, over a 15 year period of development and growth.

The first building to be constructed comprises three elements: a four-storey linear office wing for the marketing department, a two-storey square base containing training facilities, and an oval entrance pavilion which serves both elements. The building nestles in a gentle hollow between the Hotel Sonne and the Sto Design Studio, connected by footbridge to the first phase of the raised central garden. A separate lower entrance leads directly into the training reception area from a car park adjacent to the Hotel Sonne.

The office wing glides above the training building, facing the primary approach, and forming in effect a gateway to the future campus. The structure is designed to heighten the floating sensation and to minimise any obstruction of valley views from the central garden. Offices are arranged on four floors along the outer edges of the linear plan, with spectacular views across the countryside. Each floor is slipped out relative to the one just below, providing a dynamic silhouette, and the corresponding stepping back at the other end enables a link to be made to the traditional roof slopes of the existing buildings.

The oval pavilion accommodates the staff and visitor's entrance. Three seminar rooms and a large reception and exhibition area are situated at ground level, with views through continuous windows across the practical training workshop below. The partitions are flexible, allowing the whole floor to be opened up for special events. The lower entrance allows events to take place outside normal working hours when the rest of the building may be closed.

The construction is mainly of reinforced concrete, and is designed to be an exposition of the company's products, comprising a wide variety of stuccoed finishes in many colours.

Gesamtansicht   View

Eingangsbereich

Entrance and lobby

Aufsicht
Grundrisse Erdgeschoß
und Obergeschoß

Roof plan
Plans of ground
and upper floor

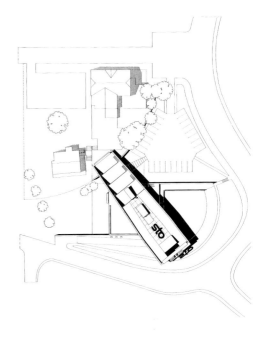

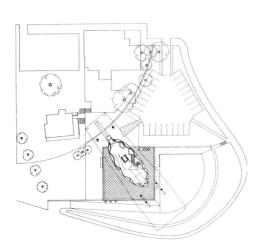

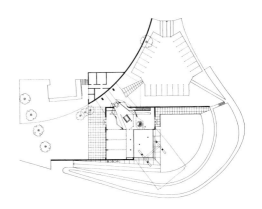

Blick auf die zurückgestaffelte Fassade

View of the staggered floors

Nachtansicht des Büroflügels

Night view of the office wing

Britische Botschaft in Berlin

Beschränkter Wettbewerb
Michael Wilford and Partners
Berlin
1995 –

Die Britische Botschaft kehrt wieder in ihre alte Position im Zentrum Berlins an der Wilhelmstraße zurück, sobald die Bundesregierung in die neue Hauptstadt umgezogen ist. Das Grundstück ist groß genug, um den Komplex mit einem Hof zu versehen, der für natürliches Tageslicht und Belüftung im Inneren des Gebäudes sorgt. Das Tor zur Wilhelmstraße leitet Besucher zu Fuß und mit dem Auto zum Eingang auf dem Botschaftsgrundstück.

Der Eingangshof wird, wie der *cours d'honneur* eines Pariser *hôtel particulier,* als Übergangsbereich zwischen der Stadt und der Botschaft fungieren, und eine Eiche in seiner Mitte soll Symbol und Erinnerung an Großbritannien sein. Bei feierlichen Anlässen werden wichtige Besucher in der Eingangshalle auf «britischem Territorium» förmlich begrüßt und die große Treppe hinauf bis zum Wintergarten im Hauptgeschoß geleitet. Der Wintergarten mit großzügigen Fenstern zum Hof und großen Dachfenstern ist der räumliche Brennpunkt im Inneren der Botschaft. An ihn grenzen der runde Konferenzsaal und der Bankettsaal, von dem man die Wilhelmstraße überblickt.

Auch die Botschaftsangestellten gelangen durch die Eingangshalle ins Gebäude, benutzen dann aber eine Sicherheitstür neben dem Fahrstuhlschacht. Durchlaufende Balkone auf dem oberen Niveau des Wintergartens bieten den Botschaftsangehörigen bei wichtigen Anlässen einen Blick auf das Geschehen unter ihnen, während sie offiziellen Besuchern Einblick in das Leben der Botschaft gewähren.

Die Straßenfassade ist 22 Meter hoch und erstreckt sich über die gesamte Länge des Grundstücks, wie durch die Bebauungsrichtlinien des Berliner Senats vorgeschrieben. An ihr lassen sich die wichtigsten Nutzungen ablesen: Empfang, Feträume und Büros für die alltägliche Arbeit. Der Einschnitt des Hofes schafft ein dynamisches Element in der sonst regelmäßigen Komposition, die sich dem Charakter der angrenzenden Gebäude anpaßt. Eine Collage von Formen wird hier in abstrakter Weise auf das Leben der Botschaft verweisen und der Neugier und Erwartung der Besucher Nahrung geben.

British Embassy Berlin

Limited competition
Michael Wilford and Partners
Berlin
1995 –

The British Embassy will re-occupy its central location on Wilhelmstrasse when the German government will move to Berlin, the new Federal Capital of Germany. The site is spacious enough to permit the adoption of a courtyard layout, allowing daylight and natural ventilation into the heart of the building. The gateway facing Wilhelmstrasse admits pedestrians and cars to a set-down and entrance point within the private space.

The entrance court, like the *cours d'honneur* of a Parisian *hôtel particulier,* will act as a point of transition between city and embassy, and an oak tree planted at its centre will function as symbol and reminder of Britain. On ceremonial occasions important visitors will be formally received on «British territory» in the entrance hall, and escorted up the grand staircase to the Wintergarden on the main floor. This space, with generous windows to the entrance court and ample rooflights above, becomes the internal focus of the embassy. Adjacent to the Wintergarden are the circular Conference Room and Banqueting Hall, overlooking Wilhelmstrasse. Staff also enter and leave through the entrance hall, but use a security door adjacent to the lift core. Circulation balconies at the upper level of the Wintergarden allow staff to glimpse important events unfolding below, while their presence allows official visitors to sense the life of the building.

The street facade is 22 metres high, and runs the whole length of the site, as required by the urban development guidelines imposed by the city of Berlin, and it expresses the main uses of the building – entrance, ceremonial spaces, and working offices. The void introduces a dynamic element into a regular composition, which otherwise conforms to the character of the adjacent buildings. Through the void will appear an abstract collage of forms, suggestive of the life of the embassy, encouraging the visitor's sense of curiosity and anticipation.

Lageplan
Modellansicht des Innenhofs

Site plan
Model view of courtyard

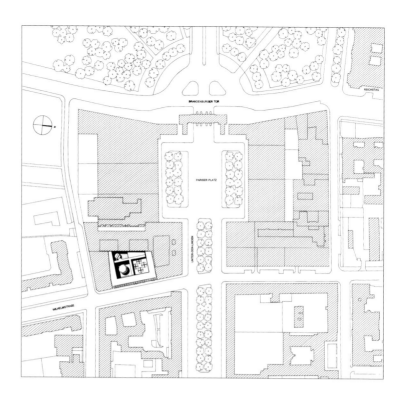

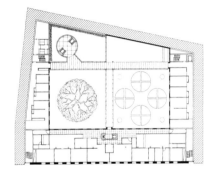

Grundrisse Erdgeschoß, 1. und 4. Obergeschoß
Modellansicht von der Straße

Plans of ground, first and fourth floor
Model view from street

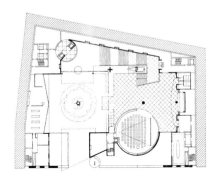

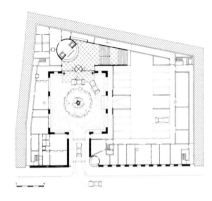

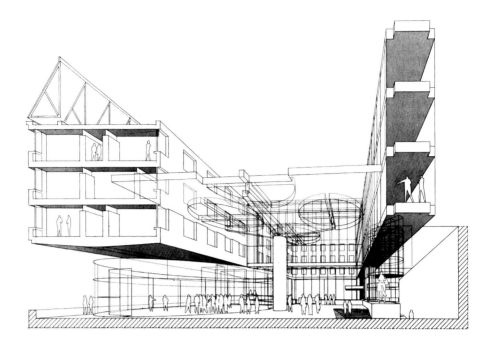

Isometrie
Modellansicht von oben

Axonometric
Model view from above

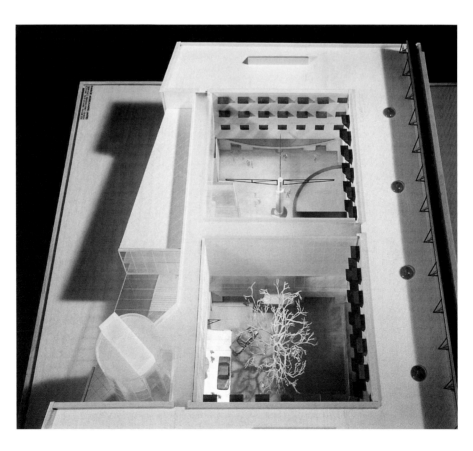

Biographie

Biography

James Stirling

1926	Geboren in Glasgow
1966	Heirat, drei Kinder

Ausbildung
1942	Liverpool School of Art
1945–50	University of Liverpool School of Architecture
1950–52	School of Town Planning and Regional Research, London

Beruf
1953–56	Senior-Assistent bei Lyons, Israel, Ellis and Gray, London
1956–63	Büro in Partnerschaft mit James Gowan, London
1964–92	Eigenes Architekturbüro (ab 1971 in Partnerschaft mit Michael Wilford als James Stirling Michael Wilford and Associates)

Lehre
1955	Architectural Association, London Gastdozent
1956–57	Regent Street Polytechnic, London
1958	Cambridge University School of Architecture
1965	Royal Institute of British Architects Dozent
Ab 1967	Yale University, New Haven, Connecticut Davenport-Professor
Ab 1977	Akademie der Künste, Düsseldorf
1977	London University Banister Fletcher-Professor
1982	American Academy, Rom Gastaufenthalt

Preise
1978	Alvar Aalto Medal, Finland
1980	Gold Medal, Royal Institute of British Architects
1981	Pritzker-Preis
1990	Praemium Imperiale Award, Japan
1992	Stirling erhält wenige Tage vor seinem Tod die Ritterwürde

Mitgliedschaften
Akademie der Künste, Berlin
Accademia delle Arti, Florenz
Accademia Nazionale di San Luca, Rom
Bund Deutscher Architekten
Honorary Fellow, American Institute of Architects

James Stirling

1926	Born in Glasgow
1966	Married, three children

Education
1942	Liverpool School of Art
1945–50	University of Liverpool School of Architecture
1950–52	School of Town Planning and Regional Research, London

Professional Experience
1953–56	Senior assistant with Lyons, Israel, Ellis and Gray, London
1956–63	Partnership with James Gowan, London
1964–92	Private practice (since 1971 in partnership with Michael Wilford, in James Stirling Michael Wilford and Associates)

Teaching Experience
1955	Architectural Association, London Visiting Lecturer
1956–57	Regent Street Polytechnic, London
1958	Cambridge University School of Architecture
1965	Royal Institute of British Architects Lecturer
From 1967	Yale University, New Haven, Connecticut Davenport Professor
From 1977	Akademie der Künste, Düsseldorf
1977	London University Banister Fletcher Professor
1982	American Academy, Rome Architect-in-Residence

Awards
1978	Alvar Aalto Medal, Finland
1980	Gold Medal, Royal Institute of British Architects
1981	Pritzker Prize
1990	Praemium Imperiale Award, Japan
1992	Stirling is knighted only days before his death

Memberships
Akademie der Künste, Berlin
Accademia delle Arti, Florence
Accademia Nazionale di San Luca, Rome
Bund Deutscher Architekten
Honorary Fellow, American Institute of Architects

Fellow Royal Society of Arts
Associate Royal Institute of British Architects

1992   Gestorben in London

Michael Wilford

1938   Geboren in Surbiton, Surrey
1960   Heirat, zwei Söhne und drei Töchter

Ausbildung
1950–55   Kingston Technical School, London
1955–62   Northern Polytechnic School of Architecture, London
1967   Regent Street Polytechnic Planning School, London

Beruf
1960–63   Senior-Assistent bei James Stirling and James Gowan
1963–65   Senior-Assistent bei James Stirling
1965–71   Assoziierter Partner bei James Stirling and Partner
1971–92   Partner bei James Stirling Michael Wilford and Associates
1992–93   Leitender Partner bei James Stirling Michael Wilford and Associates
Seit 1993 Senior-Partner bei Michael Wilford and Partners; Partner: Laurence Bain und Russell Bevington

Lehre
1968   Yale University, New Haven, Connecticut, School of Architecture
1975   Visiting Critic
1994–95   Charles Davenport Gastprofessor
            Harvard University, Cambridge, Massachusetts, School of Architecture
1968   Juror
            Architectural Association, London, School of Architecture
1969–73   Tutor
            University of Sheffield, School of Architecture
1974–79   Visiting Critic
1980–91   Graham Willis Gastprofessor
            University of Toronto, School of Architecture
1974–83   Visiting Critic
            McGill University, Montreal, School of Architecture
1975   Visiting Critic
            Rice University, Houston, School of Architecture
1978–79   Visiting Critic
1980–88   Gastprofessor
            Royal College of Art, London, School of Environmental Design
1978–79   Externer Gutachter
            University of North London, School of Architecture
1983–86   Externer Gutachter
            Leeds Polytechnic, School of Architecture
1983–85   Externer Gutachter
            University of Westminster, London, School of Architecture

Fellow Royal Society of Arts
Associate Royal Institute of British Architects

1992   Died in London

Michael Wilford

1938   Born in Surbiton, Surrey
1960   Married, five children

Education
1950–55   Kingston Technical School, London
1955–62   Northern Polytechnic School of Architecture, London
1967   Regent Street Polytechnic Planning School, London

Professional Experience
1960–63   Senior Assistant with James Stirling and James Gowan
1963–65   Senior Assistant with James Stirling
1965–71   Associate Partner in James Stirling and Partner
1971–92   Partner in James Stirling Michael Wilford and Associates
1992–93   Sole Practitioner in James Stirling Michael Wilford and Associates
Since 1993 Senior Partner in Michael Wilford and Partners; partners: Laurence Bain and Russell Bevington

Teaching Experience
1968   Yale University, New Haven, Connecticut, School of Architecture
1975   Visiting Critic
1994–95   Charles Davenport Visiting Professor
            Harvard University, Cambridge, Massachusetts, School of Architecture
1968   Juror
            Architectural Association, London, School of Architecture
1969–73   Tutor
            University of Sheffield, School of Architecture
1974–79   Visiting Critic
1980–91   Graham Willis Visiting Professor
            University of Toronto, School of Architecture
1974–83   Visiting Critic
            McGill University, Montreal, School of Architecture
1975   Visiting Critic
            Rice University, Houston, School of Architecture
1978–79   Visiting Critic
1980–88   Visiting Professor
            Royal College of Art, London, School of Environmental Design
1978–79   External Examiner
            University of North London, School of Architecture
1983–86   External Examiner
            Leeds Polytechnic, School of Architecture
1983–85   External Examiner
            University of Westminster, London, School of Architecture

1986–89	Externer Gutachter		1986–89	External Examiner
	University of London, Bartlett School of Architecture			University of London, Bartlett School of Architecture
1989–92	Externer Gutachter		1989–92	External Examiner
	University of Newcastle, Australia, School of Architecture			University of Newcastle, Australia, School of Architecture
1984	Visiting Critic		1984	Visiting Critic
1989	Gastdozent		1989	Visiting Fellow
	University of Wales, Cardiff, School of Architecture			University of Wales, Cardiff, School of Architecture
1990–91	Visiting Critic		1990–91	Visiting Critic
	University of Cincinnati, School of Architecture			University of Cincinnati, School of Architecture
1990–92	Gastprofessor		1990–92	Visiting Professor
	University of Glasgow, Mackintosh School of Architecture			University of Glasgow, Mackintosh School of Architecture
1995–96	Externer Gutachter		1995–96	External Examiner

Mitgliedschaften

Royal Institute of British Architects
Singapore Institute of Architects
Royal Institute of Arbitrators
Fellow of Royal Society of Arts

Memberships

Royal Institute of British Architects
Singapore Institute of Architects
Royal Institute of Arbitrators
Fellow of Royal Society of Arts

Werkverzeichnis/List of Buildings and Projects

James Stirling

1950	Thesis (Liverpool University)
1950	Honan Film Centre (student competition)
1951	Core and Crosswall House
1951	Stiff Domino-Housing
1951	ICA Furniture
1952	Poole Technical College (UK competition)
1953	Sheffield University (UK competition)
1953	House in North London
1954	Woolton House
1955	Village Project

James Stirling and James Gowan
Michael Wilford Senior Assistant

1955–58	Ham Common Flats, London
1956–58	Isle of Wight House
1956	House Studies
1957	Three Houses for Basil Mavrolean (limited competition)
1957–59	House Conversion Kensington
1957	Expandable House
1957–59	Preston Infill Housing (tender cost competition)
1958	Steel Mill Cladding
1958	Churchill College (limited competition)
1958–61	School Assembly Hall, Camberwell, London
1959	Student Residences for Selwyn College, Cambridge
1959–63	Engineering Building for Leicester University, Leicester
1960–64	Old People's Home, Greenwich
1960–64	Children's Home, Frogmore

James Stirling
Michael Wilford Associate Partner

1964–67	History Faculty for Cambridge University, Cambridge (limited competition)
1964–68	Camden Town Flats, London
1964–68	Student Residences for St. Andrews University, St. Andrews
1965	Headquarters for Dorman Long Steel Manufacturers, Middlesbrough
1966–71	The Florey Building for Queen's College, Oxford
1967–76	Low-Cost Housing Runcorn, Runcorn New Town
1968	Redevelopment Study, New York
1969–76	Low-Cost Housing, Lima
1969	Siemens Research Centre, Munich (limited competition)
1969–72	Olivetti Training School, Haslemere
1970	Derby Civic Centre, Derby (limited competition)

James Stirling Michael Wilford and Associates

1971	Olivetti Headquarters, Milton Keynes
1971	Arts Centre for St. Andrews University, St. Andrews
1972–77	Southgate Low-Cost Housing, Runcorn New Town
1975	Wallraf-Richartz Museum, Cologne (invited competition)
1975	Museum for Northrhine Westphalia, Düsseldorf (invited competition)
1976	Hotel Meinekestrasse, Berlin
1976	Government Centre, Doha, Qatar (limited competition)
1976	Regional Centre, Florence (national competition)
1977	UNEP Headquarters, Nairobi
1977	Revisions to the Nolli Plan, Rome
1977	Dresdner Bank, Marburg
1977	Housing Study for Muller Pier, Rotterdam
1977–84	New State Gallery and Chamber Theatre, Stuttgart (invited competition)
1978	Institute of Biology and Biochemistry, Teheran
1978	Bayer Research Centre, Monheim (limited competition)
1978	Manhattan Townhouses, New York (limited competition)
1979–81	Rice School of Architecture Extension, Houston
1979–87	Science Research Centre, Berlin (limited competition)
1979–84	Sackler Gallery, Cambridge, Massachusetts
1980	Chemistry Building for Columbia University, New York
1980–86	Clore Gallery, London
1980–94	Music Academy, Stuttgart
1981	Houston Plaza, Houston (limited competition)
1983–88	Performing Arts Center for Cornell University, Ithaca
1983	Casalecchio New Town, Bologna
1983	Villa Lingotto, Turin (limited competition)
1983	British Telecom Headquarters, Milton Keynes (limited competition)
1983	Public Library, Latina
1984–88	Tate Gallery, Albert Dock, Liverpool
1985	Museums of New Art and Sculpture Tate Gallery, London
1985	National Gallery Extension, London (limited competition)
1986–98	No. 1 Poultry, London
1986–92	Braun Headquarters, Melsungen (limited competition) with Walter Nägeli

1986	Thyssen-Bornemisza Gallery, Lugano (limited competition)
1986	State Theatre Warehouse, Stuttgart (limited competition)
1986	Paternoster Square, London (limited competition)
1986	Bracken House, London (limited competition)
1987	Kaiserplatz Aachen with Marlies Hentrup and Norbert Heyers
1987–96	Music and Theatre Academies, Stuttgart
1987	Study Centre and Library/Archive, Tate Gallery, London
1987	Palazzo Citterio Art Gallery, Brera Museum, Milan
1988	Glyndebourne Opera House (limited competition)
1988	Ballet/Opera House, Toronto (limited competition)
1988	Canary Wharf Residential Development, London (limited competition)
1988	Disney Philharmonic Hall, Los Angeles (limited competition)
1988–93	Biological Sciences Library for University of California at Irvine, Los Angeles
1988–	5–7 Carlton Gardens Apartments, London (limited competition)
1988	Stadium Development, Seville
1989	Bibliothèque de France, Paris (limited competition)
1989	Tokyo International Forum (limited competition)
1989	Opera House, Compton Verney (limited competition)
1989–91	Biennale Bookshop, Venice
1990	Cinema Palace, Venice (limited competition) with Marlies Hentrup and Norbert Heyers
1990	Channel Four Headquarters, London (limited competition)
1991	Kyoto Centre, Kyoto (limited competition)
1991–96	Temasek Polytechnic, Singapore
1991	Museum of Scotland (limited competition) with Ulrike Wilke

Michael Wilford and Partners

1992–	Lowry Centre, Salford Quays, Manchester
1992–	Abando Passenger Interchange, Bilbao
1992	Architecture School Newcastle with Suters Architects Snell
1993	Performing Arts Centre, Singapore
1993	Ty Llen National Centre for Literature and City Library, Swansea (limited competition)
1993	Sto AG Headquarters and Manufacturing Plant, Weizen, Germany
1993	Royal Library Copenhagen (competition)
1993–97	Tate Gallery, Liverpool, Phase 2
1993	Clore Gallery (Turner Collection), Tate Gallery Refurbishment
1994	British Museum, Courtyard Redevelopment (limited competition)
1994–97	Sto AG New Office Building, Weizen
1994	Campus Masterplan for Technical University, Dresden (competition)
1994–95	Sto Regional Depot, Hamburg
1994	Liverpool Museum, National Museums and Galleries on Merseyside, Liverpool
1995–	British Embassy, Berlin (limited competition)
1995	Music School and Cinemaxx, Mannheim
1995	Hanover/Laatzen Trade Fair Station, Hanover (competition)
1996	National Centre for Industrial Virtual Reality, Salford
1997	National Youth Performing Arts Centre, Gloucester (limited competition
1997	Music School, Rostock (limited competition)
1997	Hotel, Salford
1997	Hamilton Ahead Arts Centre, Hamilton, Scotland (competition)
1997	National Centre for Virtual Environments, Salford
1997	Cultural Quarter, Arts Centre, Shoreham-by-Sea

Bibliographie/Bibliography

**Aufsätze von James Stirling
and Michael Wilford
Articles by James Stirling
and Michael Wilford**

James Stirling
A representative selection of his articles can be found in:
Robert Maxwell (ed.), *James Stirling, Writings on Architecture,* Milan: Skira, 1997.

Michael Wilford
Critique of the Burrell Museum Glasgow
The Architects' Journal, 19 October 1983
«Off to the races or going to the dogs» – on development opportunities for the Isle of Dogs. *Architectural Design,* January/February 1984
Review of «Concepts of Urban Design» by David Gosling and Barry Maitland published by Academy Editions/St. Martins Press, *Architecture Review,* January 1987
«Inspired patronage» – A review of the Royal Institute of British Architects 1990 National Awards, *RIBA Journal,* April 1991
«A sense of place in Milton Keynes» – A critique of the Milton Keynes Magistrates Court. *Architecture Today,* September 1991
«An evolving design philosophy» – Introductory essay in *James Stirling and Michael Wilford,* Architectural Monographs No. 32, London: Academy Editions, 1993
Introductory essay in *James Stirling, Buildings and Projects 1975–1992, James Stirling Michael Wilford and Associates,* London: Thames & Hudson, 1994. German edition: *James Stirling, Bauten und Projekte 1975–1992, James Stirling Michael Wilford and Associates,* Stuttgart: Hatje, 1994.
«An evolving design philosophy and working method» – Introductory essay, *Wilford Stirling Wilford: Michael Wilford and Partners,* exhibition catalogue, London: E & FN Spon 1997

**Ausgewählte Monographien oder
Zeitschriftenhefte über James Stirling und/oder
Michael Wilford
Selected Monographs or Magazine
Issues on James Stirling and/or Michael Wilford**

Luigi Biscogli, «L'opera di James Stirling», *Casabella,* Milan, No. 315, July 1967.
GA – Global Architecture, Tokyo, 1971.
Domus, Milan, No. 516, November 1972.

James Stirling, exhibition catalogue of drawings, Heinz Gallery, London, introduction by Reyner Banham, 1974.
«James Stirling», *A+U – Architecture and Urbanism,* Tokyo, 75:2, No. 50, February 1975.
James Stirling, Buildings and Projects 1950–74, Stuttgart: Hatje; London: Thames & Hudson, Milan: Edizioni di Comunità; Tokyo, 1975. Reprint: *James Stirling, Bauten und Projekte 1950–1974,* Stuttgart: Hatje, 1996, text English and German, with an essay by Robert Maxwell.
Casabella, Milan, March 1975 pp. 20–48.
James Stirling, exhibition catalogue edited by Alberto Izzo and Camillo Gubitosi with essays by Marcello Angrisani, Renato De Fusco, Cesare de Seta. Rome: Officina Edizioni, 1976.
Design Quarterly, Minneapolis, No. 100, edited by Craig Hodgetts, interviews about James Stirling with Craig Ellwood, Richard Gwathmey, Philip Johnson, Richard Meier, Doug Michels, Cesar Pelli, Robert Stern, and Stanley Tigerman.
John Maule McKean, «Back with a Bang», *Building Design,* London, 7 September 1979.
John Maule McKean, «Stirling Quality», *Building Design,* London, 14 September 1979.
Architectural Design, London, No. 7/8, 1980.
Robert B. Harmon, *The Architecture of Inconsistency in the Work of James Frazer Stirling: A Selected Bibliography,* Monticello, Illinois, 1981.
«James Stirling», *Architectural Design Profile,* London: Academy Editions/St. Martin's Press, 1982, with essay by Robert Maxwell, «The architect as artist». Reprint in: Robert Maxwell, *Sweet Disorder and the Carefully Careless, Theory and Criticism in Architecture,* New York: Princeton Architectural Press, 1993, pp. 218–226.
Robert Maxwell, *James Stirling,* New York, 1983.
James Stirling, Buildings and Projects [1950–1980], James Stirling Michael Wilford and Associates, Peter Arnell and Ted Bickford (eds.), introduction by Colin Rowe, New York: Rizzoli, 1984, reprint 1987.
DB – Deutsche Bauzeitung, Stuttgart, March 1984, pp. 10–46.
Mirko Zardini (ed.), *La Nuova Galleria di Stato a Stoccarda,* Milan: Electa Periodici, 1985. (on Neue Staatsgalerie)
James Stirling Wissenschaftszentrum Berlin, exhibition catalogue, Berlin: Aedes Gallery, 1985.
«James Stirling Michael Wilford and Associates», *A+U – Architecture and Urbanism,* Tokyo, special edition, No. 194, November 1986, with essays by Colin Rowe, Robert Kahn, and John Rosenfeld.
Eine neue Galerie für die Sammlung Thyssen-Bornemisza/A New Gallery for the Thyssen-Bornemisza Collection, Lugano/Milan: Collection Thyssen-Bornemisza/Electa, 1987.

Biblioteca pubblica e giardini a Latina di James Stirling, Rome: Officina Edizioni, 1989.

Bibliothèque de France – Premiers Volumes, Paris: Institut Français d'Architecture/Editions Carte Segrete, 1989. (on Bibliothèque de France competition)

«Recent Work of James Stirling Michael Wilford & Associates», A+U – Architecture and Urbanism, Tokyo, special edition, May 1990.

«James Stirling Michael Wilford & Associates: Design Philosophy and Recent Projects», Architectural Design, London, special issue, 1990.

Werksanlagen Pfieffewiesen, exhibition catalogue, Berlin: Aedes Gallery, 1991.

I musei di James Stirling Michael Wilford & Associates, exhibition catalogue, Francesco Dal Co and Thomas Muirhead (eds.), with essays by Manfredo Tafuri, Francesco Dal Co, Thomas Muirhead, Milan: Electa, 1990. Spanish: Los Museos de James Stirling Michael Wilford y Asociados, Madrid: Electa España, 1992.

The Architectural Review, London, December 1992.

David Jenkins, Clore Gallery, Tate Gallery Liverpool, London: Phaidon, 1992.

A & V – Monografias de Arquitectura y Vivienda, Madrid, No. 42, 1993, with articles by Peter Buchanan, Francesco Dal Co, Colin Rowe, and Colin St. John Wilson.

ANY – Architecture, New York, September/October 1993.

James Stirling and Michael Wilford, Architectural Monographs No. 32., London: Academy Editions, 1993

Robert Maxwell and Thomas Muirhead, James Stirling, Buildings and Projects, 1975–1992, James Stirling Michael Wilford and Associates, London: Thames & Hudson, 1994. German edition: James Stirling, Bauten und Projekte 1975–1992, James Stirling Michael Wilford and Associates, Stuttgart: Hatje, 1994.

John McKean, Leicester University Engineering Building, London: Phaidon, 1994.

L'Industria delle Costruzioni, Rome, No. 277, November 1994, Francesco Dal Co, «Progetti e Opere di James Stirling», pp. 4–9; Michael Wilford, «Trentadue Anni di Professione», pp. 10–25.

World Architecture, Beijing, No. 79, 1/1994.

Wilford Stirling Wilford: Michael Wilford and Partners, exhibition catalogue, London: E & FN Spon, 1997.

Ausgewählte Aufsätze über James Stirling und/oder Michael Wilford
Selected Articles on James Stirling and/or Michael Wilford

Reyner Banham, «Plucky Jims», The New Statesman, London, 19 July 1958, p. 83. (on Ham Common Flats)

The Architect and Building News, London, 7 January 1959, p. 14. (on Three Houses for Basil Mavrolean)

Architecture and Building, London, May 1959, with essay by James Stirling and James Gowan, «Afterthoughts on the flats at Ham Common». (on Ham Common Flats)

L'Architecture d'Aujourd'hui, Paris, December 1959 pp. 81–85. (on Ham Common Flats)

The Architectural Review, London, January 1961, pp. 12–13. (on Student Residences for Selwyn College)

Bauen und Wohnen, Zürich, no. 3, March 1962, «Miethausgruppe in Ham Common bei London». (on Ham Common Flats)

Architectural Design, London, October 1962, pp. 480–484. (on Engineering Building for Leicester University)

Bauwelt, Berlin, No. 5, 4 February 1963, p. 142. (on Student Residences for Selwyn College)

Robert Maxwell, «Frontiers of inner space», The Sunday Times Colour Magazine, London, 29 September 1963. (on Engineering Building for Leicester University)

Architectural Design, London, February 1964, pp. 61–89, with essays by Frank Newby and Kenneth Frampton. (on Engineering Building for Leicester University)

The Architect and Building News, London, 18 March 1964, pp. 485–489. (on School Assemby Hall)

The Architectural Review, London, April 1964, pp. 252–260. (on Engineering Building for Leicester University)

Architectural Design, London, No. 5, May 1964, pp. 236–240. (on History Faculty for Cambridge University)

Domus, Milan, 415, June 1964, pp. 3–10, Joseph Rykwert, «Un episodia inglese». (on Engineering Building for Leicester University)

Domus, Milan, No. 415, June 1964, pp. 9–10. (on School Assemby Hall)

Arquitectura, Madrid, No. 67, July 1964, pp. 25–29. (on School Assemby Hall, History Faculty for Cambridge University)

Deutsche Bauzeitung, Stuttgart, October 1964, pp. 776–782. (on Engineering Building for Leicester University)

Bauwelt, Berlin, No. 43, 26 October 1964, pp. 1153–1159. (on Engineering Building for Leicester University, School Assemby Hall, History Faculty for Cambridge University)

The Kokusai Kentiku International Review of Architecture, Tokyo, No. 1, January 1965, Hiroshi Hara, «Two works by James Stirling». (on History Faculty for Cambridge University)

Bouw, Rotterdam, no. 14, 3 April 1965, pp. 508–510. (on Engineering Building for Leicester University)

L'Architettura – Cronaca e Storia, Rome, June 1965, No. 116, pp. 102–106. (on School Assemby Hall)

L'Architecture d'Aujourd'hui, Paris, July 1965.

Arkitekten, Copenhagen, 1966, pp. 361–377.

Bauwelt, Berlin, No. 31, 1 August 1966, pp. 894–895. (on Headquarters for Dorman Long Steel Manufacturers)

Werk, Zürich, September 1966, pp. 354–356. (on School Assemby Hall)

Architektur & Wohnform, Stuttgart, October 1966, p. 448. (on Student Residences for St. Andrews University)

Bauwelt, Berlin, No. 43, 24 October 1966, pp. 1230–1231. (on Student Residences for St. Andrews University)

The Listener, London, 5 January 1967, article by Nikolaus Pevsner on Engineering Building for Leicester University.

The Listener, London, 12 January 1967, letter from James Stirling replying to Pevsner's criticism.

Architektur & Wohnform, Stuttgart, February 1967, pp. 111–113. (on Ham Common Flats)

Kentiku Architecture, Tokyo, January 1968, pp. 61–90.

Architecture Canada, Toronto, April 1968, pp. 30–55.

Architectural Design, London, October 1968, pp. 475–478. (on The Florey Building for Queen's College)

Baumeister, Munich, December 1968, Paulhans Peters, «Gläserne Großform: Leicester». (on Engineering Building for Leicester University)

DB – Deutsche Bauzeitung, Stuttgart, 1 February 1969, pp. 95–99. (on History Faculty for Cambridge University)

Domus, Milan, 18 February 1969, article by Joseph Rykwert. (on History Faculty for Cambridge University)

Architectural Design, London, September 1970, pp. 447–462, with essay by Kenneth Frampton.

Architectural Forum, New York, September 1970, pp. 50–56, with essay by Charles Jencks. (on Student Residences for St. Andrews University)

A+U – Architecture and Urbanism, Tokyo, No. 8, 1971, pp. 4–16, with interview by Arata Isozaki, «James Stirling in Tokyo».

SD – Space Design, Tokyo, November 1971, pp. 18–23. (on Derby Civic Centre)

Domus, Milan, No. 516, November 1972, pp. 1–7 (on Low–Cost Housing Runcorn, Derby Civic Centre); 12–15, Joseph Rykwert, «Stirling in Oxford». (on The Florey Building for Queen's College)

The Architectural Review, London, November 1972, pp. 257, 260, 266. (on The Florey Building for Queen's College)

A+U – Architecture and Urbanism, Tokyo, November 1972. (on Low-Cost Housing Runcorn)

Architecture Plus, New York, February 1973, p. 5, 24, Robert Maxwell, « A rakish dorm confronts Oxford».

A+U – Architecture and Urbanism, Tokyo, 73:5, May 1973, pp. 37–42.

Glass Age, London, May 1973, pp. 34–39. (on The Florey Building for Queen's College)

Genghia Architecture, Taiwan, June 1973, «James Stirling: Five projects».

Domus, Milan, No. 530, January 1974, pp. 37–44, incl. Joseph Rykwert, «Lo spazio policromo». (on Olivetti Training School)

Bauen und Wohnen, Zürich, March 1974, pp. 117–120. (on The Florey Building for Queen's College)

Architecture Plus, New York, March/April 1974, pp. 96–103, incl. Charles Jencks, «Haslemere: James Stirling's corporate culture machine». (on Olivetti Training School)

The Architectural Review, London, April 1974, pp. 187, 190, 197, 200–211, incl. Reyner Banham, «Problem x 3 = Olivetti». (on Olivetti Training School)

Glasforum, Böblingen, May/June 1974, pp. 11–15.

Oppositions, New Haven, Connecticut, No. 3, Manfredo Tafuri, «L'architecture dans le boudoir».

Oppositions, New Haven, Connecticut, No. 4, October 1974, pp. 5–34, Peter Eisenman, «Real and English – the destruction of the box». (on Engineering Building for Leicester University)

2c Construccion de la Ciudad, Barcelona, No. 1, February 1975, pp. 1, 8, 20–25.

Casabella, Milan, No. 399, March 1975, pp. 40–47.

The Architects' Journal, London, 16 July 1975, pp. 104–105, 119. (on Arts Centre for St. Andrews University)

AMC – Architecture Mouvement Continuité, Paris, No. 37, December 1975, pp. 69–76, «Entretien avec James Stirling».

Building Design, London, 19 March 1976, pp. 14–17, Gavin Stamp, «Gleaming, elegant, and gay, but . . .». (on History Faculty for Cambridge University)

Progressive Architecture, Cleveland, March 1976, pp. 42–46. (on Low-Cost Housing Runcorn)

Domus, Milan, No. 559, June 1976, pp. 17–24. (on Low-Cost Housing Runcorn)

The Architectural Review, London, November 1976, pp. 282–296.

Berliner Morgenpost, Berlin, 18 January 1977, comment by Heinrich Klotz. (on Hotel Meinekestrasse)

Wettbewerbe Aktuell, Munich, No. 12, 1977. (on Neue Staatsgalerie competition)

The New York Times, New York, 26 August 1979, p. 25, Ada Louise Huxtable, «Architecture: bigger – and maybe better». (on Sackler Gallery)

The Architects' Journal, London, 16 January 1980, pp. 112–114, Peter Buchanan, «Techne in Arcadia». (on Bayer Research Centre)

Casabella, Milan, No. 455, February 1980, pp. 1, 9, 10, 12, 14–29. (on Bayer Research Centre competition)

Bauwelt, Berlin, No. 14, 11 April 1980, pp. 574–77, Gerd Neumann, «James Stirlings ‹Spree-Athen›: Eklektizismus! – ?» (on Wissenschaftszentrum)

The New York Times, New York, 16 June 1980, Paul Goldberger, «Architecture: townhouse rows». (on Manhattan Townhouses)

Architectural Design, London, 6/1981, Robert Maxwell, «The pursuit of the art of architecture».

A+U – Architecture and Urbanism, Tokyo, July 1981, pp. 87–92. (on Sackler Gallery)

Connaissance des Arts, Paris, November 1981, pp. 82–83, Philip Jodidio, «James Stirling: une dynamique dissonante».

Skyline, New York (Rizzoli), November 1981, pp. 16–20, Anthony Vidler, «Reconstructing modernism: the architecture of James Stirling».

Covjek i Prostor, Zagreb, January 1982, pp. 26–29.

Lotus, Milan, No. 36, 1982, pp. 52–53. (on Low-Cost Housing Runcorn)

Baumeister, Munich, April 1982, p. 347, «Architekturschule in Houston». (on Rice School of Architecture Extension)

Casabella, Milan, May 1982, pp. 2–13. (on Sackler Gallery)

The Architects' Journal, London, 22 & 29 December 1982, pp. 23–26. (on Neue Staatsgalerie)

G. A. Document, Tokyo, No. 5, 1982, pp. 50, 52, 56–71, Peter C. Papademetriou, «Renovations and additions to the School of Architecture, Rice University». (on Rice School of Architecture Extension)

The Architectural Review, London, March 1983, John Summerson, «Vitruvius Ludens».

DB – Deutsche Bauzeitung, Stuttgart, March 1984, pp. 7, 9–46.

Die Zeit, Hamburg, 9 March 1984, p. 16, 43, Manfred Sack, «Das Zitatenmuseum». (on Neue Staatsgalerie)

The Architectural Review, London, April 1984, pp.3, 25, 43, Michael Sorkin, «The Big Man on campus».

Building Design, London, 20 April 1984, pp. 7, 12–19, essays by Ian Latham, David Dunster, Doug Clelland. (on Neue Staatsgalerie)

Bauwelt, Berlin, No. 20, 25 May 1984. (on Neue Staatsgalerie)

DBZ – Deutsche Bauzeitschrift, Gütersloh, No. 5, May 1984, pp. 579–584. (on Neue Staatsgalerie)

Architektur & Wohnen, Hamburg, 6 June/4 September 1984,

pp. 52–57, Dirk Meyhöfer, «Ein Museum, das sich selber ausstellt». (on Neue Staatsgalerie)

Domus, Milan, No. 651, June 1984, pp. 1, 2–16. (on Neue Staatsgalerie)

Baumeister, Munich, August 1984, pp. 54–69. (on Neue Staatsgalerie)

Glasforum, Böblingen, No. 3, August 1984, pp. 13–22. (on Neue Staatsgalerie)

DB – Deutsche Bauzeitung, Stuttgart, 9 September 1984, pp. 38–47.

Architectural Record, New York, September 1984, pp. 140–150.

Der Spiegel, Hamburg, No. 10, 1984, p. 180, «Mein Gott, es ist Metro-Goldwyn-Mayer». (on Neue Staatsgalerie)

AMC – Architecture Mouvement Continuité, Paris, No. 5, October 1984, pp. 3, 4–19, incl. Claude Parent, «Opinion: une architecture moderne en liberté».

The Architectural Review, London, December 1984, Alan Colquhoun, «Democratic Monument», Reyner Banham, «Celebration of the city», Emilio Ambasz, «Popular Pantheon», Oriol Bohigas, «Turning point», William Curtis, «Virtuosity around a void». (on Neue Staatsgalerie)

The New York Times, New York, 10 April 1985, p. 22, C20, Paul Goldberger, «Architecture: Museum in Stuttgart builds a postmodernist monument». (on Neue Staatsgalerie)

Building Design, London, 5 July 1985, pp. 22–27, Ian Latham, «Latina translation». (on Latina Public Library)

Blueprint, London, July/August 1985, p. 5, 16–19, with interview by Martin Pawley. (on Latina Public Library)

Blueprint, London, September 1985, p. 5, «Stirling opens in Harvard». (on Sackler Gallery)

Architectural Record, New York, March 1986, pp. 112–123, Colin Rowe, «Who, but Stirling?». Reprint in: Colin Rowe, As I Was Saying, Vol. II, Cambridge, Mass.: MIT Press, 1996, pp. 265–275. (on Sackler Gallery)

Architectural Design, London, No. 56, 5/1986, pp. 28–39. (on No. 1 Poultry)

Blueprint, London, No. 31, October 1986, p. 24. (on National Gallery Extension)

Blueprint, London, No. 33, December 1986/January 1987, p. 8, 38. (on Clore Gallery)

The New York Times, New York, 19 April 1987, Paul Goldberger, «A Prophet honored at last in his own land». (on Clore Gallery)

Arquitectura, Madrid, No. 266, May/June 1987, pp. 116–117. (on Thyssen-Bornemisza Gallery competition)

The Architectural Review, London, June 1987, pp. 38, 45, John Summerson, «Vitruvius Ludens or Laughter at the Clore», Charles Jencks, «Clore contextualisms».

L'Arca, Milan, June 1987, pp. 32–37. (on Abando Passenger Interchange)

Architecture + Design, New Delhi, July/August 1987, p. 5, 36–49, Sunand Prasad and Satish Grover, interview of James Stirling.

Domus, Milan, No. 51, July/August 1987, p. 44, Ian Boyd White, «The Clore Gallery, Londra». (on Clore Gallery)

Architectural Design, London, No. 3/4, 1988, p. 62, 74–79. (on Disney Philharmonic Hall competition)

A&V – Monografias de Arquitectura y Vivienda, Madrid, No. 16, 1988, pp. 64–71. (on Abando Passenger Interchange)

Architectural Design, London, No. 11/12, 1988, pp. 66–75. (on Wissenschaftszentrum)

Casabella, Milan, November 1988, pp. 1, 49–62, Sebastiano Brandolini, «WZB: Osservazioni su un edificio semplice». (on Wissenschaftszentrum)

Composicion Arquitectonica – Art & Architecture, Bilbao, February 1989. (on Thyssen-Bornemisza Gallery)

The Times, London, 6 March 1989, Deyan Sudjic, «Does this estate have to die?» (on Low-Cost Housing Runcorn)

The Architectural Review, London, March 1989, pp. 3, 28, 30, 37. (on Wissenschaftszentrum)

The Independent, London, 6 March 1989, Andrew Gimson, «Mischief in Legoland».

A&V – Monografias de Arquitectura y Vivienda, Madrid, No. 20, 1989, p. 78. (on Stadium Development Seville)

Archithese, Heiden, 3/1989, pp. 59–68. (on Disney Philharmonic Hall competition)

The New York Times, New York, 23 April 1989, Paul Goldberger, «A Building with the Razzle but not the Dazzle». (on Performing Arts Center for Cornell University)

Progressive Architecture, Cleveland, June 1989, p. 21. (on Performing Arts Center for Cornell University)

A+U – Architecture and Urbanism, Tokyo, September 1989, pp. 59, 62, 70–102. (on Wissenschaftszentrum)

The Architectural Review, London, November 1989, p. 9 (on Compton Verney Opera House competition); pp. 36–47, with essay by Robert Maxwell. (on Performing Arts Center for Cornell University) Reprint in: Robert Maxwell, *Sweet Disorder and the Carefully Careless, Theory and Criticism in Architecture,* New York: Princeton Architectural Press, 1993, pp. 88–95.

The Architectural Review, London, December 1989, pp. 70–76. (on Abando Passenger Interchange)

Ambiente, Munich, March 1990, p. 44, Otto Riewoldt, «Jimmie goes to Italy». (on Performing Arts Center for Cornell University)

Architecture Today, London, No. 13, November 1990, pp. 36–55, with essay by Robert Maxwell. (on Music Academy Stuttgart) Reprint in: Robert Maxwell, *Sweet Disorder and the Carefully Careless, Theory and Criticism in Architecture,* New York: Princeton Architectural Press, 1993, pp. 96–102.

Domus, Milan, No. 724, February 1991, pp. 29–39. (on Palazzo Citterio Art Gallery)

DBZ – Deutsche Bauzeitschrift, Gütersloh, March 1991, pp. 341–348, W. Nedderhut-Heeschen, «Mozart-Goethe-Go-Go-Gown: Centre of the Performance Arts». (on Performing Arts Center for Cornell University)

Nikkei Architecture, Japan, 27 May 1991, pp. 171–189. (on Kyoto Centre competition)

Abitare, Milan, November 1991, p. 184, 186, 194–197. (on Biennale Bookshop)

Casabella, No. 585, Milan, December 1991, pp. 18–22. (on Kyoto Centre)

Werk, Bauen + Wohnen, Zürich, December 1991, pp. 8–10. (on Biennale Bookshop)

Frankfurter Allgemeine Zeitung, Frankfurt, 19 March 1992, p. 33, Michael Mönninger, «Wandelbares Monument – Ästhetik als Produktivkraft: James Stirlings Fabrik in Melsungen». (on Braun Headquarters)

Architektur und Wohnen, 4/1992, pp. 118–125, Gert Kähler, «Das Wunder von Melsungen». (on Braun Headquarters)

Baumeister, München, May 1992, pp. 40–47, «Werksanlagen in Melsungen». (on Braun Headquarters)

Bauwelt, Berlin, No. 21, 29 May 1992, pp. 1137, 1154–1169. (on Braun Headquarters)

Architecture Today, London, July 1992, p. 18, Robert Maxwell, «Masterwork at Melsungen». (on Braun Headquarters)

Architecture Interieure – Cree, Paris, October 1992, pp. 104–113, Peter Buchanan, «La complexit, une dialectique». (on Braun Headquarters)

Architectural Record, New York, October 1992, pp. 74–83. (on Braun Headquarters)

Arquitectura Viva, Madrid, November/December 1992, pp. 34–41, Robert Maxwell, «El último Stirling: una fábrica en Melsungen». (on Braun Headquarters)

Architectural Review, London, December 1992, Robert Maxwell, «The far side of modernity: Stirling's Braun HQ at Melsungen». (on Braun Headquarters) Reprint in: Robert Maxwell, *Sweet Disorder and the Carefully Careless, Theory and Criticism in Architecture,* New York: Princeton Architectural Press, 1993, pp. 236–241.

A+U – Architecture and Urbanism, Tokyo, December 1992, pp. 38–47.

Casabella, Milan, December 1992, Robert Maxwell «James Stirling and Robert Venturi: a comparison». Reprint in: Robert Maxwell, *Sweet Disorder and the Carefully Careless, Theory and Criticism in Architecture,* New York: Princeton Architectural Press, 1993, pp. 228–235.

Triennale Nara, Japan, No. 1, 1993, pp. 89–95.

DB – Deutsche Bauzeitung, Stuttgart, January 1993, pp. 25–39. (on Braun Headquarters)

A+U – Architecture and Urbanism, No. 269, February 1993, pp. 24–47, Robert Maxwell, «James Stirling, Michael Wilford: Braun Headquarters». (on Braun Headquarters)

Archis, Doetinchem, Netherlands, 3/1993, pp. 17–29. (on Braun Headquarters)

RIBA Journal, London, March 1993, pp. 24–28, Nick Wates, «Wilford plans for the future».

Baumeister, Munich, April 1993, pp. 22–26. (on Braun Headquarters)

Architectural Review, London, June 1993, pp. 33–37. (on Architecture School, Newcastle)

Casabella, Milan, No. 602, June 1993, pp. 4–19, Robert Maxwell, «Cinque architetture, un'idea: opere di James Stirling and Michael Wilford Associates».

RIBA Journal, London, September 1993, pp. 49–53, David Jenkins, «Rail links».

Techniques et Architecture, Paris, September 1993, pp. 70–77. (on Braun Headquarters)

Daidalos, Berlin, No. 51, 15 March 1994, p. 32. (on Braun Headquarters)

Archis, Doetinchem, Netherlands, No. 5, May 1994, pp. 70–80, Irénée Scalbert, «Cerebral functionalism: The design of the Leicester University Engineering Building». (on Engineering Building for Leicester University)

RIBA Journal, London, July 1994, pp. 44–49, by Robert Maxwell (on Sto AG Headquarters and Manufacturing Plant)

Wettbewerbe Aktuell, Freiburg, 11/1994, pp. 48–49. (on Tokyo International Forum competition, on Dresden Technical University competition)

Blueprint, London, December 1994/January 1995, pp. 59–63. (on Biological Sciences Library for University of California)

Kenneth Frampton, «Life Begins Tomorrow», in: *Europa nach der Flut 1945–65,* Berlin: Künstlerhaus, 1995, pp. 361–392.

RIBA Journal, London, March 1995, pp. 20–29, Naomi Stungo, «Our man in Berlin». (on British Embassy)

Blueprint, London, April 1995, pp. 42–49. (on Biological Sciences Library for University of California)

Beton – Die Fachzeitschrift für das Bauen mit Beton, Düsseldorf, 6/1995, pp. 372, 406–411. (on Music Academy Stuttgart)

Casabella, Milan, No. 624, June 1995, pp. 4–19. (on Temasek Polytechnic)

RIBA Journal, July 1995, pp. 24–33, John Welsh, «Heroic stoism», (on Sto AG Headquarters and Manufacturing Plant)

A+U – Architecture and Urbanism, Tokyo, October 1995, pp. 16–33. (on Biological Sciences Library for University of California)

World Architecture, London, No. 48, July/August 1996, Alan Brookes, «Cladding and roofing». (on Braun Headquarters)

Bauwelt, Berlin, No. 33, 30 August 1996, pp. 1848–1859 (on Music Academy Stuttgart); pp. 1860–1871 (on Temasek Polytechnic).

A+U – Architecture and Urbanism, Tokyo, September 1996, pp. 2–19. (on Temasek Polytechnic)

Architecture Today, London, No. 72, October 1996, pp. 20–30, Robert Maxwell, «Formal Inquiry: Stirling Wilford's Stuttgart Music School». (on Music Academy Stuttgart)

Architektura & Biznes, Kraków, October 1996, pp. 20–24, «Centrum Komunikacyjne Bilbao». (on Abando Passenger Interchange)

Glasforum, Böblingen, 5/1996, pp. 17–20. (on Temasek Polytechnic)

Blueprint, London, June 1996, pp. 40–43, Rowan Moore, «The genius's apprentice».

Werk, Bauen + Wohnen, Zürich, December 1996, «Passagierbahnhof Abando, Bilbao». (on Abando Passenger Interchange)

Baumeister, Munich, January 1997, pp. 40–41, Amber Sayah, «Konzertsaal der Musikhochschule Stuttgart».

DBZ – Deutsche Bauzeitschrift, Gütersloh, No. 7, July 1997, p. 19, «Schiff auf weiter Flur». (on Sto AG Headquarters)

«Wettbewerb Britische Botschaft – Architectural Design Competition British Embassy», in: Sebastian Redecke/Ralph Stern (eds.), *Foreign Affairs: Neue Botschaftsbauten und das Auswärtige Amt in Berlin – New Embassy Buildings and the German Foreign Office in Berlin,* Berlin/Basel: Bauwelt/Birkhäuser, 1997, pp. 136–168.

Bildnachweis/Illustration Credits